PARTY B
& JAPANESE
PRISONER OF WAR
PROPAGANDA

To the memory of my father, George Skalmerud Baker, 1919–1991
and my brother, Nicholas Robert Skalmerud Baker, 1959–2020

PARTY B & JAPANESE PRISONER OF WAR PROPAGANDA

BUSHIDO FOR BARBARIANS

RICHARD BAKER

Pen & Sword
MILITARY
AN IMPRINT OF PEN & SWORD BOOKS LTD.
YORKSHIRE – PHILADELPHIA

First published in Great Britain in 2026 by
PEN AND SWORD MILITARY
An imprint of
Pen & Sword Books Limited
Yorkshire – Philadelphia

ISBN 978 1 03619 030 9

A CIP catalogue record for this book is available from the British Library.

Typeset in Times New Roman 11.5/14 by
SJmagic DESIGN SERVICES, India.
Printed and bound in the UK by CPI Group (UK) Ltd.

The Publisher's authorised representative in the EU for product safety is Authorised Rep Compliance Ltd., Ground Floor, 71 Lower Baggot Street, Dublin D02 P593, Ireland.
www.arccompliance.com

For a complete list of Pen & Sword titles please contact
PEN & SWORD BOOKS LIMITED
George House, Units 12 & 13, Beevor Street, Off Pontefract Road,
Barnsley, South Yorkshire, S71 1HN, England
E-mail: enquiries@pen-and-sword.co.uk
Website: www.pen-and-sword.co.uk

or

PEN AND SWORD BOOKS
1950 Lawrence Rd, Havertown, PA 19083, USA
E-mail: uspen-and-sword@casematepublishers.com
Website: www.penandswordbooks.com

MIX
Paper | Supporting responsible forestry
FSC® C013604

Contents

Acknowledgements

I should like to thank Professor Mark Connelly, who supervised my Master's thesis on Keijo camp, and its examiner Ashley Jackson, Professor of Imperial History at King's College London, who thought it was publishable. I also thank my former supervisor, the late A.O.J. Cockshut of All Souls and Hertford Colleges, Oxford.

At the Lancashire Infantry Museum, Jane Davies was generous with her time when I visited. I also thank the staff at the International Committee of the Red Cross archives in Geneva and the librarians at the Rare Books and Music room of the British Library. Many thanks also to Nicole Allen, archivist at Churchill College Cambridge for locating a copy of Albert Nuttall's narrative of captivity; and the staff of the Liddell Hart Archives, King's College London, who allowed me access to the Proctor collection of Keijo photographs.

I am grateful to Simon Parrish, Susan Edwards and Covadonga Valdes for their thoughts on the artwork produced by prisoners at Keijo. I also thank Peter Anderson and Nick Hind for reading parts of the manuscript. I am grateful also to Martin Lewis for his practical advice.

I am particularly indebted to two independent researchers, Jacco Zwetsloot and Matt VanVolkenburg. Matt generously allowed me to make use of translations he has made from Korean newspapers, and Jacco shared relevant information uncovered by his research. In the United States, Phil Karsis provided me with copies of photographs and manuscripts previously belonging to his friend and colleague, Colonel Bill Elrington.

I also owe a great debt of gratitude to Party B family members. It was a pleasure to meet Alison Jesson, daughter of Captain John Jesson, who sent me copies of her father's journals, written at Keijo. Helen Sherpa, granddaughter of Major Conrad Rigby, provided me with a copy of his diaries. I must also thank Mark Sullivan, grandson of Colonel Vincent Sullivan, and Professor Chris Given-Wilson, son of Lieutenant Paddy

Given-Wilson. Mark offered valuable hints as well as encouragement throughout the time I was writing the book. Thanks also to Ted and Rosanne Codrington.

I also thank Merrie Frazer Bott, daughter of Lieutenant William 'Chook' Frazer, who sent me a copy of Arthur Kerr's diaries and pointed me in the direction of other useful primary sources. She also generously read portions of the manuscript.

Introduction

My father, Lieutenant George Baker of the 2nd Battalion Loyal Regiment, was a member of Party B. He had been captured at Singapore, and imprisoned at Changi camp, formerly a British military complex on the island. Here, Parties A and B were created. Party A consisted of the most senior officers and civilian officials, who were shipped to Formosa (Taiwan). Party B, numbering a thousand men, was transported to Korea, then a Japanese colony renamed 'Chosen'. Ninety per cent of the party consisted of men from two British units, The 2nd Battalion, Loyal (North Lancashire) Regiment, and the 122nd Field Artillery regiment. There were also 93 Australians from various units. On arrival, they were initially divided into two camps. The main camp was in a suburb of Seoul, which had been renamed Keijo by the Japanese, and there was a branch camp, Jinsen, located on the coast thirty miles to the west. Later, members of the party were sent to Mukden in Manchuria and, after its construction in 1943, to Konan camp in Korea. Conditions the Korean camps were the best a prisoner of the Japanese could hope for. This is the first time that their full story has been told, and the reasons for the better conditions explained.

A brief extract from my father's diary shows how the camps differed from the popular idea of imprisonment under the Japanese. In January 1944, he was found in possession of a hand-drawn map of the surrounding area. There had recently been an escape attempt at Jinsen and he was subjected to a series of interrogations:

> Summoned to the office again expecting to be questioned about the map, that very tedious subject. Captain Ushihara [the camp interpreter] held in his hand a notebook, taken off me the first day in this camp, in which was an account, just begun, on the Malayan campaign. My heart sank rather when I remembered some of the uncomplimentary remarks I had made about 'our hosts'. 'I have been making a translation of this for Colonel Noguchi [Superintendent

> of prison camps in Korea]. 'Hell,' I thought, 'the devil you have'. Ushihara continues: 'and he finds it most interesting and wishes you to continue with your writing'. Then, fingering some maps I had made he said: 'He is interested in these also.' I was astonished and rather relieved. I said I could do what I could do, that it was old history by now and I would try to reconstruct the scenes again on paper. 'If there is anything you want just say so, any writing materials, or anything.' A short silence, then Ushihara said carelessly: 'Oh by the way, don't bother about the other thing. I don't think anything is happening about the map […] I left the office with my notebook, reflecting that continuing with this Malayan battle record could do little harm and might indeed give some pleasure to old Col. Nog, who is not a bad old stick and quite kindly, tho' one of His Majesty's enemies. I had however an unpleasant feeling of blackmail.[1]

Very few prisoners of the Japanese would describe the commandant of their camp as 'not a bad old stick', and interrogations of captives suspected of planning to escape usually involved a considerable amount of violence. We can contrast his experience with that of another Keijo prisoner, an Australian, Private Clarke, who was also summoned to the office to discuss his writing activities with Ushihara. On his arrival, he was presented with a letter home he had written. Clarke had mentioned that Red Cross parcels provided a necessary supplement to their diet. Ushihara told him that this was insulting, and without further ado began punching him in the face. A colleague, Captain Terada, picked up a thick cane and joined in. They beat Clarke all over his body for forty-five minutes.[2] When he came out of the office, stunned, his face was unrecognisable. Clarke was then taken to the guardroom and made to kneel in his cell. Ushihara instructed guards to watch the prisoner and strike him if he moved.

How can we explain such a disjuncture in interpreter Ushihara's behaviour? It is true that officers at the camp generally received better treatment than the other ranks, although they could be slapped hard around the face for minor infractions of camp regulations, such as smoking in the wrong area. But it is also true that the guards at the camp victimised and bullied prisoners they took a dislike to, and that Ushihara and Terada enjoyed working together as a double act, beating prisoners up in private. My father's instinct that he was being blackmailed was correct, and offers a hint to the central fact that the more benign aspects of the camp regime and the captors' behaviour were to a large extent dictated by its propaganda function. My father's account of the debacle of the Malayan campaign and the fall of Singapore would have provided useful propaganda material and may also have offered a small addition to military intelligence. Private Clarke's letter, on the other hand, was 'off message'. Writing activities were just a very small part of the Korean camps' propaganda function. That function is the subject of this book.

For the Commander of Armed Forces in Korea, Seishiro Itagaki, Party B's primary purpose was as propaganda for the local population. In February 1942 he had written to the Japanese War Ministry asking for British and American prisoners to be sent to Korea for 'psychological propaganda' purposes, 'to stamp out the respect and admiration of the Korean people for Britain and America and to create confidence in a Japanese victory'.[3] There were no Americans at Changi at that time, and consequently Party B consisted of 900 British prisoners and ninety-three Australians, with one Canadian and a handful of New Zealanders making up the full complement. (The lack of American prisoners did not prevent the Japanese media reporting their presence in Korea from the moment the party arrived in Korea until the capitulation). As well as providing proof of Japanese superiority to the Korean people, the prisoners served as propaganda for all the Japanese territories. They provided useful accounts of Japanese superiority on the battlefield, and they appeared in newsreels and even feature films. Audiences could see the Westerners firmly under the Japanese thumb, but also as the recipients of *Bushido* magnanimity and generosity.

For the rest of the world, Party B served a greater purpose as a means of rebutting accusations of POW atrocities. The prisoners were made to write letters home and messages for radio broadcasts telling the outside world of their humane treatment. During their captivity, photographs and letters from their camps appeared in newspapers worldwide. Photographs taken at Keijo camp were the first images of Far Eastern captivity to be published in Europe and Britain. When the British and Americans made synchronised disclosures to the public of Japanese prisoner of war atrocities at the beginning of 1944, Keijo, Jinsen and Mukden were used by the Japanese as the principal evidence to rebut these accusations. The benign picture of captivity that came from the camps was accepted by the enemy, and the British government formed the completely false perception that conditions in the camps located in the northern areas of Japan's empire, which included Korea and Manchuria, were, in the words of Foreign Secretary Anthony Eden, 'generally satisfactory'.[4] The misconception arose that it was only in the southern, newly conquered territories, such as Burma and Thailand, that atrocities occurred. The worst maltreatment, it was wrongly believed, was committed by rogue elements who acted on their own initiative, outside the restraining influence of central control.

The most significant element of the Japanese POW propaganda strategy, hitherto scarcely recognised, was its successful manipulation of the International Committee of the Red Cross. Inspectors were allowed to visit the camps where Party B were held. Conditions were poor, but nevertheless far better than elsewhere, with the possible exception of two other 'show camps', Zentsuji on the Japanese mainland, and Woosun in Shanghai. With enough preparation and manipulation the camps could offer the illusion that they adhered to the standards laid down by the 1929 Geneva Convention. At the Party B camps, prisoners were given just enough to eat to stay alive, and were inoculated against the diseases – malaria, tuberculosis, smallpox and typhoid – which claimed the lives of so many other prisoners of the Japanese. The men also received far more Red Cross parcels and letters from home than their fellow prisoners elsewhere in the Far East. At some camps, prisoners could pass three-and-a-half years in captivity without receiving a single letter or parcel. The various forms of labour that the other ranks were put to caused injuries and a small number of deaths, but the mortality rate was remarkably low. Beatings were given for the smallest misdemeanours, real or imagined, with the regime at Mukden being particularly brutal. Conditions at Mukden were the most brutal of the Party B camps, but the senior British officer at Mukden, Major Robert Peaty, would later write that conditions there were nevertheless better than at most other camps, with the exception of Keijo.[5]

Japan had not ratified the Geneva Convention and it could have followed Russia's example in refusing a Red Cross presence in its territories. However, in February 1942, its diplomatic mission in Berne had responded to a request from the International Committee of the Red Cross (ICRC) to clarify its stance regarding POWs with the following statement: 'Since the Japanese government has not ratified the Geneva Convention it is therefore not bound by the said Convention. Nevertheless, in so far as possible, it intends to apply this convention *mutatis mutandis* to all prisoners of war.'[6] Historians have debated what exactly the Japanese meant by the use of the Latin phrase, but the simple fact is that Japan had no intention whatsoever of following the Convention, and the statement was nothing but propaganda.

Japan maintained this fiction of humane treatment unvaryingly and in the face of seemingly irrefutable evidence to the contrary throughout the conflict, and the ICRC was skilfully deployed as a legitimating source of its propaganda. Simply allowing the organisation into the country sent a positive message to the rest of the world, and Japan cared about world opinion. But the Japanese also provided the organisation with photographs and film footage from the Party B camps, and images suggesting humane treatment appeared in Red Cross publications across the world, reinforced by summaries of visits to the camps.

Sources

This book's origins lie in two postgraduate dissertations, written as a part-time graduate student at Oxford University and the University of Kent at Canterbury. As part of my research I made two visits to the ICRC's Geneva archives, as well as the relevant archives and libraries in this country. The Lancashire Infantry Museum in Preston holds a great deal of contemporary source material while the Liddell Hart military archives at King's College London hold a large collection of photographs taken at Keijo. Hitherto unexamined material includes a government report on Mukden camp and the activities of Unit 731, first released to the public in 2018. I have also made use of Japanese and Korean newspaper articles, some only recently re-discovered and translated into English.[7]

The chief difficulty in researching Japan's policy towards its prisoners lies in the wide-scale destruction of documents at Japanese camps at the end of the war. As defeat became inevitable, the War Ministry instructed all commandants of its prison camps to destroy documents that would be 'unbearable in the hands of the enemy', and gave permission for the guards who had been guilty of the most egregious forms of brutality to disappear immediately. At Keijo camp, Captain John Jesson, a medical officer, witnessed a succession of bonfires in August 1945. Similar conflagrations occurred at all the Japanese POW camps.

Despite this, Party B's propaganda function has meant that an unusually – possibly uniquely – large volume of primary sources remain. My father left a substantial collection of documents and drawings from Keijo camp, including a lengthy diary and several photographs. At some camps, keeping a diary could be punishable by death, but in the Korean camps it was actively encouraged. Prisoners were told that they could write what they liked with no fear of repercussions, but the camp authorities reserved the right to read them occasionally. This was in aid of a subsidiary propaganda function. By examining the thoughts of hundreds of men over a period of years, useful insights into the enemy psychology, his combat motivation and vulnerabilities could be harvested.

A family connection has enabled me to locate diaries still held by the families of other Party B prisoners, hitherto unread except by them.[8] They offer a broad perspective, encompassing the viewpoints of both British and Australians, officers and other ranks. Collectively they provide a consistent, vivid and sometimes horrifying account of life in the camps, which can be contrasted with newspaper and ICRC reports. Later testimony, in the form of published memoirs and sound recordings display less unanimity over events and personalities, but confirm significant details about the camps' propaganda function. The most striking difference between the diaries and the later memoirs is that the former contain far more raw emotion. Although the accounts often employ understatement and humour to mediate experiences, events are mostly recorded immediately after they occurred, and contain the emotion of the moment. My father, for example, records violence against fellow prisoners with white-hot fury, immediately after witnessing it. Below is a description of an assault on one of his men while out on a work party:

> The Japanese private, a short-arsed evil-visaged little runt of a being, asked him in his broken English using that vile, coarse, pseudo-domineering voice, why he had gone to the furthest benjo [latrine]. (The benjos were foully disgusting beyond description, incidentally). On being told that the man had sought a clean benjo, which happened to be the one furthest from him, the private, eyes glittering, then

> gave a most savage exhibition of vicious temper. The man was made to kneel down to attain the same height as his brutal and cowardly supervisor, who struck with clenched fists, then with a slat of wood. I tried to intervene but was brushed aside. His lips were cut and his nose bled. Then he was made to stand to attention outside for an hour and a quarter. I was boiling with hate and the exasperating feeling of my helplessness.[9]

As a child I used to ask my father about the camps. Like most former prisoners of the Japanese, he was reluctant to discuss his experiences, and what little he did say was usually recounted in a light-hearted manner. His diaries corroborate my memories of what he told me, but he gave modified accounts, suitable for children. He once mentioned, for example, that an American army tunic he used for gardening had literally dropped out of the sky. After the Japanese surrender, B29s flew over the camp to drop canisters containing relief supplies. Some of the planes flew too low and the parachutes attached to the metal containers failed to open. They smashed heavily to the ground and their contents, once opened, had become a jumbled mess of food, medicines, newspapers, toiletries and clothes. When my father received his tunic, it came decorated with chocolate, cream and toothpaste.

His diary records the incident as I remember it, but it was part of a much darker story. One of the canisters fell through the roof of a house next to the camp. At that time he was in the camp hospital. He saw a badly injured Korean woman being brought in: 'Her face was white through loss of blood, both her legs had been chopped off. She died minutes later. Another life horribly lost.'[10] The prisoners at the camps endured countless incidents over the years of captivity that they would later have no wish to recall. My father's understated recollections of camp life were corroborated by various photographs of Keijo camp, pasted in an old family photograph album. Amid snaps of holidays and picnics in the Thirties and Forties, there were photographs from Keijo, including one of him eating Christmas lunch with his close friend Captain Peter Cazalet, and another of men making bread at the camp. As a child I formed the impression that conditions at the camp had been benign. I had been deceived by Japanese propaganda.

My father did occasionally reveal glimpses of the reality, but somewhat randomly. For example, he once told me that an effect of 'going without food for some time' was to create a feeling of heightened perception, as if all one's senses had been magically sharpened. Another comment – that it is possible to die simply by giving up the will to live – must also have come from his days in Korea. Although the Party B camps were the best a POW could hope for, they were nevertheless appalling places. As one of the prisoners at Keijo, Alan Toze, wrote: 'This putrid existence, full of longing, hate, greed, hunger, meanness, pettiness and fear is surely a very near approach to hell upon earth.'[11]

Chapter 1

Overview of Japanese Wartime Propaganda

To gain a full understanding of how the men of Party B were used for propaganda, it is helpful first to place their exploitation within the context of Japan's wartime propaganda as a whole. Like Germany, Japan had been impressed by Britain's use of propaganda during the First World War, and the 1930s saw the growth of knowledge and expertise in this field in Japan, aided by the translation of key American and British theoretical works during the period.[1] Until recently, historians have generally regarded Japanese wartime propaganda as a failure, but this view has been challenged over the last fifteen years. David Earhart has drawn attention to the skill of Japanese visual propaganda, while Jane Robbins has argued that Japan's radio propaganda was successful through its diversity and adaptability.[2] Barak Kushner has suggested that if Japanese propaganda was a failure, it was at the least a successful failure, arguing that its domestic propaganda was able to maintain the unity of the Japanese people to a far greater extent than was the case in other totalitarian regimes, and that it also helped prepare the Japanese people for defeat.[3]

At the outbreak of war, Japan possessed one of the most developed mass media networks in the world to transmit its propaganda.[4] The national radio broadcasting service (NHK) reached about half the population, and the total daily press circulation was approximately 19 million, equivalent to more than one newspaper per household. During the period, Japan also made propaganda films that were the equal of anything produced by the West, although, as we shall see, its Prisoner of War propaganda newsreels and feature films by no means matched this high standard.[5] As well as the official government and military sources, independent bodies such as advertising and record companies, rakugo (comedians), storytellers, and neighbourhood associations. There were also a form of propaganda unique to Japan, *kamishibai*, literally translated as 'paper play'. At its simplest level, a performer would stand at a street corner with a set of drawings, often of great artistry, which would be shown in sequence to illustrate the storyteller's spoken narrative.[6]

But against these undoubted strengths, Japanese propaganda lacked a central coordinating authority such as Goebbel's Ministry of Propaganda, which led to inconsistencies and contradiction. The army and navy both had separate propaganda sections, for no better reason than rivalry. Japanese propaganda also suffered from ignorance of Western society and psychology, in the same way, it may be said, that American propaganda initially suffered from ignorance of Japanese society and culture. Propaganda proclaimed that the materialistic Americans would not have the stomach for a prolonged fight and that when its people started to suffer from the economic consequences of war, the Americans would sue for peace terms. This misbelief actually influenced the decision to wage war in the first place. As well as a failure to grasp the enemy's psychology, external propaganda also suffered from the more basic problem of an inadequate grasp of the English language. Broadcast messages, purportedly from prisoners, sometimes revealed their inauthenticity by simple grammatical errors or the inappropriate use of words. The English-language newspapers contained similar failings. In accordance with the Geneva Convention, prisoners at Keijo camp received censored copies of the *Nippon Times*, which provide unintended amusement for its readers. My father kept a list of mixed metaphors, which included 'The government knows which side of the fence its bread is buttered'; 'What they say cuts no ice: one swallow doesn't make a highball'; 'The Anglo-American policy of counting the chicks forgetful of the grim reaper.'

Historians have suggested that the root cause of Japanese propaganda's failure was that it was predominantly based on lies. Particularly culpable in this respect were the army and navy propaganda sections, responsible for war reporting. In the euphoria created by the remarkable early successes it was easy to believe that exaggeration would not be harmful. The numbers of enemy troops, battleships and planes wiped out by the Japanese were inflated beyond the limits of credibility. These exaggerations became unsustainable as the war increasingly turned against Japan. Nevertheless, the Japanese continued to report increasingly improbable victories. The battle of Attu in the Aleutian islands was the first 'honourable defeat' to be admitted. Defeats were thenceforth portrayed merely as temporary setbacks and strategic withdrawals. New concepts such as the 'sideways advance' came into play. War news as reported in the *Nippon Times* was, of course, continually analysed and discussed at the camps where newspapers were allowed, and the inconsistencies in the reports were easily identified. 'The Japs are rotten propagandists', wrote Lance-Bombardier Alan Toze in his diary at Keijo.

Internal Propaganda

As was the case with any belligerent nation during the twentieth century, which saw the birth of 'total warfare', it was necessary to mobilise the entire population in support of the war. A policy document issued by the Army Information Board in 1943 for the benefit of the media, 'Precautionary Measures Concerning Censorship of News of Prisoners of War', emphasises this: the principle aim of any reporting should be to 'raise the fighting spirit of the people'.[7] Initially at least, propaganda could build on strong support for the war at every level of Japanese society. The Japanese people had good reason to feel aggrieved with the West. Since its enforced emergence from isolation in the middle of the previous century, the country's ambitions to be treated as an equal of the West had met with a series of humiliating slights and rebuffs.

At Versailles in 1919, Japan's request for a declaration of racial equality to be incorporated into the covenant of the League of Nations had been vetoed by Australia; in 1921, the British government abruptly terminated the Anglo-Japanese alliance; in 1924, America introduced immigration laws which barred entry to Asiatics. More generally, Japan's attempts to emulate European imperialism by expanding their territories were regarded with great suspicion. The term 'Yellow Peril' was coined. Japan's early remarkable victories against American, Dutch and British forces were greeted with enthusiasm, and even euphoria. There was a palpable sense of revenge against past injustices.

'Precautionary Measures' also recommended obtaining accounts of Japanese martial prowess from the captives. This remained an integral part of POW propaganda throughout the conflict. As soon as Party B arrived at the Korean port of Fusan, they were met by reporters eager to hear details of Japanese military superiority in Malaya. Once they had arrived at Keijo, they were again interviewed by reporters anxious to hear about their defeat. Eighteen months later, one of the instructions in a questionnaire given to all prisoners in Korea was 'to list things admired about the Japanese army'. In its own small way, my father's account of the Malayan campaign could also have contributed.

Bushido: the Way of The Warrior

A central concept in all Japanese wartime propaganda was *Bushido*. Formerly the code of the samurai, it had become, in the words of the early twentieth century writer, Inazo Nitobe, the 'animating spirit of the Japanese people as a whole'.[8] He characterised *Bushido* as dual-natured: the masculine ferocity of the warrior, *Bushido* (武士道) was contrasted with the feminine quality of 'bushi no nasake'(武士 の 情け), the tenderness or compassion of the warrior for the defeated. Japan's prisoners benefited from this feminine quality. In his exposition of this idea, *Bushido, the Soul of Japan*, Itobe tells the reader, somewhat simperingly: 'If upright rectitude and stern justice were positively masculine, mercy had the gentleness and the persuasion of a feminine nature. Benevolence to the weak, the down-trodden and the vanquished, was ever extolled as peculiarly becoming to a samurai.' In a statement to the House of Commons, Foreign Secretary Anthony Eden offered his own definition of *Bushido*: 'a nauseating hypocrisy'.[9]

Recent research has suggested that *Bushido* was not in fact an ancient code, but dates back only as far as the 1880s, when it was concocted by various writers, journalists and intellectuals who were consciously creating an identity for Japan as it emerged from its isolation and engaged with the West and modernity.[10] There is little or no historical evidence that a group of warriors had ever adhered to a code that matched the nineteenth century invention in all its aspects. Some elements of *Bushido* may indeed have existed, but if so, it is also possible that they were honoured more in the breach than the observance.

The lack of a valid historical basis for *Bushido* meant that the concept was malleable, and by the 1930s it had evolved into a particularly harsh form, Imperial *Bushido*, mirroring the militarism of the period. Although *Bushido* generosity to the defeated was constantly cited to rebut charges of prisoner maltreatment, it was never conceptualised in terms of the feminine, nor was it ever practised. Another part of the *Bushido* code was that to surrender in battle was the ultimate disgrace. To do so brought shame not just on the prisoner himself, but also his family. It was this belief that coloured the attitude of the Japanese towards their captives.

Bushido was also used to explain the inevitability of Japanese victory. The Japanese could not claim physical, technological or intellectual superiority over their enemies, nor could they match the enemy in terms of manpower and resources. This was freely admitted. In its place, Japanese propaganda asserted the Japanese soldier's superior qualities and *Yamato-damashii*, his unique fighting spirit. *Bushido* was a manifestation of this. The uniqueness of the Japanese derived from their descent from the gods. Propaganda explained that the Japanese were uniquely pure (the word encompassing both a racial and moral sense). They were the *Yamato* race, *Yamato* being the ancient location where the Japanese had their origins. Japan also possessed a unique *kokutai* – usually translated as 'polity' – which reflected the *Bushido* principles of loyalty and patriotism, placing the nation before the individual, in contrast to the selfish individualism of the democratic system.

Despite the absence of a stable definition, we can say that a contemporary Japanese audience would have understood that *Bushido* encompassed the qualities of loyalty to one's comrades and country, self-sacrifice, pitilessness in battle, a refusal to undergo the terrible disgrace of surrender, and a severely austere manner of life. POWs are presented as the exact antithesis of the ideal. Propaganda constantly emphasised the terrible shame the prisoners had brought on themselves, their families, and their countries, by surrendering. Lacking Japan's *kokutai*, the POW selfishly put his family before his nation: he was luxury-loving (seen as an effeminate quality in Japanese propaganda), materialistic, and in awe of the Japanese soldier. Although it has been suggested that Japanese propaganda deliberately dehumanised the enemy, POWs are depicted with all-too-human failings.

Lack of comradeship was often cast in terms of resentment between different nationalities, mirroring a greater disunity between the Allied powers. Australians, for example, were offended by British snobbery and haughtiness, while Americans were unpopular with other prisoners who were envious of their higher wages and superior standard of living. The different nationalities were also assigned their own particular failings:

Americans were sentimental as well as money-minded, the British were decadent and luxury-loving, Australians were only interested in where their next drink was coming from.

There was, however, a fundamental contradiction in POW propaganda for the domestic audience. Prisoners of war were described as the beneficiaries of *Bushido* magnanimity, but at the same time, they were routinely humiliated in front of local populations. At a conference held in Tokyo in April 1942, Prime Minister Hideki Tojo had announced a policy that echoed Itagaki's earlier request for Allied POWs in Korea:

> Prisoner of War camps will be established not only in the south, but also in Japan, Korea, Manchuria and China. We will act so to create in the peoples of East Asia, who have for so many years been resigned to being no match for the white races, a feeling of trust towards Japan.[11]

As the policy played out across its territories, it was one of humiliating the prisoners in front of the local population.

As soon as they arrived in Korea, the men of Party B were paraded around the streets of Fusan. Their enfeebled, shabby appearance after a voyage in appalling conditions, was gleefully reported in Korea's national newspapers. Similar parades occurred across the Japanese territories. Americans captured at Corregidor in the Philippines fared even worse than Party B. On the last stage of their voyage to Manila they were transferred to amphibious landing craft and made to jump into Manila Bay and swim to the shore 200 feet away. They were then marched through the streets in their soaking clothes, on the verge of collapse.

Prisoners were also put to work doing menial jobs in public view. In Hong Kong, senior government officials were made to pull rickshaws; in Rangoon prisoners cleaned gutters with their bare hands, swept the streets and emptied dustbins. Prisoners in transit often formed the impression that the local population had been gathered to look at them. R. Keith Mitchell tells in his memoirs of how he was one of a party taken to a remote part of the northern island of Hokkaido. Their train stopped at a place called Yakumo: 'It was small, even for a village,' he remembered, and yet there was a crowd of people watching them as they went through the familiar routine of being lined up to be counted. 'Once again we had the general impression that the people had been ordered to be there. They showed no enthusiasm, a colourful but negative crowd although, in a place like this we must have been the first Allied prisoners they had ever seen.'[12] The locals would see groups of emaciated, malnourished men dressed in rags, as a means of instilling confidence in victory. Another British prisoner, John Fletcher Cooke, recalled how he was one of a group of men put to work at the dockyards on the island of Seto: 'Why, we asked ourselves, had a hundred or so POWs, already weakened by malnutrition and singularly lacking in the skills needed for shipbuilding, been brought thousands of miles to this little island?'[13] The answer lay in the fact that their labour was visible to the passing public.

Historian Aiko Utsumi has suggested that the starvation and general maltreatment of prisoners stemmed, at least in part, from this policy of public degradation. Due to lack of documentary evidence, it is impossible to determine its exact extent and nature.[14] But as propaganda, it was a failure. A Japanese newspaper reader would be told repeatedly about *Bushido* generosity but at the same time see – either in person or in newsreels – emaciated, sick, shabbily dressed prisoners bearing all the signs of neglect and maltreatment.

Propaganda for the Japanese Territories

The central propaganda theme for Japan's new territories and its two older established colonial possessions, Taiwan and Korea, was the creation of a 'Greater East Asian Co-Prosperity Sphere'. Japan presented itself as the liberator of the Asian people from white imperialism, and as the bearer of progress, modernity, prosperity and racial equality to its newly occupied territories. It emphasised the commonality of the Asian races and their geographical, cultural and racial ties. Working in partnership would be to their mutual benefit. As well as creating prosperity they would become a new power bloc to flex their muscles in world affairs. A representative example of Japanese propaganda for the 'New Order' can be quoted from a Filipino newspaper, *The Tribune*, purportedly the independent thoughts of a Filipino citizen:

> But today a new ideology has been brought to us in the form of the New Order, carried to these very shores by the victorious army of the Japanese Empire. Instead of devastation and

> death, murder and rape, famine and fear coming in the wake of the conquering invaders we found ourselves face to face with an army of friends who have come here to extend to us their good fellowship and fraternal equality and offer to the Philippines the privilege of membership in the Greater East Asia Co-Prosperity Sphere.
>
> We discovered that the New Order does not mean Imperialist Despotism or a regime under the iron hand of the Military War Lords, as we had been taught to believe by our Anglo-American friends. But instead it has opened up to us a new era where we would have equal opportunity to work and strive for the successful prosecution of the Co-Prosperity Sphere program. This New Order not only embodies many of the best feature of the democratic ideology, but in addition, also gives us the greatest good that man may aspire to; namely, racial equality.[15]

Japan reminded its newly acquired populations of how its own attempts to be accepted by the West as an equal had been rebuffed, and drew on a common resentment against white colonialists. To this end, propaganda pointedly contrasted the subjugated state of its prisoners with their previous arrogance. Both in Japan and its territories the conflict was termed the 'Greater East Asia War', the consequence of Western aggression. It was a war to liberate the Asian people from white oppression.

Although the construction of a Co-Prosperity Sphere was a genuine ambition, partnership and racial equality were never envisaged. The Japanese were convinced of their racial superiority over the other Asiatic peoples, whom they saw as backward. Whether the mythological explanations of superiority were believed by the Japanese as a whole or not, the greater wealth and technological achievements of the Japanese were seen as indisputable evidence of superiority.

The newspaper article describes working for the benefit of the Greater-East Asian Co-Prosperity Sphere as both an 'opportunity' and a 'privilege'. In other propaganda it is described more coercively as a 'responsibility'. In reality, working for the Co-Prosperity Sphere meant working for the Japanese war effort, to the detriment of the country's economy. The new territories were exploited as suppliers of manpower and material resources. Rather than prosperity, the Japanese brought food shortages, enemy bombs and economic disaster. Although a feature of propaganda for the newly conquered territories was to emphasise the new construction projects inaugurated by the Japanese, the most significant 'collaboration' was the construction of the Burma-Thai railway, which made use of forced Asian labour, known as *Romusha*. This group suffered a higher mortality rate than any other nationality working on the railway. Although the populations in the occupied territories were glad to see the back of white colonialists, the tentative and cautious welcome the Japanese had received was replaced by bitter and lasting hostility.[16] The various Japanese administrations exercised control over the people through repression and brutality rather than the fraternalism proclaimed by propaganda.

Japan's policy in its older colonies, Korea and Taiwan, was '*dokuashagi*', total assimilation. The idea was to turn the countries into extensions of Japan and to make its inhabitants think of themselves as Japanese. The process of 'Japanisation' began in Korea in 1937 and entailed the complete eradication of a separate Korean identity. The Korean population had to learn Japanese, take Japanese names, and think of themselves as Japanese. The historian Susan C. Townsend has justly observed that a great deal of Japan's cultural propaganda for its colonies was 'crass and insensitive', but her words are hardly adequate to describe the attempted erasure of all Korean culture.[17] The evidence of the Party B diaries is of an utterly brutal and exploitative wartime regime in both Korea and Manchuria. In the previous forty years, the Japanese had indeed wrought an industrial revolution in Korea, but for the benefit of the Japanese, not the Koreans, who mostly lived in dire poverty. In Korea and Manchuria, the presence of prisoners did not 'create confidence in a Japanese victory', as General Itagaki had confidently predicted, but instead created bonds of friendship between the local populations and the prisoners, united by their hatred of the Japanese. The prisoners often collaborated with the local population in small schemes of pilfering and deception, and the news of the outside world that the prisoners craved was often passed on by local contacts.

Propaganda for the World

The Allies soon became aware of Japanese atrocities, but until 1944 chose to keep any news of this from the public. There were good reasons for this: to publicise atrocities might hinder negotiations for providing relief to the POWs and lead to reprisals. Silence also helped sustain morale and avoid what Harold Satow, Head of the Prisoner of War Department at the Foreign Office, termed the 'fruitless worry and anxiety' that disclosures would provoke.[18] The resulting public outcry and call for action might also be damaging to the Allies' 'Germany first' policy. Instead of protesting publicly, the Allied governments lodged complaints with the Japanese government through their respective 'Protecting Powers', neutral countries that acted as intermediaries between the belligerent parties. By the end of 1943, America had made eighty-nine and Britain fifty-two. Many of the complaints were simply ignored. If the Japanese government did respond, it would either prevaricate, stating that that it would investigate the complaint when time permitted, or make a simple denial citing *Bushido* magnanimity to the defeated.

When accusations leaked into the public sphere, the Japanese responded vigorously. Early in 1942, news of atrocities committed on British fighting forces and civilians taken at Hong Kong leaked to the press, and the government's hand was forced into making a statement to the House of Commons, decrying Japanese mistreatment. Japanese media reports countered that this was simply a smokescreen to distract attention from the Allies' battlefield failures, and quoted a military spokesman as saying, 'British War Secretary Anthony Eden's purported revelations of Japanese atrocities at Hong Kong were like the howls of a third rate pugilist who drops and starts writhing on the floor claiming foul as soon as he begins losing'.[19]

When the war turned in the Allies' favour, this argument could no longer be used. Instead, the Japanese complained that Allied accusations were a smokescreen for their own atrocities against Axis POWs and Japanese internees. Specific examples were invented: in Normandy, the American troops used German POWs as human shields, binding them to the front of their tanks; in Burma, the Fourteenth Army under General Slim coerced the local population into hard labour, immediately killing any of the natives who refused to work for them.

The Japanese also invented counter narratives to explain the most notorious incidents, such as the fate of the prisoners on the transport ship, *Lisbon Maru*, which had been transporting 1,800 British prisoners from Hong Kong. In contravention of international law, the Japanese did not mark prisoner transport with a Red Cross to prevent enemy attack.

Like a significant number of prisoner transport ships, it was torpedoed by an American submarine.

At Keijo camp, Captain John Lever read an account of the incident in the *Nippon Times*, one of the two newspapers which were supplied to the prisoners. 'Emphasis was placed on the cowardly way the Yank submarine sank the ship full of prisoners of their own side.'[20] The newspaper reported that the Japanese sailors exhibited both *Bushido* boldness and compassion in their heroic attempts to rescue the prisoners from drowning, at risk of their own lives. In reality, when the ship started to sink the Japanese had battened down the hatches to block the prisoners' escape. Some of the men managed to get out by cutting the hatches' canvas covers, but the Japanese turned their machine guns on the escapees as they tried to swim to safety. Nevertheless, a number were rescued by Chinese fishing vessels and were able to tell their story.

Another staple argument was to remind the world of the exemplary treatment it had given prisoners during its war with Russia in 1904–5 and during the First World War. Japan had indeed treated its prisoners generously, but it was motivated by the ambition to be accepted by the West as an equal. That motive no longer applied. Japan also referred back to the First World War and 'the old story' of fabricated British atrocity stories against the Germans. The most successful propaganda, however, came from the show camps, especially the Party B camps, with the International Committee of the Red Cross inspectors unwittingly acted as a legitimating source for Japanese propaganda throughout the Pacific War. The mechanisms of this deception and its consequences are investigated in depth in the following chapters.

Chapter 2

Defeat and Capture

'The Army that was Betrayed' (extract) unknown member of Party B:

They smashed us back to Singapore
From Kedan to Collier Quay
And I that my tongue could utter
The thoughts that arise in me, So that I could tell the story,
Of the gallant stand that was made,
Of the army that was never beaten,
The army that was betrayed.

You'll hear of our lack of numbers
You'be told of our lack of planes
But you'll never be told in Malay grim hell
What we lacked was brains
It was in brains that they had us cooked
And not in their troops arrayed
Against the army that was never beaten
The army that was betrayed.

The enemy came at the dead of night
They attacked in swarms
Japanese HQ wanted quick results
Whilst ours wanted army Forms,
For it was Army forms we were given,
When for air support we prayed,
In the army that was never beaten,
The army that was betrayed.

And for the alibi unprepared
Just save your loudest jeers
For in the time we had to prepare defence

Which was well over two long years
But laughs won't help the dead and maimed
The heroic soldiers who paid
From the army that was never beaten
The army that was betrayed.

Lines from the poem *War* written by an anonymous member of Party B:

Stutter: Crackle, Stutter. Lewis guns and bren all around
Mortars, Sixteen inches, hold to swell the hellish sound.
Overhead the Nippon war planes, fill the skies with an angry roar,
Lie down you silly blighters, this is what the world calls war.

Men upon their bellies creeping, through the rubber and the palm,
Hungry, parched, barefoot, of sleeping, knowing not a moment calm,
Wading through swamps and marshes, clothing stiff with mud and gore,
On they go the helpless victims sacrificed to Gods of War

All around the men are lying, fathers, brothers, husbands and sons
Men are dead, and some are dying, victims all of bombs and guns.
Gasping, groaning, crying, moaning, is this nature in the raw?
Me it's simply, bloody murder, history books just call it war.

The fall of Singapore is regarded as the greatest disaster in British military history. Party B's senior officer, Colonel Mordaunt 'Bill' Elrington, would not have dissented from this verdict. He wrote two narratives of the Malayan campaign and fall of Singapore, one published in the early 1950s in the regimental magazine *The Lancashire Lad*, and another written immediately after the capitulation, with the injunction 'not to be published' on its title page. (The latter is held privately in America and I am grateful to the owner, Phil Karshis, for supplying me with a copy).[1] Elrington was a professional soldier with a distinguished career, and a family connection with the Loyal Regiment that stretched back to the eighteenth century. He had gone straight from Sandhurst to fight in the First World War, where he had won a Military Cross in Flanders. Later, he was awarded a DSO for his leadership and 'imperturbability under fire' in Malaya. After the war he received an OBE for his leadership in captivity. He had the firm respect, even admiration, of the men under his command, and it can be said without exaggeration that he was an exceptional officer. His accounts should therefore be treated with respect. He is critical of the army's performance in both narratives, but in the unpublished version he firmly points the finger of blame at the British High Command and allows full rein to his anger at their incompetence.

The 2nd Battalion Loyal Regiment, which he commanded, was a regular unit that had been sent to Singapore from Shanghai two years before hostilities broke out on garrison duties. They had the job of guarding the magnificent new naval base, completed at the cost of £60 million in 1938. He records how attempts to add to the island's defences were thwarted by both military and civilian bureaucracy, and by pervasive complacency. It was believed that it would be impossible for the Japanese to invade from the north of the Island, and that the naval base, located on the south, was impregnable.

Another member of Party B, Captain Arthur Cramsie, also recalled complacency:

> As far as the Japanese were concerned and although they were obviously in an aggressive mood, nobody took the threat from that quarter very seriously. We were repeatedly told and believed it, that the Singapore fortress with its Naval Base was impregnable and that if the little yellow men ever dared to show their noses in the area they could easily be seen off ... There was quite astonishing ignorance of Japan's military capability – this in spite of their extensive

> campaign in China and the extension of their control in Indo-China in 1941.
>
> British Army officers in those days considered it to be slightly 'not done' to be too efficient, and their cavalier attitude to their profession at times became exaggerated to the point of farce. It was quite seriously suggested Japanese soldiers and airmen could not use a bomb sight due to their slit eyes and that the physical make up of their bodies, with its long torso and short legs, would prevent a Japanese soldier from being able to endure active service for any length of time.[2]

Dr John Jesson, a medical officer attached to the 2nd battalion, was an intelligent and highly original man of strong opinions, both positive and negative. It is no exaggeration to say that he hero-worshipped Elrington, but he had equally strong opinions of an opposing nature about the average British officer stationed in Singapore. The army bureaucracy was filled, he wrote, with third-rate men who were happier circulating paper than making decisions. In the peacetime army, in his opinion, men were generally left with far too much free time on their hands. This engendered a heavy drinking culture. With a favourable exchange rate and ample free time to fill, the officers could over-indulge themselves in the restaurants, bars and night clubs of Singapore town. Too much drinking, eating and smoking, together with lack of physical exercise, meant that most of the men were nowhere near optimum fitness, and some were conspicuously overweight when they went into action. As a medical officer, Jesson's remarks can be regarded as authoritative.

Lance-Bombardier Alan Toze, a trainee architect, had enlisted with the 122nd Field Artillery Regiment. He was to become a close friend of Jesson in captivity. Toze's artillery battalion had arrived in Singapore some four months before the Japanese attack, but due to a logistics error, without its artillery. His diaries and other writings suggest an organisation which was incompetent as well as complacent:

> With the usual incredible muddle, our twenty-four 4.5-inch howitzers, limbers, tugs and transport were on another ship, which did not arrive for many weeks. Our Senior officer, Colonel Dyson, must have been at his wits' end trying to

> think of something fresh for us to do every day … The rate of exchange was so good, even for junior NCOs like myself, that we were able to enjoy quite a good lifestyle, using the cheap taxis, restaurants and entertainments, in Singapore city or Johore Bahru. As far as I can recall there was no sign of any approaching troubles, no civil defence measures and life seemed to be relaxed and going on in a peaceful manner at all levels of society. Judging by the numbers of Japanese shops, particularly barbers', there can have been no defence secrets they did not know.[3]

Even after the Japanese had begun their invaded in the north of Malaya on 8 December 1941, complacency prevailed at Gillman Barracks, the Loyals' headquarters in Singapore. Lance Bombardier Eric Wallwork wrote at the end of the year: 'Despite the news from up-country being bad, that did not prevent us from having a very good Christmas dinner, and all in all a pretty good time considering there was a war on.' One of the justifiable complaints the men were to make in captivity was that too little use had been made of them, a regular battalion that had been in Singapore for two years. They were not called into action until a month after the Japanese invasion. Meanwhile, other troops involved in the fighting were often inexperienced and under-trained.

Complacency and the priority given to the war in Europe led to insufficient weapons and equipment, despite the pleas of the Commander in Chief in Malaya, Lieutenant General Arthur Percival. Most notably his forces lacked tanks, and the elderly Brewster Buffalo planes, which tended to overheat in tropical climates, were no match for the Japanese Navy's Zero fighters. Their names alone offer an idea as to which was technologically superior. The Japanese immediately established air ascendancy, wreaking havoc on the poorly sited British airfields and aircraft during the first days of the attack. Air supremacy enabled their torpedo bombers to destroy the battleship *Prince of Wales* and battlecruiser *Repulse*, despatched to rescue the situation. Churchill described the news of their sinking as the greatest single shock he received during the entire war.

The Japanese had honed their fighting skills in China, and astonished their enemy by the dynamism and ferocity of their attack. They were far fitter and better trained than their opponents. The British had not believed it was possible for the Japanese to mount an attack through the jungles of Malaya, and consequently their men had received little or no training in jungle warfare. One of the Australians in Party B, Alec Bourne, had been given no more than six weeks' military training of any form whatsoever before being shipped off to Singapore. Alex James, a lieutenant in the Indian Army who had attached himself to Party B, wrote of his own men's lack of experience. Only recently recruited, some of them were under 18 years of age, and most had never seen a tank before.[4]

The Japanese forces deployed innovative tactics and displayed a manoeuvrability which their enemy had not bargained for. As Captain John Jesson later wrote bitterly, the British forces were unable to respond to tactics and methods that did not match those of the First World War, as taught at Sandhurst in the 1930s.[5] Certainly, the curriculum at Sandhurst would not have included the deployment of elephants to help offload tanks, nor the tactic of commandeering bicycles to advance swiftly along the jungle paths. The Japanese had also adapted their amphibious craft to make landings at locations on the shoreline which British Intelligence had determined were inaccessible by water. Another innovation was to bring soapboxes to stand on while machine-gunning the enemy, compensating for the Japanese fighting man's comparative lack of height.

In his unpublished account, Elrington attacked the poor leadership and tactical ineptitude of High Command unreservedly:

> Singapore was a disgrace to British arms which it is not easily explained away or readily excused. From lack of a military plan may be traced most of the evils that beset us in this disastrous story of military incompetence. It is true, too, that though regimental commanders in many cases did excellent work there was a noticeable lack of leadership from above ... To anyone acquainted with the art of war whose training was based on acceptable principles it is well-nigh impossible to understand why obvious courses were not followed and simple plans adhered to, instead of muddled and intricate manoeuvres, generally involving an immense amount of detailed work

by the staff and the paralysing dispersion of fighting formations.

In particular, Percival's decision to 'contest every bend in the road' seemed utterly nonsensical to Elrington. Summing up his battalion's part in the disaster he described it as:

> A tale of continuous retreat over four hundred miles of territory, of false hopes, unfulfilled promises, and of muddle unparalleled, though relieved here and there with flashes of individual heroism, gallantry and devotion to duty. The Loyal Regiment, by reason of its hard work and fighting achievements in this brief campaign has no cause to bow its head in shame at the general surrender.

It was not until 8 January 1942 that the Loyals were ordered to leave their headquarters in Singapore, Gillman Barracks, and go 400 miles up country to defend the town of Segamat. Due to what Elrington described as the 'appalling incompetence' of those who arranged their transport up the line, their journey took over twice as long as it should have. What happened next typified their experience as a whole. Eric Wallwork wrote:

> We were told our job at Segamat was to defend it to the last man and the last round, but as we later experienced, our Brigade and Divisional Commanders seemed to change their minds (from another rank's point of view) far too often, for our stay at Segamat was too short to defend it with our first round, saying nothing of the last.

The same pattern of aborted plans and poor communication was repeated during the brief few weeks that the Loyals were in action. They would be ordered to a position, but then when they arrived there, the plan would have been cancelled, or their presence would be required at another location, or the unit they were supposed to meet at the rendezvous was absent. The battalion suffered huge casualties, and lost nearly half its strength, either missing, wounded or killed. In the confusion, the Loyals were fired on by their own side, and on Singapore

Island they had their flank exposed by a supporting unit that simply withdrew from its position en masse when the stress of attack became too much for them. A great deal has been written about deserters and the extent to which they contributed to the defeat, but it is significant that Elrington withheld any blame from these men. He saw such behaviour as the inevitable consequence of placing 'untried and untested' troops in vulnerable positions. Without sufficient weapons, support or competent leadership, it was inevitable that the men's morale would eventually collapse. The fault lay with senior command.[6]

Elrington described their part in the campaign simply as one of a retreat of over 400 miles from the Segamat to Singapore Island. On 14 February, the men found themselves back at Gillman Barracks, less than five weeks after they had left it to go into action. The final order Elrington received was to fight to the last man and the last bullet: 'I shook hands with the officers and got on with it.' The noise inside the barracks as it was bombed and fired on by artillery was astonishing. Elrington wrote of the 'zip-zipping and phut-phut of bullets from all angles, the hiss and scream of shells, blasting of brick and cracking cement' with cracks and holes appearing in the walls and ceilings. But the men held their nerve while the barracks literally collapsed around their ears. The Second-in-command, Major Watkins, impressed my father with his sangfroid when a bomb came close to killing them both:

> A bomb from the air landed in the middle of the gym, whose floor was a smooth parquet and the pride of the second-in-command. He was silent for a second viewing this destruction through a thick cloud of dust: 'Good God, to think of all the time and bloody trouble I spent trying to stop the men spoiling that blasted floor with their cigarette ends and hobnails.[7]

At that point, death seemed the most probable outcome. Senior medical officer Major Conrad Rigby stopped bothering to take cover as he went to the aid of the wounded. His death seemed inevitable and seeking cover was a waste of his time. The Loyals stood their ground and returned fire with such ferocity that after the surrender a Japanese commander congratulated Elrington, as one professional to another, on the fight his men had put up. The last shots in the campaign were in fact fired by the

Loyals under the indefatigable leadership of their senior officer. But in the evening of 15 February 1942, the message came through to lay down their arms and surrender.

Japanese prisoner of war propaganda began at the very moment of surrender. Lieutenant General Arthur Percival, commander in chief of the defeated British forces, was ordered to report to the Ford Motor factory at Bukit Timah, accompanied by men carrying a Union Jack and the white flag of surrender. As he approached the factory, Japanese photographers, cameramen and war artists recorded the scene. The potency of the image as propaganda is proved by its enduring familiarity: it has become emblematic not just of the fall of Singapore but of the demise of the British Empire in the Far East. As well as being photographed and filmed, the surrender party was also rendered in water colours with various additions to emphasise the ignominy of the defeat. In one adaptation the smouldering ruins of Singapore town are visible in the background. As part of its campaign to turn India against the British, posters were distributed with the derisive caption in English and Urdu 'How Glorious Retreats End'. The image of defeat infuriated Churchill, who apparently never forgave Percival for allowing himself to be photographed with a white flag.

Chapter 3

Party B at Changi

It was not until two days after the surrender that the defeated soldiers were rounded up and, to their relief, discovered that no one was to be killed, at least for the moment. During the fighting, men who had fallen into the hands of the enemy had been machine-gunned, burned alive or beaten to death. Lance Corporal Busby had made a near-miraculous escape after he and a party of seven other Loyals had fallen into Japanese hands. (He lived to report that his comrades had been machine-gunned as he escaped from the party into the jungle.)

The prisoners were marched to their new home, Changi, a large complex of buildings recently constructed at great expense by the British as their base in Singapore. The Japanese exploited the propaganda opportunities the march offered: members of the local population were made to gather at various points along their route, waving Japanese flags. The Rising Sun was also flown from buildings which, until just a few days earlier, had displayed the Union Jack. A few days later the prisoners themselves would be made to line the streets of Singapore as a cavalcade of expensive modern cars – until very recently for the exclusive use of senior British officials – drove slowly past, with newly attached Japanese pennants and flags gently fluttering in the breeze. In the front of the cars were senior Japanese officers sitting next to their chauffeurs; in the rear were Japanese cameramen and photographers capturing this moment of Japanese glory and British humiliation. The scenes immediately appeared in newsreels and later in a Japanese feature documentary, *Mare Senki Shingeki No Kiroku.* Prisoners, including officers, are also seen clearing up the damage done to Singapore by Japanese bombs.

More photographs were taken on the morning after Party B's arrival at Changi. The prisoners – some 50,000 at that moment – were assembled on the vast parade ground. The spectacle rubbed salt into the men's wounds. 'Where were all these men when the fighting was taking place?' thought

Eric Wallwork.[1] 'Goodness knows where they were when the fighting was taking place, for anyone would have thought that there were only a couple or so battalions on the island before the capitulation.' Many had in fact deserted. Captain Jesson shared Wallwork's dismay: 'It was rather like fool's mate in chess, where the game ends at the fifth move due to a faulty opening by the loser, who finds himself still possessing a strong, well-equipped force.'[2] Photographs of the assembled prisoners appeared in Japanese newspapers. An image of the men sitting huddled together in long rows which seem to stretch back endlessly into a far horizon was accompanied in one newspaper with the caption: 'A pathetic spectacle of complete shamelessness'.[3] Japan's visual propaganda was at least as good as anything the West could produce.

These first newspaper reports repeatedly referenced the ideology of *Bushido*, both in the kind treatment the prisoners were receiving, and by the absence of *Bushido* in the captured men, who lacked any sense of shame:

> Perhaps the prisoners' dictionaries contain no such sayings as 'men should die for the nation's cause' or 'it is most dishonourable for a samurai to be taken prisoner' which every Japanese soldier keeps in mind. Their state of mind which is quite indifferent to their own shameful condition, seems to provide the reason for their defeat.

The British prisoners, both officers and other ranks, are depicted somewhat along the lines of the drones of P.G. Wodehouse's stories: empty-headed, feckless and even carefree, despite their circumstances. They are preoccupied by trivialities: some of them have brought their pet dogs along with them, others strum jazz tunes on their banjos. One reporter related the reactions of a visiting Japanese official:

> Apart from the kindness of the Japanese authorities the thing which interested and at the same time baffled him the most was the nonchalant, happy-go-lucky, devil-may-care attitude of these soldiers who are actually proud of being prisoners. He was appalled by their lack of real comradeship and patriotism. These Tommies seem far more at home playing than fighting.

Colonel Elrington was later to write that the Japanese were indeed genuinely astonished by the prisoners' cheerfulness in the circumstances. The idea of remaining cheerful as an expression of indomitability – 'they can't stop us from smiling' – was entirely alien to the Japanese way of thinking.

An effeminate love of luxury is also referenced in the reports. The victorious commander-in-chief of the Malayan campaign, General Yamashita, spared time to give an interview:

> There are over 200,000 prisoners of war, but by the generosity of Japanese *Bushido* spirit, each and every one of them is spending a carefree life without the slightest inconvenience, though, of course, it is hardly possible to supply them with high-priced perfumes and hair-oils so they can spend nearly an hour on 'make-up'.

Photographs of the prisoners were reproduced on the same page as Yamashita's interview with the following commentary:

> The prisoners are enjoying a happy life, playing water-polo in the warm waters and strumming on guitars and singing in chorus under the coconut palms in the cool of the evening. Seen in the pictures above are some of the 73,000 war captives taken in the Malay campaign, and a glance at the happy looks on their faces corroborates General Yamashita's statement.

The same carelessness over numbers can be found in all Japanese war reporting. The newspaper also carried a brief item on the same page from the Berlin correspondent of the news agency, *Domei.* It implicitly makes the contrast about fighting spirit, proclaiming:

> **Reich finds Reason for Japan's Power, Germans admit that 'Spiritual strength is at bottom of victories'**
> For the last two and a half months not just Germany but all of Europe has been struggling to explain the astonishing series of Japanese victories on land and sea and air.
>
> The answer lay in the *Bushido* spirit of attack, which was now being studied intensively by the Germans.

Although these reports would have been well-received by a Japanese audience at the time, they were poor propaganda, as they would make the task of explaining away subsequent Allied successes more difficult. Readers who remembered accounts of the enemy living in idleness and comfort might also wonder why they had been allowed to do so when they themselves were enduring ever-increasing privations caused by the war. A reversal of strategy was to appear in 1943's 'Precautionary Measures': 'Accounts of prisoners being too well treated' were henceforth forbidden, along with accounts of them being badly treated.

There were perhaps some aspects of the first weeks at Changi which may have offered stimulus to a propagandist's imagination in creating a vision of leisured ease. Overwhelmed by the unexpectedly large number of men captured, the Japanese initially left the administration of the camp to the British High Command, while they busied themselves with rounding up and executing the thousands of Chinese in Singapore who were suspected of harbouring hostility towards the new regime. As a means of raising morale and keeping the men occupied, a wide range of educational and recreational opportunities were organised. There were football and cricket matches, and as well as communal sing-songs the prisoners could go to hear bands and choral groups at the open-air theatre, which also put on a new theatrical production every month. For the first few weeks, there was no wire around the perimeter of the camp, and prisoners were able to go down to the sea for a swim every day, if not to play water polo.

But all these events were merely temporary distractions from a nightmarish reality. Alex James recalled a swimming trip:

> One morning, several of us were bathing and were surprised to hear the sound of intense machine gun and Tommy gun fire coming from behind a clump of bushes, not a hundred yards away. On approaching to investigate we were shooed off in no uncertain manner by Japanese with rifles levelled at us.[4]

The next day, men were permitted to return to the same location as a burial party. They discovered over a hundred Chinese lying dead on the beach, their hands tied behind their backs.

It was at Changi that the men were first introduced to the evils of their lives that would torment them over the next three-and-a-half years. Disease and sickness would become constants in their lives. Many had come into the camp with untreated wounds from the fighting, and soon after their arrival a dysentery epidemic broke out. The men also suffered from the diseases caused by vitamin deficiency: beriberi, scurvy and pellagra. The hospital building had been bombed, and as the one Canadian in Party B, Doctor Harry Morris, recorded: 'There was no lighting, no arrangements for cooking, washing, laundry or disposal of excreta.'[5] It would be five months before the hospital had running water and electricity.

Along with illness came 'hunger, real hunger, that type that gnaws at your belly' as Elrington put it. The men's meals consisted mainly of small portions of rice, 'invariably contaminated with weevils and mealworms'. according to an unnamed officer, who added: 'As an indication of the state of affairs, it is worth mentioning that all dogs and cats in the vicinity disappeared and several units ordered parties to collect snails from the local hedges'.

Changi also gave the men their first taste of what would become other constant features of their lives: humiliation and violence. The world was turned upside down for Colonel Elrington when Sikh soldiers took up new roles as camp guards. According to Alex James, many of the Sikhs were formerly civilians, but a good number had turned sides, thereby avoiding the particularly cruel treatment the Japanese meted out to Indian POWs. The prisoners were forced to salute their former comrades, and if they were slow to do so, might receive a powerful slap round the face or kick on the shin from one of these 'bearded beauties', as Elrington called them.

The men were naturally traumatised by the slaughter they had witnessed, and felt all the bitterness and rancour that defeat brings. This manifested itself in fierce resentment among the other ranks at the behaviour of the officers and the army administration generally, both before and during the campaign. The British officers continued to insist on their privileges, to the disgust of their men. They allowed themselves better accommodation and food, and even required batmen to do chores for them. By contrast, the Australian officers were on first name terms with their men, and shared the same meals and accommodation.

The resentment felt by the other ranks is expressed by an anonymous member of Party B in 'The Ballad of Changi'.[6]

> The Officers lived in married quarters, row after row,
> They had to have the best, for they were gentlemen you know
> The Troops lived in barracks, wherever they could squeeze
> They were so crowded out they hardly had room to sneeze
> The Officers had batmen to look after them day and night
> To do their washing, clean their rooms, and put their kit right
> Fatigue parties dug their gardens, their seeds they did sow
> The officers just sat back and watched the flowers grow
>
> Men should help each other in adversity
> Sharing out tasks and doing them with equality
> But the Officers in Changi made the men do all the work
> They would not soil their hands, all labours they did shirk

Among my wartime father's papers are notes taken at a court martial held at the camp. The defendant had been a member of a working party assembled for a day's labour. On the officer's command to march off, he had muttered the words 'fuck off'. Unfortunately, his response had not been inaudible to the officer who issued the command. He was found guilty as charged but the punishment he received is not recorded. Many of the men were infuriated by the officers issuing punishments and commands as if they were still free men. There were many cases of men refusing orders, and several larger incidents that were classified as mutiny. A lot of the other ranks felt that now they were all prisoners, they shared the same status and that distinctions of rank should be abandoned. Elrington admitted that it was sometimes a difficult job to uphold discipline over the ensuing years of captivity, but argued that discipline was essential, as it was the 'cement' that held the men together. Although he and his officers succeeded in keeping order, in some camps it would break down entirely. One of Elrington's men, Private Arthur Christie, wrote later that the Americans and Australians were able to maintain discipline without the need for the parade ground 'bullshit' that some of the British officers insisted on maintaining. His view was widely shared. Although the Japanese would deliberately attempt to set men against officers in other camps, it can be suggested that the Japanese missed a profitable propaganda target at Changi.

After the first few months of its existence, Changi's function would change. There would be no further propaganda visits, and the camp would become essentially a holding area for a reservoir of labour that could be deployed in various parts of the Japanese empire. Many of the men would be sent to work on the Burma–Thai railway; others would construct airfields or work in particularly appalling conditions in the copper and tin mines of Taiwan and Japan.

Exactly six months after the men's arrival at Changi, Party B was formed. Volunteers for Japan, rather than Korea, were asked for. Colonel Elrington consulted his officers, who were in favour of a move. They would escape the tropical climate, and it would allow the battalion to stay intact as a unit. With rations becoming ever more inadequate, there was little to keep them at Changi. Elrington conferred with Colonel Dyson, commanding officer of the 122nd Field Artillery Regiment, and they decided to volunteer their units together. The 122nd had arrived in Singapore several months before the Japanese invasion, and friendships had been formed between the two groups of men. Other prisoners – those of an adventurous disposition like Alex James, or those who simply wanted a change – were permitted to join them. In retrospect it proved to be a good decision, as it meant that they avoided the drafts later that year to Burma and Thailand to work on the railway. But it was a decision that would cost Colonel Dyson his life. The conditions on the ship that took them to Korea would kill him and fifteen other men.

Chapter 4

The Voyage of the *Fukkai Maru*

'We were treated like animals, with animals as our keepers'.
Lieutenant A.F. Douglas Allison

On the morning of 14 August 1942, parties A and B were assembled outside the camp on Artillery Square to be given a brief medical examination. There were two tests: one involved a jab in the ear with a needle; the other, in Colonel Elrington's words, was 'a jab with a glass rod up the fundamental orifice' to check against intestinal infection. The tests were carried out in full public view in strict order of rank. The generals were thus the first to bare their bottoms. Elrington wrote that their faces 'became nearly as red as their hat bands'. The procedure was enacted publicly on other departing parties, and prisoners later formed the opinion that its intention, at least in part, was to humiliate the prisoners. Certainly, the passing public enjoyed such scenes. The fact that the men of Parties A and B were taken from Artillery Square to Keppel harbour without waiting for the results of the tests might also be seen as evidence.

At the harbour the men underwent a fumigation procedure on board the *Elisinor Maru.* This involved bathing in warm water that had been treated with various chemicals, and was actually a moment of enjoyment. It was their first hot bath in over six months. Afterwards, the two parties were given tea and led to a location at the water's edge between two burnt-out warehouses. Here they sat down and waited. It was an afternoon that was indelibly imprinted in my father's memory. He spent it staring out to sea, wondering what lay beyond the horizon, both literally and figuratively. Uncertainty imposed its own stresses on the prisoners. As Elrington wrote: 'This state of ignorance about the future is a continual one in a prisoner's life and though after a time he gets used to it he cannot avoid the effect on his outlook.' The prisoners held no illusions as to what their captors were capable of.

It was not until the early evening that their transport ship, the *Fukkai Maru*, came alongside. One of the prisoners, Lieutenant A.F. Douglas Allison, later wrote a published account of their six-week voyage.[1] He describes the ship as a 'dirty, rust-streaked 3,800-ton run-down cargo vessel'. Elrington was horrified: 'No, this could not be the ship, not our ship! It was little more than a tug!' The men were pushed and shoved aboard without any regard for rank and one of the senior officers, Brigadier Williams, fell between the wharf and the ship's side into the water. He would have been disappointed had he known of his men's reaction to his mishap.

The ship carried a cargo of 5,000 tons of bauxite in its lower holds. There were four upper holds, each measuring approximately 15 yards square, which were to be the prisoners' accommodation for the next six weeks. Platforms had been constructed around the sides of the holds to squeeze in as many men as possible. Each platform was eleven feet wide and was designed to house two rows of men lying feet to head, one row of heads against the ship's side, the other overlooking the central space. The men had a personal space just six feet two inches long to fit themselves and their personal belongings into. Douglas Allison wrote:

> The congestion was similar to the underground at rush hour. The heat and atmosphere were infinitely worse ... Those holds resembled dungeons, gloomy and airless, with a temperature that hovered permanently around one hundred degrees Fahrenheit ... The accommodation might have been sufficient for Japanese troops about five feet in height, but tall Europeans like ourselves suffered agonies of cramp. Being over six feet myself I had to pass the whole six weeks' voyage curled up like a snake.[2]

Elrington remembered: 'As nearly as possible, we became inanimate objects that took in rice twice daily, frequent mugs of Japanese tea, hot and weak and a little air occasionally.'[3]

The guards had tried to cram both parties into the one ship, but the senior British officers resisted. After prolonged argument from Party A, their group of 400 was allowed off the boat to spend the night sleeping on the harbour. The remaining men had to wait in a nightmarishly claustrophobic environment for three days before setting sail, sharing their accommodation with rats, lice, flies and various other unknown creatures. Many later recalled the voyage as the worst period of their captivity. There were just twelve latrines for the 1,000 men, and no washing facilities, apart from a communal hosing down with salt water on deck every evening. They were allowed two one-hour breaks on the deck per day. The smell in the holds soon became almost unbearable.

The men's rations were even more inadequate than the diet at Changi. There were two meals a day, at 9 am and 5 pm. Both consisted of a very thin stew and a small portion of rice. The stew came from British meat and vegetable (M&V) tins. Initially, each man's ration was one-tenth of a tin but this was later reduced to one-twentieth. The ship's purser – 'a drunken swine' according to Elrington – held back a significant proportion of the rations intended for the prisoners so that he could make himself a tidy profit by selling it on. Water was strictly rationed, but there was a regular supply of hot tea, although it carried the tang of the rusty pipes through which the hot water flowed.

After three weeks at sea the ship harboured at Takao in Formosa (Taiwan) to unload the bauxite. By this stage, a number of the men were suffering from dysentery, and the worst cases were taken to hospital. There were also two cases of diphtheria. About half the men were suffering from diseases caused by vitamin deficiency, particularly scurvy and beriberi. For the next three years beriberi, caused by a lack of thiamine (vitamin B1), would be a continual scourge of their lives.

All of the men suffered from it to a greater or lesser degree at some point in their captivity. 'Wet' beriberi affects the heart and circulatory system and can cause heart failure. 'Dry' beriberi causes damage to the peripheral nerves. Mental symptoms include confusion and irritability; its most common physical symptoms are tingling sensations in the hands and feet, akin to minor electric shocks. This particular symptom was christened 'happy feet' or 'electric feet' by the Far Eastern prisoners. Beriberi also made the skin unbearably itchy, particularly the scrotum, hence the term 'Changi balls'. Later in their captivity, some of the party would suffer from one of its most extreme symptoms, paralysis. Douglas Allison described the first symptoms of the disease on board the *Fukkai Maru*: 'Accompanied by a feeling of complete inertia, it took the form of a spongy swelling of the legs. Slight pressure with the thumb around the ankles would leave a small hollow in the flesh, and in very bad cases the flesh could be kneaded like dough'. The men also suffered from vitamin A deficiency, which affected their eyesight, causing blurred vision or even blindness. Although it appears that the cases of complete loss of vision reported by Party B were temporary, in other Japanese camps, men went blind permanently.

The stop at Takao provided a brief respite. The men spent two weeks unloading and taking on cargo, and were able to commit small acts of sabotage as they went about their work. Then the ship embarked on the final leg of its journey to the port of Fusan in the south of Korea. They were hit by a storm and sea-sickness became an additional problem. There was also food poisoning caused by pork that had gone off. Many of the men, particularly those suffering from dysentery and diarrhoea, eventually became too weak to drag themselves to the latrines.

On arrival in Korea, the men were instructed to write an essay: 'Your Opinion of the voyage to Chosen'. The Loyals' medical officer, Captain Jesson, was somehow able to retain a draft of his essay, which is valuable as a contemporary account of conditions by a medical professional:

> It is impossible to discuss on one page many of the things that struck me during the six weeks, and as a doctor I feel that I should confine myself to medical matters; I regret that my comments must consist of criticism. During our six months at Singapore, a widespread outbreak of dysentery caused considerable sickness and many deaths, and so we were particularly careful to exclude all possible causes of diseases from the party. As we underwent two careful medical examinations and a thorough disinfection before leaving, it seemed that due regard was to be paid to our health, and I was therefore dumbfounded when we embarked upon the *Fukkai Maru*. I noticed with apprehension the absence of any sick bay or isolation space, the twelve latrines of most primitive type for a thousand men, and the overcrowded conditions in the holds, all circumstances ideal for the spread of an epidemic.... The eventual result was of course inevitable and we reached Chosen [Korea] with a considerable number of dysentery cases and severe diarrhoea; more came to light as we arrived in camp. These sick men had to endure many hardships due to their

> cramped ill-ventilated accommodation, the lack of bedpans and washing facilities and the unsuitable diet, and some were so ill on disembarkation that it is no wonder that they subsequently died. It can only be regarded as a most lucky chance that the diphtheria which started at Takao [in Taiwan] did not lead to a further disaster onboard, though many cases have occurred since. A lot of skin trouble resulted from the totally inadequate ablution arrangements.[4]

Bad as they were, conditions on the *Fukkai Maru* were in fact significantly better than those on other 'Hellships', as they became known. The death toll of sixteen out of a thousand men was unusually low.

Chapter 5
Fusan Victory Parade

> 'Behold the vivid sight of the defeated and shabby-looking American and British barbarians!'
>
> *Keijo Nippo* 25 September 1942

Forty-one days after leaving Singapore, the prisoners at last arrived at the port of Fusan on the southern tip of Korea, early in the morning of Friday, 22 September 1942. They were weak through lack of food and sleep as well as illness. 'As the voyage neared the port of Fusan,' Elrington remembered, 'some of the men had entered a state of impassivity where nothing registered.' A few of the very sickest – those suffering from dysentery, enteritis and 'blue typhus' – were immediately taken to Fusan hospital. The less urgent cases, including Lance Bombardier Alan Toze, were driven away in an open lorry: 'We were dumped in a wooden hut with six blankets apiece and no medical attention, or medicine at all. Food was an improvement but quite unsuitable, being always vegetable stews. Hot water was the only drink available for days.'[1] As soon as they were well enough, the men were made to write another essay, 'Your opinion of Japan and the Japanese people'.

The rest of the prisoners remained onboard another two days, and by the evening of the second day were, in Elrington's words, 'fretting themselves silly'. But the Japanese had scheduled their parade through the streets to coincide with *Chusoek*, a major Korean festival marking the autumn equinox, which fell on the Sunday after their arrival. Korea's sole remaining Korean language newspaper, the *Maeil Sinbo*, reported on the preparations for the event and the city's keen expectation:

> On this day of excitement, the port of Fusan was completely ready to receive the prisoners of war, and everywhere you went in the city there were stories about them. At the Arai Ryokan guest house in front of the station, where Colonel

> Atsuchi of the Korean military press office was stationed, groups of newspaper reporters, photo crews, and news cameramen came and went, busy communicating with each other so that the exciting news of the arrival of the prisoners of war could be communicated behind the front lines. The port of Fusan was filled with the excitement of the century.[2]

Advance notice of the route of the victory parade was also given:

> At midday on the 24th the POWs will land at Fusan wharf and then eat lunch, and after that will march through Fusan's downtown, passing through the large streets Choryang-Jeong and Yeong-Jeong, and will again come to Fusan Station, pass in front of the Post Office and at 1pm will reach Number 1 and Number 7 Elementary schools ….
>
> **Caution**
> Do not talk to POWs or adopt a kind attitude toward them.
> Do not take or give any objects to the POWs.
> If you discover a POW who has escaped, immediately report them to authorities, military police, or police.
> Do not aid POWs in escape or hide them.

Later that morning, the prisoners slowly filed down the gangplanks. On the dock, *Kempeitai* officers (the Japanese military police, often referred to as Japan's Gestapo) searched them and confiscated gold rings, packs of cards and cameras. Before the search, some of the prisoners had wisely jettisoned items they had managed to smuggle onboard, including a dagger and a revolver. Contrary to the timetable given in the newspapers, the prisoners did not eat lunch. Instead, they watched the Japanese and Korean guards eating lunch. Elrington made a particular point of this; it was torture for the ravenously hungry men to see food being consumed by others. When their captors had finished eating, the prisoners were lined up in columns, four abreast, and told that they would now march to the railway station. Their route took them through the business and shopping centres, but when they reached the outskirts of the town they were wheeled back round to return to the docks. In all, they marched for three-and-a-half hours, with a short break allowed at a school playground. On their journey they were flanked by journalists, photographers, Korean guards, military police and a selection of Japanese officers on horseback. Lieutenant William Frazer AIF recorded how one of them 'appeared to derive great enjoyment from stepping his horse almost onto the heels of the rear men and having the animal snort and slaver over their shoulders'.[3] This was Major Okuda, commandant of Jinsen camp, later to be christened 'the Mad Major'. In an interview he gave to the *Maeil Sinbo*, he explained that he had grown impatient with the prisoners' 'dawdling':

> The POWs' movements are generally not very quick. Something that the Japanese Army can carry out in nine minutes takes as long as thirty minutes, which is truly pitiful. They pester us with 'Give me cigarettes' or 'Give me apples and beef', and having already asked for rice naturally they have diarrhoea, and they are greedy.[4]

It seemed to the men as if the entire city had turned out to watch them. The crowds stood four to five deep on the pavement, dressed in their national costumes for the festival. Captain Ivor Thomas remembered feeling a sense of utter humiliation as the Koreans stared at them.[5] Parading in full kit in the heat of the day, several of the men fainted and were dumped onto the back of a lorry. No doubt others in Party B felt his sense of humiliation, but they were surprised by the faces of the crowd, which were in the main expressionless. There was a little jeering from Japanese civilians, and when they stopped for a rest at a school playground they were spat at by a group of children. But for the most part the crowd seemed almost indifferent to the parade, although the tartan kilts of the Highlanders and the slouch hats of the AIF were of interest. In reality, the prisoners were at least as interested in the crowd as the crowd in them. The diarists recorded how the women wore pink, sky-blue and magenta dresses, while the men were immaculately dressed in white and black. The older men wore their country's miniature top hats made of horsehair with a ribbon tied under the chin, and traditional long white jackets and voluminous white trousers. There were also Japanese women and children among the crowd, distinctive in their brightly-coloured kimonos.

The Fusan parade was deemed a great success by the Chief of Staff of the Korean army, Hijura Ibara, who sent a report to other military leaders, 'Reactions among the Public following Internment of British POW's'.[6] He was of the opinion that the victory march had made a real impression upon both the Korean and Japanese bystanders. 'Many of them sneered at the disgraceful behaviour and utter indifference of the British displayed before their very eyes by the prisoners and thought it quite natural that an army so lacking in patriotism should be defeated by the Imperial Army.' The report concluded confidently: 'As the effect of propaganda gradually tells upon them when the prisoners are put to labour, we may expect much greater results which will contribute greatly to ruling Korea'.

The problem with Ibara's report as a historical document is that it was written several weeks before the prisoners had actually arrived in Korea. It is dated 13 August, and was received by the Vice Minister of War, Hyotaro Kimura on 22 August. Further copies landed on various desks at the War Ministry at the end of that month. There is nothing in the report to pin the remarks to the actual march; there is no mention, for example, of men fainting, or of the kilts which attracted the interest of the crowd. It is valuable instead as a record of Japanese propaganda aims, and there is a close correlation between its contents and the newspaper reports of the event.

Ibara appended a long list of onlookers' comments for use by his colleagues. As well as the reactions from Korean spectators, there were also comments from a variety of nationalities. A White Russian interpreted the prisoners' whistling as a sign of indifference: 'They whistle and don't seem to care a bit. It seems that being a prisoner of war is no disgrace to them. The clothes that they wear are ragged and their physique is poor.' A French citizen reported that the spectacle made him ashamed to be European, while a German took a sterner line: 'I hope you will be cruel to them. The war is being prolonged on their account, they should be worked to death.' The general reaction of the Japanese in the crowd was reported as being one of 'sober anxiety'. Despite the manifest uselessness of the enemy, this was no time for complacency. 'They have no shame, but some arrogance still, so they must be treated firmly,' said one of them.

The newspaper reports also carried the comments of as many different nationalities as could plausibly be claimed to be present, repeating the same propaganda themes. The *Keijo Nippo*, Korea's main Japanese language newspaper, carried an interview with a local man, Mr Baigudin Gusman:

> Mr Gusman (45) who has lived in Japan for twenty-one years and now runs a clothing business in Okura-machi 3-chome, Fusan, has a very pro-Japanese family. He is a Turkish Tartar with the same red blood of the Orient running through his veins as ours. Mr Gusman praised the greatness of Japan as follows: 'I think it is a natural judgment of God that America and Britain who did not realise Japan's fundamental strength and underestimated its economic power, were defeated without a moment's hesitation and came ashore as pitiful prisoners of war.'

The report added that his family were currently fasting in observation of Ramadan. Money saved on buying food would be donated to the National Defence fund and they would also be offering prayers for the establishment of the Greater East Asian Co-Prosperity Sphere.

The wooden language of the purported onlookers does not suggest authenticity; but the *Keijo Nippo* descriptions of the parade nevertheless contain details that indicate that they are true eyewitness accounts, although the reported presence of American prisoners in Korea was simply a fabrication that would consistently be repeated over the next three years. A distinctively Japanese sense of humour is apparent in the reports: sly, derisive and cruel, with a keen eye for the ridiculous, as in the deliberate misidentification of the prisoners' kitbags as bags of flour.

The kilts of the Highlanders were a particular target for ridicule. Under the headline 'A rare sight: soldiers in women's clothing', readers were told that 'some of the prisoners wore navy blue and red women's clothing, perhaps given to them as mementos of their wives, and some even wore red flowers in their hats'. As in the reports from Changi, the prisoners are depicted as essentially ludicrous figures, hopelessly unsuited both physically and mentally to waging war:

> There was also an old prisoner of war who looked like a tourist in khaki shorts and hat, carrying a large trunk with labels stuck all over it. There were some wounded soldiers who were carried away in trucks. This was the pitiful state of the British prisoners of war, who had always been proud of the British Empire with its immorality and cruelty. In the past, British troops ran rampant in the world, treating it as

> if they owned it, but once the Imperial Military arose, they raised their white flags.
>
> The British prisoners of war, who we can only assume had been educated to follow the motto, 'If our enemy is strong enough, we should surrender, then our lives will surely be spared', were sent here with facial expressions that almost looked as though they had never been involved in war. The words and deeds of these captives, who were uneducated and had a false world view imprinted in them, were full of bittersweet smiles from ignorance. Here are a few glimpses that we caught at the landing scene:
>
> The prisoners of war afflicted by ringworm were dangling canvas bags resembling first aid kits on their backs and in front of themselves, clinking aluminium lunch boxes and thermos cups made out of coffee cans, and carrying flour bags under their arms. A young military doctor disinfected them with a sprayer at the bottom of the ramp as the prisoners of war with the ringworm walked about. The young military doctor then made a hand gesture instructing them to show him the palms of their hands, but instead they let go of their luggage under their arms and raised both hands. It seems they were only taught to surrender.

Another new element of the reports is to place the absence of Bushido spirit in the broader context of moral degeneracy, which Japanese propaganda asserted was a defining feature of British and American society: 'Then came the inspection of their belongings. Every playing card they showed us was soiled and worn. These were the tools of gambling. There were many letters sent from the delinquent young women at the ports. Their blue eyes were darting about desperately throughout all this.'

The parade served a dual propaganda purpose. As well as its goal of eradicating respect for the enemy, the victory parade was also used to support Japan's policy of *kominka*, or assimilation of the Korean people, by showcasing the newly recruited young Korean prison guards. As we have seen, in 1937 the Japanese had introduced a scheme of assimilation aimed at the complete annihilation of Korea's national identity, with the long-term ambition of persuading the Koreans to think of themselves as Japanese. Korean culture, religion, and even its language were suppressed. The Koreans were given Japanese names and became, officially, Japanese. Korean palaces and temples and other buildings, signifiers of a Korean identity, were demolished and Japanese Shinto shrines were built across the country to replace the Korean places of worship. Young Korean women were encouraged to marry Japanese soldiers.

The programme was underpinned by a concocted mythology which argued that in fact the Koreans had been part of the Japanese race throughout their history. Korea had been founded by a nephew of the founder of Japan, the Goddess Amaterasu and over the centuries, Japan had acted as a kindly big brother towards Korea, solicitous of its well-being and ever ready to come to its defence when threatened by hostile neighbours. These ideas were propounded repeatedly and forcefully by the Japanese Governor General of Korea, Kuniaki Koiso, appearing in newspaper reports of the governor's speeches. According to him, the two nations were as inseparable as 'lips and teeth'.[7] The term 'Korean' was replaced by a new phrase, 'The people of the peninsula'.

As well as providing much-needed manpower, the recruitment of Koreans as guards was also seen as useful propaganda for the young men themselves and the Korean population as a whole. By guarding Westerners, Koreans would realise that the Japanese were now top dogs and be grateful to share a place in the new world hierarchy. According to Ibara's report, the spectacle of Korean guards was deeply moving. One Korean shed tears of joy at seeing 'the young men of the peninsula' guarding the prisoners. Another spoke of the wonder of the spectacle: 'It seems like a dream to see the British and Americans, who used to make light of us and thought us an inferior people, as prisoners. Koreans have felt pride in being Japanese. Their feelings have completely changed.' Newspaper reports reiterated the message of the Ibara document: 'Wearing field caps with their uniforms and powerfully wielding bayonets, the peninsula youths guarding the POWs wore an energetic expression on their faces: from that day forward they would carry out their sublime duty as Imperial subjects.'[8] In reality, the Korean people continued to harbour the deep hatred towards the Japanese which had existed since Japan had annexed Korea, against the wishes of its people, in 1910.

Party B finally reached the railway station in the early evening, with many on the verge of collapse. Here, they were told for the first time that they were to journey overnight to their final destinations, Keijo and Jinsen. Elrington recorded that they were met by a new set of guards who seemed particularly excitable and jumpy, manhandling the men onto the train as if expecting resistance. These were also young Koreans on duty for the first time. But once on board, the prisoners received their first pleasant surprise: they were given ordinary third-class seats in a heated modern carriage. There was another surprise: their rations. They were given two lunch boxes, each containing the best food they had eaten in months: 'good quality rice and a cold collation of fish, sausage, vegetable and pickle,' Elrington remembered. But the special treatment was for the benefit of the reporters and photographers on the train. Prisoners who were transported from Changi to Thailand and Burma were crammed into cattle trucks with little or no sanitary facilities.

The train halted at every station during its 280-mile journey to Keijo. On the platforms were groups of locals. The *Maeil Sinbo* reported that these were people who had interrupted their sleep to satisfy their curiosity: 'Employees from government offices, members of patriotic associations, elementary school students and ordinary residents who had come out to have a look at the prisoner train, their eyes wide open in wonder.' It can be suggested that their presence was the result of coercion.

Journalists interviewed both the prisoners and the Korean guards. Although proud to serve Japan, the guards were unimpressed by the prisoners, who gave the impression of being 'really disorderly' and 'more like delinquents than soldiers'. There was also an untypically impressionistic piece on the captives from special correspondent Kim Jung-wan in the *Maeil Sinbo*:

> Stepping on land for the first time, seeing unfamiliar scenes along the train line, what thoughts are coming and going in their heads? Caught after abandoning their weapons, the POWs take in the atmosphere and don't talk with each other, seemingly lost in meditation. When the train arrived at Kamrangjin, already the mantle of twilight had fallen and the bright harvest moon was shining through the train

> window. Seeing the moon floating in the clear, azure sky, they may have been crying as they thought of their wives and children waiting in their hometowns.

This was not meant to evoke sympathy, but contempt. The reader would have known that the way of the samurai was death. He forgot about his family as soon as he went to war.

The following morning, the train divided at the junction before Keijo. The Loyals continued on the main line, arriving at Keijo at midday, while the men of the 122nd Field Regiment followed a branch line to Jinsen. The Australians were divided equally between the two British parties. There were further victory parades in front of the local population in both cities, with photographers and journalists on hand to record the event, and crowds of curious citizens. But to the prisoners' relief, neither parade lasted more than half an hour, and in the early afternoon they entered their new homes. Some of them would die or become permanently disabled there, a few would lose their sanity, and all of them would suffer from starvation and illness. Many of the party would find it difficult to adjust to civilian life on release, and some never did. Images of the men would also appear in newspapers worldwide over the next three years, as illustrations of Japanese humanity.

Chapter 6

First Weeks in Korea

Located in a residential area in the south-east of the city, Keijo camp had previously been a silk mill. Other, more suitable buildings had been suggested to General Itagaki for the prisoners, but he rejected them on the grounds that they were too good for prisoners of war. The camp's position in the middle of a suburb was also good for propaganda, as the locals would be able to see the men each day as they went out on their work parties. Colonel Elrington's first impressions were not positive:

> Confronting us as we turned in at the gate was a high, ugly, brick building with a few obviously new huts about its base, and passing through here we pulled up in a yard about 60 yards by 30 yards. The whole was surrounded by a high stockade, wired and pronged. Was this dirty, ramshackle compound to be our new home? God forbid! Yet it was borne in upon us as we eased our equipment and gear onto the broken rubble surface that this fly-blown, poxy dust heap in the midst of a filthy, evil-smelling slum area had been partially cleared and specially reserved for use as a prisoner of war camp.[1]

A more objective but equally negative description of the camp is found in an intelligence report produced by the liberating American forces in September 1945:

> The prisoners were housed in a large four storey building with wooden floors and stairs. Each floor was divided into four rooms. Heating was satisfactory between December and March, but in early and late winter there was no heat [...] The lighting in the room was poor. All windows were glassed and of the shuttered type. In the summer

> the ventilation was almost non-existent and in winter the inside temperature was often below zero at night. No beds were available and the prisoners slept on straw mattresses. Cells used for punishment were 8 feet by 10 feet, with no windows and a small door. The fence surrounding the camp was of six-foot pickets, in close formation, on top of which were sharpened bamboo sticks. The only entrance to the camp was a double main gate. The entire area was about 67,840 square feet. The hospital consisted of a small hut. In the winter the temperature would often be at freezing point and many cases of illnesses were concealed and nursed in the barracks as conditions were more favourable than in the hospital There were two Japanese-type lavatories with twelve cubicles in each. There were also a sufficient number of the standing-up type cubicles but the drainage was very poor.[2]

Similar disappointment was in store for the Jinsen party. They travelled a further thirty miles, eventually coming to a halt in a siding just outside the town. After a few minutes, there was a salvo of shouting to herald the arrival of a very short man with a small moustache and big sword, yelling orders at the Japanese and Korean guards, who were obviously frightened of him. The men recognised Major Okuda from the Fusan march. Captain Ivor Thomas later described him as 'intelligent but borderline mad'.[3] 'If this was the man who would hold the power of the life and death of the men during their imprisonment,' he added, 'then our troubles had really begun.' The men were marched two miles to Jinsen camp. It was newly built, consisting of wooden huts set in four acres of grounds. But in some respects it was even more unsatisfactory than Keijo, having no flooring and very little furniture. Like Keijo it would prove to be cold and unhygienic, with insufficient toilet and bathing facilities. As at Keijo, the washrooms often became completely frozen over during the winter. The perimeter fence was 10 feet high, with barbed wire and electrified wire covering its top, giving the prisoners the unpleasant sense of being completely cut off from the outside world.

The first few weeks were a period when morale was at its lowest. There was disappointment at the new accommodation. The long lists of regulations that were issued at the camps, threatening dire punishments for trivial offences, gave no cause for an uplift in spirits. Most of the men continued to suffer from the ill effects of the voyage. At Jinsen, there were twenty-one cases of diphtheria and several cases of malaria. Most of the men were suffering from beriberi, and scabies spread rapidly during the first few days. As at Keijo, there was also a dysentery epidemic. There was little medicine available and men started to die.

Rations were also a disappointment. 'We had expected that when we had arrived in this camp we should receive more adequate food but it was still insufficient and I felt I could, with beneficial effect, have eaten about three times the quantity,' wrote Captain John Lever at Keijo.[4] 'Some fellows have changed so much as to be unrecognisable as they were before the capitulation of Singapore.' The men were weighed on their arrival at the camps, and again a month later. The prisoners had lost an average of half a stone during the first month in Korea. At Jinsen, the men were as much as three stone under their normal weight.

At Jinsen, the address Major Okuda gave the prisoners reinforced their fears of what the regime under him might be like. It was more a harangue than a speech, they thought. Although a Japanese victory was ordained by God, Okuda told the prisoners, they had irredeemably disgraced themselves by surrendering. They were the 'lowest of the low, lower than animals; lower, even, than Indians.' They should expect to be treated as such. Privately, the prisoners ridiculed their captors. Citing Major Okuda, Captain Thomas described the prisoners' perception of their captors at Jinsen as dual-natured: the Japanese were both ridiculous but at the same time frightening. 'Little more than five feet tall, he always dressed scruffily, usually wearing Wellington boots. Whether calm or in his more usual state of anger, there was always a grin on his face.'[5] In general, camp commandants were not selected from the most able officers, and the position was neither prestigious nor popular. Okuda addressed the men through the camp interpreter, 'Yokohama Pete', and together they became a comedy act. Before the war, the interpreter had worked as a docker at Yokohama Bay and had learnt his English largely by mixing with American sailors, from whom he had picked up a great deal of slang, including obscenities. Like most interpreters at Japanese camps, his English was insufficient for his job. Okuda would stand on a box on the parade ground and rail angrily at the men for several minutes without pause. The translation that followed was often a précis of no more than a single sentence, such as 'You guys, watch your step'! Sometimes, if Captain Thomas is to be believed, the cue for the interpreter to translate would be a slap on the top of the head from the major.

But the major had an alarming side as well. Too short to be able to strike the men around the face with his fists, he used to work off his anger by beating men around the head with his sword or a pole. At both camps, the men were introduced to Japanese violence. The punishment for the most minor infractions of camp rules – for example, mislaying a cup, or smoking in the wrong area – was a 'binta', or hefty slap around the face. There was nothing gentle about these slaps. But an obvious irony hangs over the complaints about violence the men recorded in their diaries. Their treatment was the best a prisoner of the Japanese could hope for. At other camps, the men would not find it possible to extract any humour from their captors' behaviour.

Party B Perceptions of the Koreans

On the train from Fusan, Colonel Cardew of the Loyals was interviewed by special correspondent Kim Jung-wan. In the 25 September edition of the *Maeil Sinbo* he is quoted as saying:

> While it can't be said that Fusan's streets are magnificent I was surprised that even though the war has been going on for five to six years the stores are full of supplies. And we saw that not only Japanese people, but Koreans as well wore colourful clothes and happy expressions and were full of energy, and also that many boys and girls were playing.[6]

The words are an almost exact inversion of the truth. During the first weeks in Korea the prisoners were shocked by the depths of poverty and destitution they came across when they went out on work parties. Eric Wallwork noticed that even if the Koreans had enough money to make purchases, there was hardly anything to buy in the shops. The Koreans appeared to the men to be 'down-trodden', subdued and ever-cautious of the Japanese, with good reason. When Arthur Kerr went out on a work party on a public holiday marking the New Year, he was surprised to see children playing in the snow. 'This was the first time I had ever seen the children looking at all happy and enjoying themselves.'[7]

The Japanese exercised control through extreme violence. Alan Toze recorded several horrific incidents:

> During the morning there was a hue and cry and exciting chase along the road above the garden; a Korean thief or summat came steaming along chased by a string of officials. He was run to earth in the gardens in the hollow, frightfully mauled and kicked by his captors, and finally flung twice down a forty-foot bank before being taken away … At Keijo station Stan [Strange] saw a Korean cart driver who failed to show his pass being beaten and mauled with iron bag hooks. He was taken away an hour later, apparently dead.[8]

Another of his entries provides an example of how the 'young men of the peninsula' were treated by their Japanese brothers: 'A Korean guard who (report states) got drunk on his monthly half day off was beaten up by six of his comrades in the Jap enclosure: knocked and kicked unconscious three times, then carted, bleeding profusely from many wounds. Bloodstains on the ground covered with two buckets of sand.'[9]

What shocked the prisoners most was the sight of the corpses of the destitutes who had lived and died on the streets. Arthur Kerr recorded that after two months out on working parties he had 'come across four stiffs lying in public places'. One morning, Alan Toze passed the body of a young female, aged about 15, lying in the gutter: 'Poor mite, she is one of the many in this inhuman part of the world. No one did more than cursorily glance at her. On our return in the evening, she had been dragged on to the pavement, and her mud-caked feet laid upward between two piles of refuse.'[10]

During their stop-off at Formosa, the other long-established possession of the Japanese, Arthur Kerr had been surprised by the poverty he saw there. But he remarked that it was nothing in comparison with Korea. He wondered how the population managed to survive through the winter months:

> The lack of clothing seems to be a very predominant feature. Their clothes are patch on patch. I have counted as many as five different ones on the one spot. Children

> have a minimum of clothing. I could count on one hand the number of children with leather shoes. Many of the adults wear footwear of plaited straw, totally inadequate in the ice and snow. Some live in semi-European style houses and are fairly comfortable, but most live in absolute hovels made of mud and thatched with rice straw. Sanitary conditions are hopeless, in the lesser homes it seems to be let nature call where it may, one place is as good as another. In the larger places the cesspool comes into its own and here the human wastage lays till it is boiled and carted for use as fertilizer. Household dirt and waste garbage here is very hygienically dumped on the sidewalk in heaps to be cleared up whenever it seems to suit.[11]

Japanese propaganda boasted of how it had modernised and transformed Korea for the benefit of its people. Japan had indeed brought industry, railways, ports and other infrastructure to the country, but not to the benefit of the Koreans. They mostly worked in extremely poor conditions on low wages. By 1942, nearly all the industry in the country was owned by the Japanese. They had also bought up farmland, with many former owners reduced to the status of tenants or forced off their land altogether. When war broke out, Japan began to strip the country of its resources in aid of Japan's war effort, with citizens scouring the country to collect iron for the war effort, and crops being shipped to Japan to feed its people. The Korean people themselves were coerced into playing a major role in the war. Young males were conscripted into the army, many of them, as we have seen, to be deployed as guards at POW camps. Over 2.5 million Korean men and women were sent to Japan as forced labour. Most terrible of all, young Korean women were forced into sexual slavery as 'comfort women' for the Japanese troops.

The media was entirely controlled by the Japanese, and their newspapers display an instinctive contempt for the Koreans. Sometimes a chiding tone is evident, as if the writer were scolding recalcitrant children. Concerns over tax evasion, for example, provoked a bullying editorial in the *Keijo Nippo*:

> Keijo's tax delinquency rate averages twenty-five per cent, which means that as many as twenty-five out of

> every hundred people in Keijo are feckless people who are delinquent in paying their taxes. The people of Keijo, who brag that their city is the 'Capital of Chosen', have the distinction stuck on the tips of their noses of being the laziest people not only in Imperial Japan, but also in the whole world when it comes to paying their taxes.[12]

Japan became increasingly desperate to increase the country's productivity. The *Keijo Nippo* reported a 'round table discussion' of senior Japanese business managers, who had met to share ideas about achieving this. Takeo Yoshida, manager of the Greater Japan Riken Research Institute explained a routine procedure at his office:

> If a worker is lazy, he is punished by being made to run at full speed. When people run, all unfocused thoughts disappear (laughter). So, whenever I feel that the heat is getting to them and they are feeling a little dozy, I immediately make them go for a run (laughter).[13]

When the prisoners went out on work parties, they were always accompanied by guards under the pretence that they were needed to protect the men from the animosity of the local population. But the Koreans reacted with kindness rather than hostility. The Koreans' initial interest in the prisoners was identical to the curiosity the onlookers at Fusan had aroused in the prisoners: they were an interesting, almost exotic, spectacle. Soldiers with red hair attracted particular interest. But the Koreans also felt sympathy, and the evidence of the diaries is that a bond was forged with the prisoners as fellow sufferers under Japanese oppression. One of the men's first jobs at Jinsen was to excavate ground for a new railway track. As the Japanese had hoped, the workers attracted a large crowd of spectators. But it was a friendly crowd. The children threw cigarettes, apples and turnips down to the prisoners until the guards intervened. Throughout their time in Korea, the prisoners were continually offered small gifts such as these, from people who themselves possessed almost nothing.

Alan Toze's diary records other acts of helpfulness. Out on a work party, he was struggling to put a heavy load over his shoulder when a Korean woman dropped the pack she was carrying to come to his aid.

He also sustained a non-verbal friendship with a Korean family whose backyard was visible from the second floor of the main prison building. Although looking out of windows was forbidden, Toze started waving at them: '[a] Korean family including four wenches "over the fence" have been providing innocent entertainment. A couple of nights ago I stood and waved, while they beckoned me down, offered me their young puppy, dishes of food etc, and generally showed signs of being thrilled.'[14] On a more practical level, some of the Korean guards were happy to pass on war news, or could be persuaded to smuggle cigarettes and food into the camp at a price. From 1944 a young Korean male smuggled newspapers into Keijo camp, risking his life on a daily basis for twenty American cigarettes.

Propaganda for the Prisoners

It is likely that in the euphoria of its early successes the Japanese may also have decided to experiment with a programme of assimilation targeted at the prisoners themselves. Lieutenant Arthur Cramsie was to write:

> As the weeks at Jinsen went by it was obvious that our hosts were anxious to make a bid to turn us all into Japanese. They wanted us to bow to the Emperor's palace, learn Japanese, and study Japanese history. Did they think we would be with them for ever as cheap labour and the sooner we were absorbed into their way of life, the better, or what? We never really discovered.[15]

At Keijo, Elrington remembered: 'In retrospect, it is fair to say that the Jap did all he could to impress upon us his superiority in culture, in military prowess, in science and medicine. He bribed us to learn his language and tired us with his propaganda, but all to no purpose.'[16]

Camp commandants throughout the Japanese territories referenced the code of *Bushido* continually, reminding their captives of the superiority of the Japanese military and the kind treatment that they were getting, even though they didn't deserve it. But Keijo and Jinsen were exceptional in the amount of time and effort devoted to propaganda, and the structured manner in which the Japanese attempted to inculcate a knowledge of Japanese culture, values and history.

At Keijo, lessons in Japanese mythology began with Colonel Noguchi's first speech to the prisoners. He followed a standard propaganda line in that he explicitly discounted the idea that the enemy was less powerful than the Japanese, instead explaining that supernatural aid made victory inevitable:

> I think these war results do not signify the inferior power of our enemy but rather owe to our absolute indomitable power, the power protected by Kami [Heaven]. Wherever Nippon navy and army advance, Tenu Sinjo [Special Providential help] always follows, you should recognise the fact and consider the reason: Nippon army and navy are under the Imperial Command of Tenno [Emperor] who is the personification of the Kami [God] so that the Imperial Troops are to be called the troops of God.[17]

Most unusually, all the prisoners were given a translated copy of his speech in English. They decided that 'Special Providential help' sounded like an insurance company. Japanese propaganda was simply another target of ridicule.

There were several activities at the camps in the early days which were unusual, possibly unique, features of the Korean camps. These included formal lessons in Japanese language, history and culture. Although attempting to learn Japanese could be punished by death at other camps, Japanese language lessons were at first compulsory for all the officers, and at Keijo the prisoners were promised the reward of a radio if they became fluent. Lessons were of a high quality, given by a civilian, Mr Sato, and 'Prof' Ukai, a lively and friendly Japanese corporal who had previously been a lecturer at Keijo University. There were tests, and prizes of cake and sake for those who did best. At Jinsen, Major Okuda interested himself closely in the lessons, but in a characteristically unpredictable manner, according to one of the prisoners:

> One morning he came into one of the prisoner's huts before reveille, dressed only in a nightshirt, with an assistant carrying a blackboard. He chalked up the Japanese for 'the

> small flower is very pretty'. *Chīsana hana wa totemo kirei desu.* The normal routine of washing and breakfast was abandoned and Okuda spent the next five hours explaining the various grammatical points the sentence illustrated.[18]

Unsurprisingly perhaps, none of the prisoners at Jinsen mastered the language. At Keijo, my father saw the benefits to be gained from learning the language and he and another young officer, Tom Henling Wade, spent up to four hours a day studying it. His diaries reveal it was not an easy task, and at times he wondered whether there was any point to it. But by 1944 he had acquired a good reading knowledge of the language, and was able to translate newspapers smuggled into the camp.

At the same time as the language lessons, there were lectures in Japanese history and culture. The prisoners at Jinsen were allowed to submit questions at the end of each session, which would receive a typewritten response a week later. This was not taken seriously. One of the men's questions was to ask whether they could be allowed out on weekly trips to Jinsen's cinema to study contemporary Japanese culture. There is little information about the lessons at Keijo, but even as late as 1944 my father's diary indicates that they were still being given.

Another unusual aspect of this first period at the camps was the length of time devoted to drilling. Prisoners at all Japanese camps had to number off in the Japanese language, but in Korea the prisoners spent six whole weeks learning to drill in the Japanese fashion. Alex James at Jinsen wrote:

> It was like depot days again with a difference. We were on parade from 8.30 till 12 noon in the morning and from 1 pm until 4.30 pm in the afternoon. All commands were given in Japanese; we learnt how to salute with the palm of the hand facing down, standing to attention with the fingers splayed and at ease with the weight on one foot. We were also taught to adopt the curious Japanese form of goose-stepping march. Our problems with mastering this new form of drill provided the Japanese guards with a lot of amusement, but if a prisoner was thought not to be trying hard enough, he would be slapped sharply round the face.

Despite the tedium and punishments, the prisoners were again able to find humour in their situation. At Keijo, John Lever found the Japanese manner of marching and drilling inherently ludicrous:

> To see Japanese soldiers 'marching' was a comic sight to us as they shuffle and shamble along with no idea of keeping step. When drilling they have a peculiar step which isn't quite the goose-step. They lift their knees well up, stamp their feet down and do a very exaggerated swing of the arms. They made us learn this and to see some of the comedians making it look still more ridiculous than is strictly necessary was enough to make you split your sides laughing. CQMS Collins was the star turn, though there were some who ran him close without trying to be funny.[19]

At Jinsen, the prisoners asked why they were being taught Japanese, and received the disheartening answer that, as they would be spending the rest of their lives as prisoners, a knowledge of the language would be indispensable. They were also told that they were to follow a process of assimilation. Once a correct attitude had been successfully instilled in them, they would then have the honour to serve alongside the Imperial Japanese Army. It is impossible, of course, to know the extent to which this actually reflected Japanese thinking, if at all, but undoubtedly there is ample evidence to suggest that a scheme of assimilation had at first been seriously envisaged.

Chapter 7

Filming at Keijo

During the first weeks in Korea, men continued to die from the ill-effects of the voyage on the *Fukkai Maru*. Private Parkinson of the 2nd Battalion died of dysentery on 2 October, followed by Private Metcalfe of the Royal Pioneers, who died of the same disease on 15 October. The commanding officer of the 122 Field Regiment, 56-year-old Colonel Dyson, had begun to recover from diphtheria, but died in the camp hospital hut from heart failure. A few days later John Lever's close friend and bridge partner Jackie Whiting developed what seemed at first simply a bad cough. Lever wrote in a mildly teasing but nevertheless sympathetic tone that his friend had 'got a cold and decided to go into hospital for a few days'. But his next entry reads:

> I got a horrible shock a few days later. Jackie Whiting died on the night of 1 November with diphtheria. I had no idea that he was really ill, I just thought that he would be better off in hospital than a cold cheerless room in which it was too cold to sit about reading or writing.[1]

Lever's prose is the most understated of all the prisoners', expressive of a cool, ironic cast of mind. When he writes 'I got a horrible shock,' the full power of the word 'horrible' is felt by the reader. In all, sixteen men were to die from illnesses they had developed during the voyage to Korea.

The deaths provided an opportunity for propaganda, however. At the newly created prison cemetery, the Japanese organised a filmed memorial service. It was an elaborate affair, and was attended by senior officers of the Imperial Japanese Army, including a major general. The prisoners selected to attend borrowed items of clothing from those who would not be going in order to look their smartest as a mark of respect for their comrades. All the Japanese officers from the camp attended, and Noguchi gave Colonel Elrington a lift to the cemetery in his car. It was a nice gesture by the commandant, the men thought.

At the cemetery, the Japanese army had donated eight large wreaths which were displayed to striking effect on trestles. A variety of religious ministers were present. As well as the Anglican chaplain, Peter Cazalet, there was a Roman Catholic priest, a Methodist minister and two Shinto priests, who wore masks and shook horsehair whisks at various points in the ceremony. After a brief service led by Cazalet, white boxes containing the men's ashes were placed in graves, a foot below the surface. The Last Post and Reveille were played and then a group of prisoners shovelled earth into the graves. All the while, a cameraman filmed the spectacle. Colonel Cardew made a short speech which was translated into Japanese, and a Japanese major general offered a brief response. The service ended, in Lever's words, when Colonel Cardew 'did his grovelling salute-cum-bow which we all disliked so much.'[2] Any gestures which might suggest an obsequious attitude towards their captors had now become anathema to the prisoners. There was another moment of awkwardness: the Japanese had placed tangerines and biscuits on the graveyard altar, a symbolic act that was part of traditional Shinto burial rites. They were shocked by the prisoners' request to take the food away to give to sick prisoners at the camp. Such a request was sacrilegious.

The prisoners were puzzled at the degree of respect shown their dead comrades. Had a similar amount of attention been given to these men when they were still alive, it might have saved them from dying, they thought. But if something didn't feel quite right, at this stage the prisoners were able to mark it down as another example of weird Japanese behaviour. Two of the artists among the prisoners, Alan Toze and Stan Strange, had been allowed to draw sketches. In 1947 they published a collection of their wartime drawings, including one of the memorial service with an explanatory note beneath: 'Mass burial of Prisoners of War who died at Keijo camp. Propaganda screen and artificial wreaths were for press purposes. Later, in Kobe, men who died were broken into crouching position and put into soya barrels' [3]

The respect shown to the dead prisoners at Keijo by the Japanese was not in fact entirely anomalous. According to *Bushido*, the prisoners had redeemed their disgrace by dying for their country, removing the stain of surrender. Funerals carried a different cultural meaning for the Japanese, and it can be suggested that the mistaken assumption that these beliefs were shared by the West explains why services for the dead appear in at least four propaganda films. The function of memorial services in Japanese theology was to allow the bereaved to uphold their family's honour, and to celebrate the nobility of the dead, rather than to mourn their loss. Local ceremonies for the war dead were held in schools and village halls throughout Japan, with national ceremonies at the Yasukini Shrine in Tokyo broadcast live. Prisoner memorial services were also filmed in Java and Thailand, and even when one of the prisoners died at the civilian gaol in Keijo, the mourners at his funeral included a Buddhist priest and a cameraman. But even taking this into account, it can be said that Japanese funerals for their own men were far less elaborate.

After the ceremony, the prisoners were told that an investigation would be held into the conditions on the *Fukkai Maru*, and that the deceased prisoners' belongings would be sent back to their relatives, along with letters of condolence. Colonel Elrington wrote a letter of thanks to Noguchi after the service. A knowledge of Elrington's dealings with the camp authorities during captivity makes it possible to suggest that its real purpose was to obtain photographs of the event to send to the families of the deceased, but he could nevertheless offer his sincere thanks without compromising his integrity. The letter very soon found its way to the ICRC headquarters in Geneva, where it remains in the organisation's archive.

> Sir,
>
> I have the honour to convey to you the thanks and appreciation of all officers and men of this Camp for the honour done to our dead comrades at yesterday's ceremony. We were all very gratified at the excellent arrangements made and at the attendance of representatives of the Imperial Japanese Army. The kindness and sympathy shown by yourself and the camp staff in many ways, including the gift of the floral tributes, are much appreciated and will be remembered.
>
> It would be an added kindness if some of the photographs could be made available, as in due time they will be of great interest to the parents and families of the deceased soldiers.

> May I add a personal word of thanks to yourself for so kindly taking me in your car.
>
> M. Elrington
> Lieutenant Colonel.[4]

Along with the letter, a large selection of photographs of the event were received by the ICRC via the *Huryojohokyoku*, the Prisoner of War Information Office. Eight of the photographs were published in the April 1943 edition of its monthly journal, with an accompanying expression of thanks to the *Huryo* for kindly allowing them to be reproduced. These were the first images of Far Eastern captivity to be published outside Japanese territories, and their publication was reported by the news agency *Domei,* quick to capitalise on the *imprimatur* of the ICRC. All the photographs of Far Eastern captivity published by the Red Cross over the next three years would be Japanese propaganda.

The second major propaganda event of the year was Christmas Day. Perhaps surprisingly, prisoners were allowed to celebrate Christmas at nearly all the Japanese POW camps, and they were usually allowed extra rations as well. If one photograph of a camp survives, it is of Christmas Day. At Keijo and Jinsen, Christmas 1942 was celebrated in a manner that both pleased and surprised the men.

Major Conrad Rigby's diary provides the details:

> A fortnight before Christmas we were asked to submit a list of extras we wanted. We therefore submitted a list which would have provided a really good peacetime Christmas on the grounds that if we got half of it we should not do badly. And after telling us it was out of the question they really did very well for us. We all expected a very poor Christmas. It is bad enough away from home in the best circumstances, but as prisoners of war it seems very much worse. We couldn't write home, or send presents or receive any mail and it is now a year since most of us had any news of home. Our only interest therefore was in food and as we are always more or less hungry the idea of feeling well fed for a day was in itself most attractive. The canteen supplied us with the following:

4 tins of fish
6 oz of ham
1/4 lb of butter
2 oz of marmalade
2 bags of cakes
4 apples
50 cigarettes
1/2 bottle of claret
1/2 bottle of saki
1 bottle of beer
1 tin of pineapple'

> We each got the above, and as a tin of fish serves four we got sixteen meals supplemented. The pineapple is enough for four also. All this is extra to the ordinary ration, and a special day's ration was issued. For breakfast we had rice and a very good stew. For midday was another very good stew, and 8oz loaf of bread, ½ oz of butter and in addition two good slices of ham and vegetable salad. In the evening we had rice, a plain stew of vegetables and a decent helping of pork in fried butter. So we not only did very well for food, but can live very well for some days on our extras.[5]

Early in the morning there was a light sprinkling of snow. Through the snow came a Japanese propaganda unit bearing cameras, lights and sound-recording equipment. There was a power cut across the entire city while it installed its lights, suggesting that the film crew was not stinting on their resources. The prisoners got up early as usual and exchanged presents and Christmas cards. Alan Toze was thrilled to receive a British Navy Cut cigarette from the padre, a considerable luxury in the circumstances.

The first event to be filmed was the Christmas breakfast. The extra rations of food that the men received came as a delightful surprise, and the cameras would have caught the undernourished, hungry prisoners at their happiest. After breakfast there was a carol service, followed by Holy Communion. For Toze, a devout Christian, the film crew was an unwelcome distraction, 'leaping about with their powerful lamps and buzzing cameras.'[6] But at midday there was a lunch of unusually good stew accompanied by bread, butter, ('pure elixir' for Henling Wade) vegetable salad and two slices of ham. The prisoners had also made paper hats and Christmas crackers for themselves and used sheets for table cloths. There was a small amount of alcohol, which promoted a festive atmosphere.

Then followed the day's main event, the Christmas Show, *Chosen Calling.* The cast had been preparing the show for several weeks. The initial plan was to perform it in one of the squad rooms, but shortly before Christmas Colonel Noguchi came across the prisoners rehearsing and took an interest. He offered them the use of an unoccupied downstairs room, and its partitions were altered to enable the creation of a theatre with stage and curtains. Materials for props and costumes were also provided by the Japanese, and the camp band received a brand new side-drum from Noguchi as a Christmas present.

The show was directed by Jack McNaughton, a professional actor who had produced shows at Changi. Lance Bombardier Arthur Butler also resumed his Changi persona as 'Gloria D'Earie'. As a singer and female impersonator, Arthur Butler was to lighten the lives of many of the men at Keijo. In the POW camps in Europe and the Far East, drag artists were prized not so much for how well they exploited the comic elements of cross-dressing, but for how realistically they approximated an attractive female. The variety of responses to female impersonators at the camps was complex. Some of the men let their imaginations take full flight and allowed themselves to view the performers as actual women, but for others, cross-dressers such as Arthur Butler were sexually exciting because they were men dressed as women. Some of the archival material relating to Keijo includes notes and drawings which express unambiguous sexual interest in him. Off the stage, Arthur Butler was a good-natured and generous man. He and Alan Toze were particularly good friends, and when Toze fell sick, he could always rely on Butler's sympathy and practical help in the form of cups of tea or making up his bed for him. On stage, his impersonation of the actress Diane Wynyard's performance in Noël Coward's *Cavalcade* was apparently his *pièce de résistance.*

Before being allowed to stage the show, censors had scrutinised the script very carefully to check for anything that might be considered subversive, and during the performance interpreter Ushihara 'listened very attentively for anything untoward, but there was nothing to cause offence, except possibly for a few gags about the camp food'.[7]

It is possible that film of the show may survive somewhere today in Japan or Korea, although nothing has yet been discovered. But several photographs of this show, and 1944's production, *The Curate's Egg*, are held in archives and private collections. The lyrics of the opening number of *Chosen Calling* have also survived:

> Come to our show in Keijo,
> We have some laughter for you
> New songs, new jokes, and some new sketches,
> Each one a tonic for your blues,
> Gloria's skirts will be shorter
> Crowd in a get a lovely view,
> We'll make you forget your sorrows,
> Chosen is calling you.
>
> Chosen is calling from Keijo,
> Chosen is calling to you,
> Bring all your cases from the Benjo,
> Put down your bowls of turnip stew
> We know what we'll have for our dinner,
> Face it and never feel blue,
> Cheer up and say as you bango,
> Chosen is calling you.

A collection of comic sketches and light-hearted musical items, the show ran for nearly two hours. It was greatly enjoyed by all the prisoners, and was apparently an equal success with the guards Afterwards, Colonel Elrington got up to offer his thanks. As well as making the usual acknowledgements to the director, cast and band, he also thanked Colonel Noguchi for allowing the performance. He then led a round of 'For he's a Jolly Good Fellow', also directed at Noguchi as well as the cast. After the show, the musicians were asked to record some Christmas carols. To bandsman Eric Wallwork's excitement, they were told that they would receive copies of the recordings and be allowed to see the finished film. At that early stage of their captivity, the prisoners still believed some of the things the Japanese told them.

The men were aware that the day had been used for propaganda, but there were no complaints about this. John Jesson had enjoyed his activities as stage manager for the show and his occupation as manufacturer of Christmas crackers and hats:

> Sank back into the old flea bag happily mulled from an unaccustomed stretch of vigorous activity and unaccustomed ration of wine of beer, saki and white wine. As regards the fare, the few extras obtainable were infinitely more welcome after ten months of a rice diet than the traditional dishes are in times of comfortable abundance.[8]

Major Rigby also went to bed happy: 'Far better Christmas than any of us had expected, feeling full and satisfied and having the satisfactory feeling of knowing we had a nice reserve of food. The only unpleasant thought we had was whether we may still be here next Christmas.'[9] For some of the men the day brought on feelings of homesickness and isolation. The group photograph of the officers, taken on the stage in the afternoon, shows something of the variety of emotions.

Stills from the filming were immediately despatched by the *Huryo* to Geneva and footage appeared in newsreels across Japan and its territories. In March 1943, a feature film, *Huryo Chosen ni Kita* ('The Prisoners who came to Korea') was released. Posters for the film carried Korea's Japanese Governor-General Koiso's personal recommendation. A flyer for the film depicts a woebegone POW wearing a skirt, holding his hands up in surrender. It may be that the film followed the Fusan newspaper reports in presenting the prisoners primarily as objects of ridicule.

In all, four POW propaganda films appear to have been made by the Japanese during the war. Keijo stands apart from the other films in that there was no overt faking. Filming also took place at Zentsuji, but the prisoners were made to act a part. They were filmed, for example, collecting rations of fruit and cigarettes, which were immediately retrieved by the guards as they stepped out of camera shot. Another prisoner, Captain 'Stew' Nottage, AIF, had a blanket stuffed under his tunic to make him look appropriately bulked out by the prison diet.

The one film that does survive is *Calling Australia.* Here, every scene is faked. It was made over a period of six months at an internment camp in Batavia, the capital of Java. The idea for the film was conceived during the early days of Japan's successes and its main purpose was to soften up Australia for invasion. Instead, it illustrates the depths of crassness and cruelty that Japanese propaganda could plumb. As well as a large contingent of Australian POWs, the film made use of women and children, all of whom had been coerced to appear on pain of starvation. *Calling Australia* was deception on a grand scale; we see the men relaxing in a bar, eating steak and drinking beer, then going for a swim at the beach and playing cricket. In a domestic scene, a woman complains to a friend that, despite her best efforts to control her diet, she is putting on weight. The zombie-like performances of the enlisted actors are not merely entirely unconvincing, but also disturbing.

Senior Japanese propaganda officials viewed all four films and decided that this one was the best. In the event, the film was never released: as the war turned against Japan, the invasion of Australia was forgotten, and the idyllic lives of the prisoners may not have appealed to domestic Japanese audiences who were enduring ever-worsening conditions. After the war, the film was used in a documentary *Nippon Presents*, where extracts from the film were contrasted with the testimony of the surviving participants. The documentary was shown at the Tokyo War Crimes Trials. Far from helping the Japanese cause, it apparently had a profound effect on the judges. The testimony from the survivors was heart-rending. One of the prisoners who appeared in the film as a housewife, 'Mrs Johnson', told the trial:

> For the first few months conditions were really not bad in our camp. It was pleasantly placed, the food was good enough, and we had reasonable enough freedom. We lived in fact in a fool's paradise. When the Japs had made the scenes you have just seen, well, that was the end. We were whisked off to the germ-laden, rat-infested, filthy, slummy, bug breeding slums you see of Batavia, a forlorn mess of misery, of brutal beatings and indignities, of degrees of fever, weevils, lice, weevily rice, and utter hopelessness. That is what Java meant to us from then on.

Chapter 8
Photography

More photographs of Keijo exist than of any other Japanese prisoner of war camp. Collections of them can be found at the Imperial War Museum, the Lancashire Infantry Museum, and the Liddell Hart Military Archives at King's College London. Many other photographs are still held by the families of the men who were at Keijo. As well as the professional photographers from the propaganda corps who visited the camp, several of the camp guards took photographs, including Sergeant Kobiashi, rumoured to be a *Kempeitai* spy, Dr Uchida and the violent Corporal Takuma. Prisoners could buy copies and enclose them in letters home. Other copies were passed to the ICRC, who published selections in their journals. The first photographs of Far Eastern captivity to be published in the British press were of an open-air Keijo, taken soon after the men's arrival in October 1942. They were a simple but very successful form of propaganda. Men were keen to be photographed, and Captain Lever expresses his disappointment when he misses out. The photographers took pictures of individuals and small groups for the men to send home in their letters. Christmas celebrations and camp shows were always photographed to show the men in good spirits, and the message that the men were getting enough to eat was reinforced by photographs of Red Cross parcels, the Keijo vegetable garden and the camp's rabbits.

Red Cross Parcels

Pleasant feelings in my tummy,
Taste of marge and cheese,
I feel full now, isn't that funny,
Must be with 10 o'clock teas,
Meals I've seen at nights in my dreams,
Dreams of bacon and pork,

Of sugar in tea and tins of Peak Freans,
And of half pound blocks of plain York,
What should I eat first; I think I will toss,
My thoughts far from rice now have gone,
But before I begin I'll give a thought to
The Red Cross and profoundest thanks to St Johns

Eric Wallwork, Keijo, February 1942[1]

One of the central messages of Japanese POW propaganda was that Red Cross supplies were being received at the camps. In reality, if parcels did get through to Japanese territories, there was no guarantee that the prisoners would ever see them. After the Japanese surrender, large consignments were found unopened in warehouses at the docks where they had been offloaded. If parcels did reach the camps, it was not unknown for the commandant to refuse them. If he accepted them, medical supplies were retained by the camp authorities and the food parcels were routinely pilfered by the camp staff. At the time of the Japanese surrender, the men at Nakhom Nayok camp in Thailand were near death through starvation and so short of clothing that they went about their daily lives almost naked. But now they discovered large quantities of shirts, shorts and towels, and bulk supplies of sugar, beans and peanuts, crates of drugs and medical equipment. Dozens of lives might have been saved at the camp had the Japanese been willing to issue the supplies. At Keijo, Adjutant Takeo Terada had Red Cross parcels directly delivered to his personal quarters. Items in the parcels that did not appeal to the Terada household were thrown into the dustbin rather than returned for distribution. In August 1945 at Mukden, ICRC inspector Junod caught sight of American Red Cross parcels piled high in a storeroom. When he asked why they had not been distributed, he received the improbable reply that the commandant had been saving them for Christmas.

Throughout the war, the ICRC struggled to get relief supplies to the prisoners in the Far East by ship or rail. Their attempts to get the Japanese to allow inspectors to buy food, clothes and medicines with cash transferred internationally to local banks were continually frustrated. Linda Goetz Holmes tells how the ICRC negotiated an agreement between the Allied governments and the Japanese whereby the ICRC could deposit cash donated by the Allied governments into an account created by the Swiss National Bank. The bank had several branches in Japan and its territories, where inspectors would be allowed to withdraw cash and buy supplies locally. The Japanese then reneged on the agreement and insisted that the funds be held by the Yokohama Specie Bank. Once the funds were received, the Japanese instructed the bank not to release them.[2]

There was no limit to the budget that the Allied governments were willing to set aside for their prisoners in the Far East, and thousands of lives could have been spared if the Japanese had been willing to respect the Geneva Convention. Requests were simply ignored, or if an answer was given it would be that there was no need for supplies, as the prisoners were well looked after. Fritz Paravicini, the head of the ICRC delegation based in Japan, was responsible for establishing supply routes for Red Cross aid and ensuring that medicine, food and clothing reached the prisoners, where necessary. Paravicini wrote to Geneva advising that the basic problem was that the Japanese viewed relief supplies as a form of propaganda, indicative of the enemy's abundant resources and logistical capabilities. When Prime Minister Tojo and the head of the *Huryo*, General Uemura, discussed this issue they had agreed that there was no need to pamper prisoners who had disgraced themselves by surrendering, when Japanese soldiers were enduring privations. Had the prisoners received their Red Cross supplies in the quantities requested, they would indeed have enjoyed a better diet than the Japanese servicemen and the civilian population.

The Japanese placed seemingly insurmountable obstacles in the way of deliveries by ship. In August 1942, they had decreed that no neutral ship, even if it flew the flag of the Red Cross, would be allowed in Japanese waters. To his great credit, Paravicini's suggestion that the exchange vessels carrying interned Japanese nationals back home could also carry relief supplies was accepted by the Japanese. Thereafter, irregular supplies reached the prisoners. In 1944 the ICRC believed that at last a regular route had been established. Supplies from America were to be shipped to Vladivostok in a Russian ship, where the goods would then be transferred to Japanese vessels. This worked on one occasion only, and in January 1945 Party B received parcels which had travelled from San Francisco to Fusan via Vladivostok. Unfortunately, one of the unmarked Japanese ships carrying supplies to the southern occupied territories, *Ayo Maru*, was mistakenly torpedoed by an American submarine, and the scheme was cancelled. The ship was off course and not showing its lights, and it has been suggested that the vessel was attempting to deliver ammunition to local Japanese forces.

On average, a prisoner of the Japanese in the southern territories received the equivalent of half a parcel over three years. By comparison, in January 1944 John Lever recorded that each man had received the equivalent of seven-and-a-half parcels. With the parcels came receipts to be signed by the camp commandant and the senior officer among the prisoners. Very few of these receipts were ever returned to the ICRC, but the Geneva archives contain several signed by Noguchi and Elrington.

The opening of the Red Cross parcels generated anticipation and excitement akin to opening Christmas presents. At Jinsen, some of the prisoners could not sleep for excitement on the eve of their first distribution. At Keijo, the prisoners saw the first consignment of parcels being delivered on 15 February 1943, but they lay unopened in the camp office for nine days. The men's excitement turned to frustration and then fury as the days passed. The men later formed the opinion that this was one of the smaller cruelties the Japanese enjoyed: they would let the prisoners find out that letters or parcels had been delivered, then delay their distribution, sometimes for months.

When the parcels were finally opened it was a moment of pure delight commemorated in prose and poetry, by sketches, cartoons and photographs. As well as the benefits of nourishing and familiar food, it gave the prisoners the comforting sense that they had not been forgotten by the outside world. The wrappings and the familiar brand names of Peek Freans and York were also a delightful reminder of home. Eric Wallwork recorded that he received:

> ½ lb tin of biscuits
> 1lb tin curried mutton
> ½ lb tin bacon
> 10 oz.tin meat Gelatine
> 10ozs tinned tomatoes
> ¼ lb (Rowntrees) York Chocolate
> 2ozs (Hunters) Boiled Sweets
> Large tin Nestles milk
> ½ lb tin margarine
> 12ozs (Mortons) Red Plum jam

2ozs (Twinings) tea
2 x 2ozs tins sugar
3ozs Tin beef paste
2ozs (C & G) Farmers wife Cheese
1 tab unscented soap
10 ozs tin treacle pudding pre-war price approx. 7s-10d, about ten pounds in weight.[3]

The parcels were all the same size and weight, but their contents varied according to three categories: those designed for invalids, others for 'semi-invalids' and the healthy. A complex bartering system evolved, as described by John Lever:

> Powdered milk was valued most highly at 100 points. ½ pound of cheese was worth 50 points, a 12 oz tin of meat was valued at 45, a 6oz tin of coffee was valued at 20 points and so on. Coffee was the rather to be despised item at first but later on it rallied to 30. By a stroke of luck Duggie Stewart and myself were able to swap an invalid parcel for a non-invalid so we were able to come in for a bit more of the meat stuff. As there was nothing in the parcels I wasn't fond of, and preferring variety, I didn't swap very much. The parcels provided much fun and games, and much needed nourishment.[4]

Most of the men carefully rationed their supplies as occasional treats, but others managed to eat the entire contents of their parcel in one sitting, with dramatic ill effects on their digestive systems later.[5]

As well as the parcels there were bulk supplies of cocoa, bully (corned beef) and sugar. Colonel Noguchi kept these supplies back and issued rations when he saw fit. In September 1944, at a time when the prisoners were receiving less than 1,800 calories a day, Elrington was allowed to meet Noguchi to plead for more food. Lever wrote:

> On Sept 7th the C.O. had one of his rare interviews with Noguchi, the camp superintendent. They discussed many things but the only thing of interest we got out of it was an agreement to issue some Red Cross sugar every Sunday henceforth instead of every ten days. This wasn't as good

> an improvement as it promised to be as they made the issue smaller. We reckoned it worked out at 23 per cent more but the next issue was smaller still so the gain isn't very much at all.

The meeting had followed a familiar pattern, with Noguchi adopting the persona of a generous benefactor acting in the best interests of the men despite their ingratitude, when in fact he did little or nothing in their favour. One of the reasons he gave for the lack of food was the strength of public opinion against the prisoners: increased rations would excite anger and unrest in the local population. It is true that those of the local population who lived on the verge of starvation envied the prisoners' superior diet, but the blame for the dire poverty in Korea lay entirely with the Japanese and their exploitation of the country for their war aims.

Vegetable Gardens

Both Keijo and Jinsen had officers' vegetable gardens which the inspectors were always guided to when they made a visit. The Keijo garden was photographed several times, not just by the usual camp photographers but also by visiting professionals. No photographs of the gardens at Jinsen appear to have survived, but there are many descriptions, both in letters and diaries, of the pleasure and interest that the gardens at both camps brought to the prisoners' lives.

In March 1943 the officers at Keijo were allocated an area about the size of a football pitch outside the camp. The men supplied the money to buy tomato plants and set about levelling and draining the area. They divided the ground into one communal plot and private plots to be shared by small groups of three or four men. The diaries record the progress of the vegetables and their harvesting in very considerable detail. It provided a point of interest in their achingly monotonous lives. 'If it wasn't for the garden, this existence would be well-nigh unbearable,' wrote Alan Toze, one of a party of five other ranks seconded to work there. He drew bar graphs to record the amounts harvested each year. The produce included cabbages, lettuce, corn, daikon, pumpkins, onions, carrots, spinach and cucumbers. Peter Cazalet added aesthetic interest to the garden by creating lawns and flower beds, with my father acting as his assistant. There was a great deal of enthusiasm, knowledge and expertise to call upon. The chief advisor was an Australian, Alec Bourne, who had worked in agriculture before the war. Australia also provided the acknowledged tomato expert, Corporal Barnes.

For my father, simply the change of scene provided by getting out of the camp was a huge relief. Of all the diarists he most gives the sense of being caged in, and of the 'terrible restlessness', as he described it, that confinement caused. He was aware though, that most of the produce was for the benefit of the camp staff, and wrote that after a year's gardening 'not much of its produce has appeared on our plates yet'.

At Jinsen, one of the officers recalled how much he relished the fresh air, exercise and sunshine that a trip to the garden offered. The garden produce did not in fact result in greater calorific intake, as the camp officials ensured that there was a reduction in the daily rations to counterbalance the additional calories provided by the garden, From March till the end of November, gardening was the main leisure activity for several officers. Inside the camp's ground, they cultivated half an acre of gravelly soil. In 1944 they were allowed a larger area outside the camp.

One officer remembered:

> Escorted by two Korean guards and one Japanese, the officers were marched 300 yards to our garden, which covered about an acre and a half of good ground. There were five or six regular workers, and then twelve more who came when they felt like it….
>
> Our normal routine was to work all morning, then to return to camp in time for a cold bath before lunch. The Japanese made repeated efforts to make us work in the afternoon, but only met with success when we felt inclined, which was not very often. Our big lever was that gardening was a voluntary effort on the part of the officer, and the slightest suggestion of a direct order put us on a strike at once. When the order was put in the form of a respectful request from the Commandant – and not until – we usually complied. (This state of affairs was frankly disbelieved by prisoners from camps in Japan, where such action would have been ruthlessly punished).[6]

Livestock

Keijo and Mukden both possessed various animals, but at Keijo the animals were merely 'eye wash for the inspectors' in Lever's opinion. From the inspectors' first visits to Korea, Colonel Noguchi had advertised his intention of introducing livestock, but at the end of 1943 this only amounted to the rabbits that were kept at Keijo. Lever was not impressed:

> We have about seventy or a hundred rabbits; we thought these would be for us to eat from time to time and for the skins to be dried and used as earmuffs. The policy seems to be to underfeed them and let them die of pneumonia etc … So far about two have been eaten.[7]

In fact, a maximum of ten rabbits could be killed at a time, not a great addition to the diet of a camp population of over 200 men. If we believe one of the prisoners' tales, subterfuge enabled an increase in number:

> The Japanese never knew the rabbit strength, as they had been told that the does were likely to eat their young if frightened by strangers. The fact that the strength was unknown made it possible to increase the numbers ordered for the cookhouse by up to fifty per cent, provided the skins were not found.[8]

The photographs taken of various officers, including Colonel Elrington, holding the rabbits, might well have made good domestic propaganda as well as showing Japanese willingness to supplement the prisoners' diet with fresh meat. It is impossible to define the significance that rabbits hold for the Japanese: if you visit Tokyo today you can find rabbits in their hutches at cafes and hotel lobbies. It can be said, at least, that the Japanese would not have considered tending rabbits a worthy occupation for a samurai in wartime. Late in 1944, the hens and pigs promised by Noguchi in his conversations with the inspectors, arrived at Keijo. Again, strict limits were placed on breeding them. It was one of the minor cruelties that stoked the men's hatred of their captors. It was only when the food situation became desperate in 1945 that restrictions were finally lifted.

At Mukden, one exceptional member of Party B illustrated how livestock could make a significant difference to the men's diet, if sufficient subterfuge was deployed.

Albert Nuttall, the 'Pig Man of Mukden', had not given his true occupation to the Japanese when asked. He was a professional mechanic, and did not want to employ his skills on behalf of the Japanese military. As he had been born on a farm, he gave his occupation instead as a farmer. In an account he wrote immediately after his release he tells how 'an old man looked me up and suggested I kept pigs in the factory' and was assigned about half an acre of ground at the rear of the factory cookhouse:

> I had six pigs and one sow to begin with and in two years I managed to produce six tons of dressed pork and finished the war with a hundred and six pigs. Among them were two pedigree Hampshire, and Yorkshire boars and a Hampshire gilt. The old man and I stole all our building materials and built a fine pig pen. We were constantly enlarging it until I can say it really was a model, even for a civilised country. The old man saw that we had our share of the pork, but after a while we were given only the heads. Of course I was able to slip quite a lot across for the midday meal which was eaten in the factory. My pig pen soon served a second purpose as a clearing house for stolen goods. The Chinese offered good prices on the black market for stolen goods. I had made a secret compartment in one of the pens; the pens were fitted with electric light so that the sow might be able to see her farrow at night and not crush her. Mine, of course, was not the only crime ring, there were others, and a rival gang. An American supervisor, disappointed in getting no cut from a deal in which he claimed a share, informed on us.

His written account describes, with remarkable nonchalance, the 'clubbings' and the appalling conditions of solitary confinement he suffered. When he came out again he was sent back to his old job, as no prisoner of comparable ability could be found. He became something of a legend. A fellow prisoner, Arthur Christie, remembered him many years later in his memoirs as 'a man who had come to terms with Hoten. For the security of his pigs he built a world of his own where he could shut out all the obscenities going on around him.'[9]

Chapter 9

Dr Paravicini Visits Keijo

The key element of the Japanese POW external propaganda strategy, and the one that the Japanese devoted most time and resources to, was its successful deception of the International Committee of the Red Cross. It allowed the organisation to visit a small number of show camps under heavily manipulated conditions, and disseminated propaganda photographs, film footage, radio messages and letters from these camps. As part of its pretence that it was following international law, the Japanese created a Prisoner of War Information Office, the *Huryojohokyoku* or *Huryo* as it was referred to in ICRC correspondence, ostensibly to satisfy Article 77 of the 1929 Geneva Convention. Its function, as formulated by the Convention, was to operate as an independent body, receiving and supplying POW information. It was also responsible, with the Japanese postal service, for coordinating prisoner mail. At the same time, another supposedly independent organisation required by the Geneva Convention was created, The POW Management Office, responsible for camp administration, discipline and prisoner transfers. Although historians have discussed the two bodies as separate entities, it can be suggested that there was just one office masquerading as two. Its main functions were to fulfil prime minister Hideki Tojo's decision to exploit the prisoners as slave labour and propaganda. They shared the same building and the same staff, including the same head of staff, General Mikio Uemura. The chief was known for his dislike of foreigners and is on record as stating that 'within the bounds of humanity', prisoners should be treated severely. His organisation was not independent, but reported directly to the Army Ministry.

From the beginning of the conflict until the Japanese capitulation, many constraints were placed on the ICRC's work. The southern, newly occupied territories which held nearly 90 per cent of the Allied prisoners were forbidden to the ICRC on the grounds that they were war zones. All waters surrounding Japanese territories were also out of bounds to neutral ships, thereby preventing aid supplies reaching the prisoners. The ICRC was also limited in its number of accredited delegates. In comparison to the thirty permitted in Germany, only three delegations were initially allowed into Japanese territories, which occupied an area as large as Europe.

Dr Fritz Paravicini, a society doctor who had lived in Tokyo since the early years of the century, became the head of the Japan delegation. He had acted in the same role during the First World War and had many useful contacts among the diplomatic community and the higher echelons of Japanese society, including its royalty. (The Japanese royal family had interested itself in its national Red Cross society since its creation in the 1890s, a connection which still exists today.) Their humanitarian impulse was genuine, but like its German counterpart, the Japanese Red Cross was now bereft of any independence and completely under the control of the Japanese government. Following its usual procedure, the ICRC sought the Swiss consul's advice for the names of suitable Swiss nationals to take on the two other permitted positions, in Shanghai and Hong Kong. Eventually Edouard Egle, a director of a firm of importers and exporters, took up the role of delegate in Shanghai, and Rudolf Zindel, an employee of a trading company in China for the previous twenty years, took the position in Hong Kong. The ICRC already had delegates in other newly occupied countries, but the Japanese refused to recognise them. With great bravery, these delegates attempted to help the POWs in an unofficial, clandestine capacity, but they ran very great risks. The delegate in Borneo, Dr Mathaeus Fischer, a doctor and missionary, was beheaded, along with his wife, on fabricated charges of espionage.

In the previous conflict, Paravicini had relied on support and practical assistance from the Japanese Red Cross and the *Gaimusho*, the Japanese Foreign Office; but although these two organisations remained courteous they ceased to offer help, and directed Paravicini to the *Huryo* as his contact for obtaining prisoner lists and setting up inspection visits. The office's policy was one of stalling and deception. As Sibylla Jane Flower has noted, it was official policy to conceal the location of prisoners in areas regarded as strategically significant but the ICRC remained entirely unaware of this.[1] A trickle of prisoners' names slowly seeped out from the *Huryo* over the three-and-a-half years of the Pacific war, but even at the end of the conflict, the fate of a large number of prisoners was still unknown. The office claimed, falsely, that it was almost impossible to obtain accurate information about the widely dispersed prisoners due to the difficulties in communication created by wartime conditions. But in fact Uemura's office kept detailed records of the individual prisoners at least until 1944, enabling prisoners to be transferred across the empire to locations where their skills matched particular labour requirements.[2] It released just enough information to the enemy to be able to claim it was acting in good faith. Apart from the slow release of prisoner lists, nearly everything that came from it – letters, photographs, radio messages and film reels – was misinformation and propaganda.

Paravicini's relationship with the *Huryo* caused him agonies of frustration. In an official account of its activities during World War II, the ICRC recalls its dealings with the organisation in a tone of hurt indignation. 'From the outset the bureau was very unwilling to cooperate with the delegation. Personal visits were discountenanced: the delegates were even asked to deal with all questions only by correspondence. Over the period it issued the least possible information concerning PW.'[3] On 12 January 1943 Paravicini wrote to Geneva: 'If I look back on the first year of my activity I am most disappointed with the results; no delegate in the South, no Red Cross ships admitted, enquiries, correspondence, lists, distribution etc. very unsatisfactory.' The situation did not improve. In December of that year he wrote again: 'have sent *Huryojohokyoku* by cable or letter several thousand enquiries on missing or unidentified POWs – so far, very few answers received.'

But Paravicini's requests for inspection visits or suggestions for establishing supply routes were rarely refused outright. The Japanese held out the possibility of them being enacted at some unspecified date in the future. It also reminded the delegates that they had no legal basis for their presence, and that any complaints from them would lead to their immediate expulsion. It was an effective form of blackmail because Paravicini believed that with sufficient patience, results might be obtained. He saw procrastination as typically Japanese, as he explained to Geneva: 'although the Rising Sun only allows fruit to ripen very slowly', progress was being made, he assured them.[4] The slow, incremental approach he was willing to adopt was entirely in keeping with his organisation's *modus operandi*. At the outset he also believed that the Japanese were genuine when they held out the prospect of future improvements for the prisoners: he advised Geneva that they should be conscious that the Japanese were a people who were used to making do with very little themselves, and therefore found it hard to understand the necessity of relief supplies. During wartime, he added, anything which did not concern the progress of the war was low priority.

A variety of bureaucratic obstacles were placed in the way of the inspectors when they attempted to set up camp visits. They had to obtain photographic passes and permits for the areas they passed through, and negotiate the difficulties of finding transport and permission from a range of authorities. Not infrequently, inspections were cancelled at the last minute. In reality, there was little or nothing that was random about where the inspectors finally went. They were steered to the Party B camps, to the two other show camps, Zentsuji and Woosun, and were allowed two visits to the camps in Taiwan where senior officers were held under the better conditions allowed by the Japanese for the most senior public officials and military officers. Other camps on the Japanese mainland were permitted a single visit, but out of the approximately one thousand camps that came into existence in the Japanese territories, only forty-three received an inspection.

Manipulation did not end on the day of the inspection. When the inspectors came to write the reports, there was considerable pressure placed on them to avoid criticism. The Japanese reacted badly to less than positive remarks. As Paravicini wrote to Geneva, 'the mildest criticisms are met with expressions of outraged hurt'.[5] Once the reports were written, they were doctored by the Japanese, as the ICRC's report on its activities during the Second World War makes clear:

> The Committee's correspondence, too, either by letter or by telegram, was subject to censorship under conditions which severely hampered it. Thus, in March 1944, a telegram from a delegate giving an account of his visit to the POW camp Fukushima was considerably amended by the military authorities, who were unwilling for the delegate to report the unsatisfactory details he had noted concerning the rations, sanitary conditions and discipline of the Allied soldiers detained in the camp.

Abundant evidence of doctoring can be found in the Geneva archives. It was not confined to minor alterations either, but also the addition of lengthy passages written by the Japanese. For example, there is a letter from Inspector Egle in Hong Kong to Paravicini which begins with the news that he has 'casually overheard a conversation' between German soldiers in a bar discussing the bravery displayed by the Japanese in their efforts to save drowning POWs from the torpedoed *Lisbon Maru*. As we have seen, this was the fictitious Japanese narrative created in response to a protest by the British government.

Paravicini was radically shocked by the hostility and suspicion he encountered, the complete reverse of the courtesy and helpfulness he had met with during the First World War. But the ease with which he was able to arrange a visit to the Korean camps gave him grounds for believing that despite all the delays and obstacles, he was slowly making progress.

On his arrival in Korea in December 1942, the doctor was surprised and delighted by the warmth of his reception. The importance attached to POW propaganda from the Korean camps is evidenced by the attention he received at the highest levels: some of the most senior officials, both public and military, took the trouble to welcome him. Writing back to Geneva, he reported happily to his colleagues: 'The hospitality and generosity of the Governor-general, the Supreme Commander of the Army, his chief of Staff, the President of The Red Cross Society of Chosen (Korea), and other dignitaries were overwhelming'.[6]

Although the close involvement of senior figures was unique to Korea, Paravicini's visit followed a pattern that was repeated every year at the camps that were permitted inspections. In the days preceding a visit there was a noticeable relaxation in camp discipline. Red Cross supplies or letters were often released just before the inspection, lifting the men's spirits as well as enabling the inspector to confirm that relief supplies had reached the camps. Small repairs and minor cosmetic improvements were made to the parts of the camp the inspectors would be shown. The day before the inspection, the prisoners were sometimes given a holiday to clean the camp, 'as if the Japs were expecting a visit from the Emperor', as a prisoner at Jinsen later wrote.

My father's diary provides details of the typical preparations that occurred before a visit. In November 1943 he wrote: 'For the last three days we have been allowed to keep the lights on until 12. Noticed general mildening [*sic*] in attitude towards us.' Two days before the inspection, the officers were offered the chance to buy pot plants, including palms, aspidistras and 'dwarf fir trees' to brighten up their squad rooms. Red Cross parcels were delivered on the evening before the inspection.

'Hungry POWs flock to see the lorry up at the entrance being unloaded by the Korean sentries. What joviality, what geniality pervades the camp, eyes alight with expectation.'[7]

Some of the supplies would be used to stock the camp's canteen, an amenity stipulated by the 1929 Geneva Convention. It was envisaged as a store where prisoners would be able to buy items such as toiletries, cigarettes, stationery and small snacks. However, the Keijo canteen was for most of the year 'an empty room with the sign "canteen" on the door' according to Captain Lever.'[8] As at other camps, it was stocked up before the inspections, but the goods were usually removed immediately after the inspection had finished. If they were conspicuously malnourished, prisoners were given extra rations in the days, or even weeks, before an inspection, so that they could regain some weight and create a healthier appearance. At a senior officers' camp in Formosa, General Lewis Beebe wrote: 'We had an inspection on 8 November [1944]. Prior to the inspection we had been receiving about all the rice we could eat, and the soup was also nourishing, but following the inspection there was a cut in food for some reason.'[9]

The inspection followed the same timetable at each camp. The visit was never to exceed two hours and the first hour was taken up with an interview with the camp commandant, who parried awkward questions by stating he did not have the authority to answer them, or in more extreme cases, threatening to terminate the visit there and then. Inspectors would also be reminded that they had no legal basis for their presence. But Paravicini was evidently impressed by Colonel Noguchi, and wrote back to Geneva that 'he was like a father to his prisoners'.[10] At each visit, Noguchi would show his concern for the men by outlining various intended schemes for their benefit. In 1942, Noguchi was aiming to have showers installed and to set up recreational Sunday walks for the men. The next year he had a more ambitious but equally chimeric project, the installation of a cinema. At Mukden the commandant also offered illusory plans: in 1944 he was hoping to introduce horses and cows into the camp for the men's recreation, although he did not specify what recreational opportunities the cows would offer.

After the interview the inspector would be shown those areas of the camp which could bear inspection. They would be hurried along by Japanese officials, acting as a shield against prisoners who might wish to approach them. Those rooms which would reveal something of the reality of the men's lives were never open to inspection. In 1943, Alan Toze wrote: 'Today is a holiday on account of the Red Cross representative. To our disgust, he did not come into our room – the darkest, coldest and most miserable in the building.'[11] When Paravicini's successor Marcel Junod visited the hospital at Mukden in 1945, he wrote that it was the first time an ICRC inspector had ever been allowed into a hospital or sick bay. This is hard to believe, but the inconsistencies in the reports from Keijo suggest that its own 'hospital' was out of bounds. The hospital hut never held more than ten beds, yet in 1942 it was reported that the 'infirmary' had fifteen. In 1944 this had increased to twenty, with both isolation and convalescent wards. Another routine deception was to supply detailed statistics on the prisoners' diet, itemising the exact weight of each type of food provided in the ten days prior to the visit. They would also see the prisoners having lunch, which would be a very significantly larger and more nutritious meal than the usual fare. There would be a compensatory reduction in their rations on the day following the visit.

The final part of the inspection was an interview with prisoner representatives, termed 'men of confidence'. The Geneva Convention stipulated that these should be conducted privately, with no interference from the camp officials. This was never allowed; there were always Japanese officers in attendance. The men of confidence were instructed as to what they could say, and any deviation from this would be severely punished. Before the 1942 visit to Keijo, the men were asked to submit a list of the questions that they wanted to ask the inspectors. It was returned with unacceptable questions crossed out. In 1943, the senior officer at Jinsen, Major Holohan, dared to tell the inspector that the prisoners needed a more balanced diet. He was sentenced to ten days' solitary confinement in one of the unheated punishment cells for 'ingratitude'. Out of desperation, prisoners sometimes did tell the truth, regardless of consequences. At Zentsuji in 1944, the prisoners had not been allowed to get near the inspector, but as he left some of the men called out to him; 'We are dying of hunger!'[12] They endured particularly savage beatings afterwards.

1942 Inspection of Keijo Camp

Paravicini was surprised to find that a Swiss diplomat based in Tokyo, Heinrich Angst, had arrived at the camp at the same time as him. Switzerland was Britain's 'Protecting Power' in the war, and as such it had the right to visit camps independently of the Red Cross. It was not a coincidence, and when Paravicini mildly observed to the Japanese that it was the usual thing for the Red Cross and the Protecting Power to visit independently on different dates, he was not telling them anything they did not already know.

Very few inspections were actually made by the Protecting Powers, but their reports could be sent back to Switzerland using the privilege of the diplomatic bag. Angst sent Paravicini's report to Geneva under diplomatic protection, and consequently it can be used as a case study in the knowledge that it escaped doctoring by the Japanese. The entries under the various categories suggest humane conditions, although the authenticity of the report is enhanced by the inclusion of two complaints: the men lacked adequate underclothes for the cold climate, and there was nothing to buy in the canteen. A summary of the various sections of the report is given below and contrasted with the reality.

Diet

Prisoners received a balanced diet including meat, sugar, vegetables, soya beans and bread. On average a prisoner received 3250 calories a day.[13]

The men lived in a state of almost constant hunger from their arrival in September 1942 until August 1945. The medical officers among them calculated that rations added up to about 1,800 calories or at most 2,000 calories a day, rather than the 3,250 stated in the report, and in 1945 their diet sometimes dropped to no more than 1,500 a day. By comparison, the Australian army gave men on active service 4,200 calories a day, and health organisations today suggest 2,400 calories as an average amount for an adult male. There were three periods during Party B's captivity in Korea where the rations became so inadequate that the medical officers became worried that there would be deaths from malnutrition. Their diet was nevertheless far better than at most camps. Bread was a very rare item on prisoner menus in the Far East, but occasionally available at the Korean camps. The Japanese made sure to exploit its propaganda value not just through inspection visits but by taking photographs of the men making their own bread at Keijo.

There were three meals a day: at 8.00am, midday and 5.30pm.

John Lever made a note of what the prisoners were eating in the weeks before Paravicini visited:

> We usually got rice and a pint of thin stew, or at lunchtime a small loaf with a little grease on it instead of rice. Occasionally the stew contained a very small amount of meat or fish, but the main ingredient was usually a vegetable: spinach, sweet potato, daikon (a kind of cabbage) or seaweed.

At breakfast and lunch the prisoners were also allowed a cup of Japanese tea, 'little more than hot water with a slight tea flavour' Lever complained. He estimated that to feel full he would have needed to eat three times the amount he received.

As well as the diet being inadequate and monotonous, some of the staple foods were so repellent that many of the men could not eat them. My father, however hungry he was, found the seaweed that was often served for breakfast totally uneatable. Alan Toze describes other food that most could not bring themselves to eat: 'Every day for the last week we have had a lunch of scaled fish soup which has been made from a stock got in about twelve months ago. And which is going rotten. The stench and taste are appalling. Hardly anyone can face it.'[14] Equally unappetising was chrysanthemum-leaf stew, which apparently had a very bitter taste and stained the teeth.[15]

The diaries illustrate the obsession with food that comes to those living on the verge of starvation. The contents of each Red Cross parcel are always written out in full in every diary, and Major Rigby wrote a record of every single meal he ate at Keijo. In a letter to his parents written on Christmas Day 1943, my father finishes with an apology: 'I am afraid this letter rather resembles a menu. I shall do better next time.' He had listed every item of food he had eaten that day, and also mentioned the items of food that featured on the hand-drawn Christmas cards he had received. At Jinsen, Alex Johnstone started a recipe book, 'Dream Dishes'.[16] By December 1942 there were already a hundred of them, and eventually it ran to over 600 recipes, each dish carefully indexed under the appropriate category. He allowed full rein to his culinary imagination, offering recipes for banana soufflés and a variety of exotic cocktails.[17]

Heating, Lighting, Ventilation

Ventilation is adequate, although the windows are small. Electric lighting is installed throughout. The building is heated and room temperature was 16 degrees Celsius on the day of the visit.

Ventilation, heating and lighting were all utterly inadequate. In summer, the prisoners sweltered in the heat. Lighting was also poor: the men continually complain in their diaries about not having enough light to read by in the squad rooms unless they were close to a window. The hours during which electric lights were allowed on were severely limited. However, the greatest affliction the prisoners had to bear, along with hunger, was the Korean winter, which lasted for over four months of the year. In January 1943, the temperature dropped to -19°C. The diaries for the first months of imprisonment record a growing surprise, turning to fear, at the intensity of the cold and the inadequacy of the heating and clothing for the malnourished men. The first snowfall was on 8 November. Some of the Australians enjoyed the sight; it was the first time in his life that Arthur Kerr had seen snow. The novelty rapidly wore off. During the winter months, the temperature in the squad rooms often dropped below zero at night. The men at Keijo would wake to find frost on the walls, and at Jinsen there would be icicles hanging from the ceiling.

Stoves were allowed in the squad rooms from the middle of December to the middle of March. The heat they generated was inadequate, and the temperature recorded by Paravicini appears unique for a December day inside the camp. The prisoners agreed that the worst periods at the camp were the weeks just before and after the stoves were allowed. Lever's diary entry for 15 March 1943 reads: 'It becomes too warm for us to have stoves officially. The fact that you have to wrap yourself in blankets or wear an overcoat if you stay in the room has no bearing on the matter.' There were heavy snowfalls in April, and the next month Lever complained 'Although it's well into May the weather isn't really warm yet and we are still wearing winter clothing.' The suffering caused by the winter climate should not be underestimated.

As the cold weather began again in November 1943 Toze wrote:

> The most unmerciful and terrifying winds and frosts that were ever let loose make our lives a continual misery,

> numbing bodies, minds – even our will to carry on and live. The Siberian wind of unbelievable coldness is whistling through the ill-fitting doors and windows, penetrating our clothes – our very flesh – as tho' it was not there. Another twelve months of this life under summer or autumnal conditions would be bearable, but, God in Heaven! How we fear and loathe the winter here.[18]

Sanitation

Everything is in working order and clean. The Japanese issue essential supplies such as soap, toothbrushes, toothpaste, razor blades, etc.

The conditions at the camp were unhygienic in all areas. The squad rooms were lice-ridden and verminous, and in summer they were invaded by swarms of fleas and mosquitoes, bringing disease. My father's opinion that the latrines and washrooms were 'foully disgusting beyond description' needs no elaboration. In winter the pipes often froze, and the washrooms would become, as Toze found one morning, 'a quagmire of excreta and filth'. Even if the pipes were not frozen, washing yourself during the winter months was an ordeal. In January 1943 my father wrote: 'Baths on 5th Wed, fortitude required for participation: ice on floor and in washing tubs.' The razor blades, soap and toothpaste listed on the inspection report were always scarce items, and sometimes supplies of soap ran out completely. When an unexpected consignment of toothpaste arrived at Jinsen in 1944, the men were so hungry, they ate it.

Health

The medical, surgical and dental equipment is adequate for minor cases. More serious cases are taken to the local hospital.

The cold, poor diet and squalid, unhygienic living conditions meant that there was constant illness at the camp. The diseases were the common ones of Far Eastern captivity, malaria, dysentery, diphtheria and those caused by vitamin deficiency such as pellagra and beriberi. There were also the illnesses that were prevalent in camps in colder climates: pleurisy, bronchitis and pneumonia. Although on a smaller scale than elsewhere, there were also serious workplace injuries resulting in permanent disablement and death. Some of the more minor complaints were a continuous presence in each prisoner's life throughout his time at Keijo. Toze, like many others, suffered unremittingly from diarrhoea throughout his captivity. Most of the men suffered from worm infestations, and all of them from diseases caused by vitamin deficiencies.

Although the report said that medical, surgical and dental equipment was adequate for minor cases, there was virtually none. Captain Charles Mummery was a dentist, but the only form of treatment he appears to have been able to provide was to extract teeth with a pair of pliers. There were a lot of teeth to be pulled – one of the effects of an inadequate diet was gum disease, and the slaps around the face from the guards sometimes left broken or loose teeth. The men took this in their stride; on board the *Fukkai Maru* the tooth pulling had become a form of entertainment – men gathered around to watch and cheered at the moment of extraction.

The prisoners were, however, fortunate in that serious cases were taken to a civilian hospital, as recorded in the 1942 report. But Arthur Kerr, who had first-hand experience, described the surgical treatment as 'butchery'. One of the Loyals, Harry Kingsley, had been buried in an earthfall at work and emerged with a crushed leg: 'Kingsley's pelvis arranged without Thomas splint, and apparently without anything else; leg is about 2" shorter than other, and sciatic nerve is gone. Foot is raised for walking by means of string in hand.' Later, the leg had to be amputated.

Two of the great cruelties which seem to have been common to all the camps, including those in Korea, were to withhold available medicine and to compel sick men to work. After the war, Colonel Cardew testified that during the first year at Keijo he constantly made requests for available medicine, which were invariably denied. They received next to nothing. Red Cross medical supplies were commandeered by the Japanese, and released only in very limited quantities, after considerable pleading. In 1945, this directly led to the deaths at Jinsen of two Americans, part of a group that had been transferred to the camp from the Philippines. At Keijo, Ushihara served as a medical orderly as well as the camp interpreter, and used to assault prisoners who came to him to report sick. He was not above striking sick men as they lay in their beds.

Camp Regime

Relations with camp staff: 'Actually cordial'

As this early stage the prisoners still had a positive attitude towards Colonel Noguchi, and believed his assurances that he was doing all he could for the prisoners. Captain Lever was willing to concede, in characteristically lordly manner, that among the Japanese there were 'one or two you could take for gentleman if you were prepared to overlook a few things'. It would have been foolhardy and pointless for the prisoners to complain about their captors, but Paravicini's statement that relations at the camp were 'cordial' reflected something of the truth at that time. Later, the diaries express hatred.

The violence committed on the prisoners appears negligible compared to other Japanese camps, but this highlights the extremities of cruelty that existed elsewhere rather than the beneficence of the captors in Korea. Slappings occurred every day at the Korean camps, although officers were struck less often. A 'binta' might leave the victim with a black eye, broken nose or missing tooth. At all the camps there were bullies and sadists who would knock the men around on the slightest pretext. One of the main perpetrators was the adjutant, Captain Terada, the most 'heartily detested' man in the camp, according to John Lever. He used to encourage the junior guards going out on work parties for the day to give the men a good slapping if they were not up to scratch. Among them, Corporal Takuma became notorious for his rages. He was given the nickname 'Scoops', to commemorate the occasion when he had attacked a group of men with an improvised soup ladle, made from a stick and a tin can attached to it with protruding nails. The attack left the men with deep grooves on their faces. 'Kicker's' nickname needs no explanation, other than that his usual target was the men's shins.

Work

Officers did not have to work, but other ranks could choose from a variety of jobs.

This statement is false; the other ranks had no choice in the work they were assigned. Officers did not have to work, although they had initially been ordered to do so. Elrington recorded how their refusal to work resulted in 'spilt teeth and black eyes' but, remarkably for a Japanese camp, the officers won the argument.[19] Prisoners at Keijo and Jinsen were made to work in sight of the public as part of the policy of humiliation. At Jinsen, men were made to dig a channel for a new railway track and worked at the docks as stevedores. As well as attracting Korean onlookers, in the first days they were also sketched by a Japanese war artist. At Keijo, the diaries make constant reference to 'the farm' and 'the warehouse' located near the station. Here they shifted, packed and unpacked goods. Another job was 'knots', which simply involved sorting ropes and untying knots in them. Occasionally they were lent out to civilian contractors, when they might be in luck and receive better rations. The most popular job appears to have been 'sew sew', working as tailors in a workshop at Keijo mending Japanese military uniforms. The officers were used as overseers of the men's labour. My father particularly disliked this, especially in winter, when he would have to stand around doing nothing all day in sub-zero temperatures. The work was tedious and exhausting for the malnourished and hungry men, with the only satisfaction coming from the occasional opportunities to pilfer food, or small acts of sabotage, such as swapping the destination labels of various items at the railway station. There were workplace injuries, with broken bones and men losing fingers or toes. There were frequent slappings for unsatisfactory behaviour, and sometimes the men were made to slap each other. Alex Johnstone injured his legs permanently when he slipped trying to climb onto a railway truck. Nevertheless, in comparison to the prisoners working on the railway, or in the mines of Japan and Formosa, or men constructing airfields in Borneo, they were undoubtedly fortunate. But if the men were lucky compared to other prisoners of the Japanese, they were unaware of it. The sheer, grinding boredom and discomfort of performing physical labour while suffering from malnutrition, hunger and a variety of diseases was an ordeal that came increasingly unbearable as the years passed.

Living conditions also became increasingly irksome. Alan Toze's diary offers a very vivid account of what being a prisoner at Keijo was actually like:

> I am heartily sick of this place, the stinking benjos [latrines], the dusty, draughty, crowded, humanity-reeking squad rooms, the mess and muck and poverty, and extreme stinginess of everything Asiatic, of burning my fingers every meal time on the ridiculous aluminium eating utensils, of having to eat stew with a fork, of travelling down to drain off rice water two or three times a night … of our humourless jabbering custodians, their scruffiness, their face-slapping, empty promises, pilfering of Red Cross parcels etc etc ad lib, of the soul-wrenching contrast of eating one of the 'meals', then immediately afterwards reading one of the books in which an English meal is described. Compared to a POW's life a spell in gaol would be nothing as you know the most important thing, i.e. when it is going to terminate. It is a most appalling vista to contemplate now, the possibility of even another year only of this appalling, soul-destroying existence, cut off from the world, our kith and kin, from news, deprived of even such simple pleasures as an evening walk or a game of football, not allowed to sing, or have a talk or lecture, having to watch every move for fear some innocent action will be misinterpreted by our ever watchful custodians and we are subjected to the indignity and mortification of corporal punishment.

Chapter 10
Mukden

Although Seishiro Itagaki was disappointed in his plans to bring American prisoners to Korea, Mukden in Manchuria fulfilled his ambition to have a propaganda camp where both British and American prisoners were held. It served a dual function and also provided manpower for the *Manshou kosaki kai Kibasha ki Kaisha*, the 'Manchurian Tool Manufacturing Company', known to both the captives and Japanese by the abbreviation 'MKK'. Owned by Mitsubishi, it was a tool and dye factory where machine parts were manufactured to aid Japan's war effort. These included parts for the Zero fighter planes. In 1944 the prisoners would also be allocated to other, smaller factories: *Nakayama Steel*, *Manchu Leather*, and *Manchu Cloth.* American prisoners who had the particular types of skills and experience necessary for this type of work were transported from the Philippines. Their selection offers proof that the Japanese held central records for their prisoners.

At 11.30 am on 8 November 1942, fifty of the men left Keijo for Mukden, a 400-mile train journey to the north. The band played 'Auld Lang Syne' and Colonel Noguchi shook each man's hand as he bade them farewell. He assured them that they had all behaved like true English gentlemen and that he was grieved to lose them, but hoped that they would all meet up again under happier circumstances. The men joined a contingent from Jinsen at Keijo railway station then boarded the train for Manchuria. Here they met up with the American prisoners for the first time, a party of over a thousand men. To the Americans, the malnourished members of Party B looked relatively well-fed. The British and Australian troops for their part were shocked by the condition the American troops were in and by what they told them about their experiences. They had been shipped from the Philippines on the *Tottori Maru* in conditions which made the voyage on the *Fukkai Maru* 'look like a pleasure cruise', to quote Eric Wallwork. Forty Americans had died on the ship and, as was the case with the

Fukkai Maru, there would be more deaths from the ill effects of the voyage during the ensuing weeks.

For the first months, the prisoners were housed in a temporary camp, and later moved to a newly constructed building in a suburb of Mukden, Hoten, which was closer to the factories. (For simplicity's sake I follow the usual custom of referring to both as Mukden, although the latter is also referred to as 'Hoten'). The regime was harsher than at the Korean camps, with worse living conditions. The Japanese had taken nineteen huts that had previously served as Chinese army barracks, to house the men. The huts were of an unusual construction in that they were partially submerged into the ground, which did not help sanitation and heating. The roofs were made of wooden boards covered with mud. 'What a dump,' was Australian Des Brennan's first reaction. The senior British officer, Major Robert Peaty, was equally unimpressed: 'I would not keep my garden tools in such a hut.'[1] On arrival, the prisoners were made to stand outside in the freezing weather while the camp commandant, Colonel Matsuyama, delivered a greeting which was the opposite in tone of Colonel Noguchi's valediction: 'The yellow and white man are eternal enemies, and as long as the white man is in Asia, there will be no peace in Asia.' he told them. 'I will not rest till all of you are dead.'[2]

Keeping a diary was forbidden, but Major Peaty did so secretly using a code of his creation. He also wrote a lengthy debriefing report on his arrival in England. They both depict a barbaric regime, with conditions closer to the popular conception of Far Eastern captivity than the Korean camps. His report states: 'Beatings were of such frequent occurrence that one ceased to take note of them being anything out of the ordinary run.' The diary entries suggest that he was keeping a record of prisoner abuse to be used after the war. On 20 February 1943 he wrote:

> Sergeant Woolham, 3854639, 2nd Bn. The Loyal Regiment, was beaten up with a shovel in my presence, by the Superintendent Officer, Lt. Miki, and Corporal Noda of the Japanese Pay corps. They alleged that he was about to strike one of them, but the whole thing took place before my eyes, and the actual facts are that Sgt Woolham, during the course of an investigation into a supposed breach of camp regulations, was struck by Cpl. Noda. The unexpected blow

> nearly threw him off his balance, and he swung his right arm back to maintain it. The Japanese at once seized on this as an excuse, and Miki went berserk, and picking up a shovel, laid into Woolham with the edge of it as hard as he could go. This lasted for a full ten minutes.

Peaty also recorded men dying from their beatings: 'Two Americans who were badly beaten up died about fourteen days later. They were perfectly hale and hearty before being beaten up, and on coming out of the guardhouse they just took to their beds and died.'[3] Punishments for minor offences were also savage:

> It was a regular thing for men to be made to stand with arms outstretched holding a bowl of water, and to receive a clout from a 'Kendo Stick' or wooden sword if they spilt any water. Men were also made to hold their hands above their heads and at the same time adopt a 'knees bend' position. As soon as the muscles tired and the position could no longer be held, a whack across the back of the legs was handed out. Similarly the 'press-up' attitude would be ordered, and as soon as the arms gave out, the 'kendo stick' came into use.

Unsurprisingly perhaps, the most obvious contrast between Mukden and the Korean camps lies in the much higher death toll. Between 11 November 1942 and the end of March 1943, 235 American prisoners perished. During the winter the ground was frozen solid and their bodies were simply stacked up in a warehouse. Medical care was totally inadequate. The 'hospital' was no more than one of the huts set aside for that purpose. It had only one bedpan at a time when there were a hundred patients within the hospital suffering from dysentery. Many died from the pneumonia they caught from having to go outside to the latrines when the temperature was several degrees below zero. Major Peaty was scathing about the Japanese medical personnel:

> Many of its practitioners were only one degree above witch doctors. Among the medicines was powdered rhinoceros horn. Milk was regarded as a medicine but was only given in teaspoonfuls. In cases where they wished to give opium for

> dysentery, the doctors only allowed one hundredth of what we considered the minimum. They regarded this as a fatal dose and were deeply suspicious of our doctors' request. Where we take two aspirins, the Japanese doctor would give half a tablet of about one twentieth of the strength of ours.

The prisoners who worked as medical staff did their best with totally inadequate resources, under the heroic leadership of Des Brennan. He later recollected that the temperature inside the hospital could be as low as -20°C. Inside the infectious diseases ward where he worked there were ninety men in a space which should have held no more than forty. But as in all the Party B camps, there were also Japanese who acted with compassion and humanity. Among the medical staff was a Dr Otki, 'a short, tubby man with glasses', remembered medical orderly Arthur Christie. At considerable risk to himself, Otki used his own money to buy medicines and soup bowls to be used as bedpans. But there was also his antithesis, a Captain Kawashima, 'almost certainly the most evil and sadistic unmentionable piece of humanity that ever posed as a doctor. He was responsible for more beatings than any other Japanese in that camp.'[4]

Conditions were less harsh in the factories. Here, the men worked a ten hour day with two days off per month. They were under the supervision of Japanese civilians who did not hesitate to beat their charges if they were unhappy with them, but because their skills were valuable to the Japanese and not easily replaceable, they did not have to suffer the extremes of ill-treatment that occurred elsewhere.

No amount of window dressing would ever have made the temporary camp suitable for a Red Cross inspection, but in the summer of 1943 the prisoners moved into a newly constructed building with a new commandant, Colonel Matsuda. Like the Korean camps, Mukden received three inspection visits. The fact that a brand-new prison had been built for the prisoners with no expense spared was of course emphasised to the ICRC inspectors on each of their visits. The first inspection report gave a very positive account of the building:

> The barracks, or quarters for the prisoners, are of brick and newly built. They contain electric lights and heat. Ventilation is satisfactory. Each prisoner has one mattress, six army blankets, two sheets, and one pillow case. In summer

> they are issued mosquito nets. The officers and men have separate sections. Sanitary facilities are connected to the barrack buildings. Privates and non-commissioned officers are allowed a hot bath every other day, and officers every day.[5]

This can be contrasted with Major Peaty's description:

> Our Ministry of Health would not pass such buildings as fit for human habitation. There were no damp courses, for one thing, and no gutters for another. So the rain off the roof ran straight down the walls, and the wet came through. The roofs leaked, so it was always damp inside. The windows were quite inadequate, and as lights were forbidden during the day, it was always dark inside.

For the first few months the camp lacked running water. As at the Korean camps, the men shared their accommodation with flies, lice, fleas and vermin. The sanitary facilities were infested by maggots. Requests to be allowed to clean the latrines were refused.

Given the brutal conditions at the camp, it is perhaps surprising to note that Mukden received more visits from film and recording units than Keijo. Major Robert Peaty gives an idea of what interested them in his debriefing report:

> I formed the opinion that it was a propaganda camp, for we received so many visits from the Japanese Propaganda Corps, who brought cine cameras and took reels of baseball games, the men marching to work, (with all Japanese guards well out of sight), quizzes, spelling bees, camp orchestra, sing songs at Christmas.

Musical and sporting activities were the main focus of interest. As well as a camp orchestra there was a choir, with Peaty retaining command in the role of choirmaster. On 18 December 1943 the propaganda unit came to make a sound recording of their Christmas service: 'We are going to celebrate by singing carols, if I can teach the Americans not to relapse into their usual mournful dirge-like singing', he wrote.[6] Matsuda knew the value of these propaganda activities. At Easter 1944, the Vatican was able to send money to the camps to be spent on relief supplies. Despite pleas for it to be spent on food and medicine, Matsuda bought clocks for the squad rooms, baseball gloves, two violins, two guitars and an accordion.

In July 1943, the propaganda corps spent a whole week at the camp. As at Keijo, there were attempts to lighten the atmosphere. The propaganda team distributed cigarettes and sweets, and broadcast the latest Hollywood and sports news. There was a holiday for all the men on 22 July, with concerts and a baseball match. The 1943 ICRC inspection report mentions 'a large sports ground', a slight exaggeration. Nevertheless, the space was very much larger than Keijo's yard and the prisoners were able to play baseball, basketball, rugby and football. The British had their own baseball team but it was over two years before 'The Limeys' actually won a match, beating the US Navy 5-3. Unsurprisingly, the inspectors were not informed of some of the other 'games' the Japanese made the prisoners play on the sports ground. As a punishment for minor offences, men were made to run around the perimeter of the ground naked in freezing weather. On one occasion, men who had reported sick with severe diarrhoea were sent to run laps clad only in their underwear. Those who soiled themselves were excused work, the remainder were sent to the factory. This was exactly the sort of humiliation that the Japanese guards found amusing.

As at Keijo, one of the major filming events involved the commemoration of dead comrades. At Mukden it took the form of an opening ceremony for the new camp cemetery. Major Peaty played his part by laying flowers at the cemetery's main cross: 'They were only a bunch of thistles and stunted wild gladioli but flowers they were, nonetheless. Prayers were said and hymns were sung.'[7] As Colonel Cardew had done at the Keijo memorial service, Major Hankins, the senior American officer, made a short speech to the assembled company, thanking the Japanese for the 'consideration and the care with which 218 individual crosses were constructed for each dead man'. Like Noguchi, Colonel Matsuda enjoyed receiving written expressions of appreciation from his prisoners. He ordered Major Hankins to put his thanks in writing. Shortly afterwards *Domei* released details of his letter for worldwide distribution: 'Major Hankins, who is acting as leader of the American prisoners in the camp, delivered an impressive dedication speech as well as writing a letter of thanks to the chief commander of Mukden camp'. Some of the prisoners criticised their senior officer for his speech, but Peaty knew that Hankins was a quick-witted man and guessed his purpose. He had sent a message to the outside world that 218 of his men had died at the camp since their arrival.

Unit 731

Mukden has become notorious for the visits of the biological and chemical warfare research group, Unit 731. Under the leadership of microbiologist General Shirō Ishii, Unit 731 perpetrated some of the worst atrocities of the twentieth century. They were based in Manchuria and experimented on the local population. Whole villages were infected with cholera and plague. In the 1980s a British biological warfare expert wrote in a confidential Foreign Office report:

> The activities of Lt Gen Ishii and his team are well known to me from a previous posting at DNBCC CDE Porton.[8] In the whole saga of war crimes and inhumanity his activities are without peer; the hypothermia and tissue transplant experiments at Auschwitz pale into insignificance.

Their headquarters were located in Manchuria in a suburb of the city of Harbin, so Mukden camp was conveniently close for them. There are widely accepted claims that prisoners at Mukden were deliberately injected by the unit with infectious diseases as part of the unit's research. The conspiracy theory as it exists today partly depends on a significant misquotation from Peaty's diary. The Wikipedia entry under Hoten camp perpetuates this error, telling the reader: 'In a secret diary, Peaty recorded inmates being given regular injections of infectious diseases, disguised as harmless vaccinations. On 23 February 1943, his entry read: 'Funeral service for 142 dead. 186 have died in 5 days, all Americans.' Peaty in fact wrote **105** days, not 5 days.

There is no doubt that the unit visited the camp, but a lot of the 'evidence' used to support the theory in fact relates to the camp's propaganda function. It has been claimed, for example, that the Propaganda Unit was in reality part of Unit 731, and was filming and recording the men to observe the effects of the injections. The claims had originated in America in the 1970s, and were taken up in Britain by journalists who produced a documentary for television and an accompanying book.[9] Both made a deep impression on the British survivors from Mukden. Arthur Christie organised a campaign for compensation, enlisting the support of his constituency MP. The result was a lengthy and wide-reaching government investigation making use of documentary evidence and testimony from this country and America. Files relating to the investigation were only made public in 2018.[10] The report concluded that there was no evidence that British POWs had been injected with infectious diseases.

Various aspects of Mukden were claimed to be unique and thus could be proffered as evidence of Unit 731's experiments on the men. The report lists them as follows:

(a) the number of vaccinations
(b) the fact that a new camp was built for prisoners
(c) the weighing and measuring of the prisoners
(d) the presence of permanent medical staff
(e) the falsification of medical records
(f) the number of inoculations

Each claim is analysed and rejected in turn. There was nothing unique about the construction of a new camp, nor the presence of permanent medical staff. The facilities at the hospital were in any case totally inadequate for the type of research the unit performed. The report also conjectures, correctly, that the new building may have served a propaganda purpose. Neither the weighing or measuring of prisoners nor the vaccinations and inoculations were unique to Mukden.

The report makes no reference to the Korean camps, but knowledge of the propaganda activities in Korea strengthens its findings. The men at the Korean camps received the same types of inoculations as the prisoners at Mukden. There was a propaganda motive for keeping the men alive, and at Mukden there was the additional factor that the prisoners were a skilled workforce and not as easily replaceable as the men on the Burma–Thai railway. The claim that medical records were falsified is correct, but both medical orderly Arthur Christie and Major Peaty believed that the records were doctored to create a good impression for the ICRC inspectors, who visited shortly after the falsification occurred. It is certain that inspector Max Pestalozzi was shown the medical records.

The visit of a group medical officers to measure the prisoners' limbs certainly mystified Dr Brennan. As well as being measured with callipers, the prisoners had to walk on footsteps painted on the floor of the room where they were examined. They were asked about their ancestry. The hand of General Ishii has been detected in these examinations, but Keijo was also visited by civilians who carried out similar examinations. Over several days a group of civilians filmed and photographed the men, and made detailed measurements of their limbs and torsos. They also took samples of hair from various parts of the body. The prisoners were then interviewed and questioned on their ancestry. Although Jinsen did not receive a visit from this group, the prisoners were required to provide samples of hair to be sent away for analysis. (Some of the men were able to sabotage the exercise by submitting hair taken from dogs and rats.) At both camps, the prisoners were told that they were taking part in 'racial comparison' tests. Similar tests were also carried out at other camps across the Japanese territories. Eugenics was still a respectable scientific discipline at that time and it was a field in which Unit 731 held a particular interest. The visiting groups of civilians may well have been associates or even members of Unit 731, but the tests caused no ill effects.

There is no doubt that Unit 731 visited the camp, but they did so at the request of the camp commandant, Colonel Matsuda, who was alarmed at the high death rate of the skilled workforce that had been shipped from the Philippines to help the Japanese war effort. The various activities undertaken by these visitors included autopsies, the burial of the stacks of dead bodies, the inoculation of the prisoners and tests to detect which of the prisoners were suffering from, or carriers of, dysentery and diarrhoea. These all served the purpose of stemming the flood of deaths. As the government report notes, they were successful in this. Following their visits the deaths tailed off and the only Americans to die later in the camp's history were the ones beaten to death by the camp guards. So the visits from Unit 731 had the opposite effect to what was claimed: instead of causing deaths, it prevented them.

In a letter he wrote to Prime Minister Margaret Thatcher as part of his campaign, Arthur Christie posed the entirely reasonable and deeply poignant question about the British members of Party B at Mukden: 'Why have many of our group of seventy-eight died early in our fifties? Those still alive mostly in very poor health?' Sadly, there was nothing unusual about these early deaths. In his study of Keijo camp, Chris Given-Wilson writes that his father, Lieutenant Paddy Given-Wilson, died at the comparatively early age of 57, adding that 'Not many prisoners of the Japanese survived into old age.'[11] My mother mentioned to me once that a lot of Keijo prisoners died in their forties and fifties. It is impossible to verify this with statistics, but of the members of Party B mentioned in this book, those who died before their sixtieth birthday include Peter Cazalet, Wilf Fawcett, Alex Johnstone, Harvey Muir-Hardinge, William 'Chook' Frazer and Captain Proctor. Poor health and a shortened life-expectancy were the legacies bequeathed to the survivors of all the Japanese camps.

Despite the government report's rejection of the claims made to support the theory that Unit 731 carried out biological warfare experiments on the prisoners, it nevertheless concludes that the Americans at the camp may well have been used for a single experiment. It states:

> There is one important strand of hard evidence: that of Major Karasawa, a Tokyo subordinate of General Ishii, who was held and tried by the Soviets for war crimes. A summary of his affidavit was given in the US Legal Section's 7 June 1947 telegram:
>
> Karasawa affidavit states that Ishii experimented as to the most effective germ cultivation; the way of infection; dispersing germs as means of attack; large-scale production of virus; preservation of virus; and discovery of preventative materials. ...in the section on germ cultivation Kurasawa states, 'A Mr Minato, a technical expert, examined the blood of American prisoners of war, who were held near Mukden about the summer of 1943. About this Minato told me that as a result of the study of the blood which was started simultaneously with the experimental research of strengthening the power of bacteria, no distinction had been found in serum immunity between races.' Although we believe that the statements about 'blood serum' could refer to

> laboratory tests on normal blood taken from the US POWs, which was then exposed in the laboratory to the bacteria, it could be read another way, i.e. that the men were injected with bacteria and their blood level examined subsequently to this … At that time, little was known about the human immune system. It was a commonly held belief that the different races had different susceptibilities to diseases … this belief was strongly reenforced by ideological belief, i.e. *untermenschen.* Thus it is probable Lt Gen Ishii *et al* would consider that an organism which was potent against Japanese would not necessarily work against Americans and vice-versa. Therefore he would perform blood tests on Americans in an attempt to ascertain their infectious vulnerabilities.

The investigation concludes:

> There is sufficient evidence to make it probable that on at least one occasion, samples taken from the POWs were taken away to be used in the context of bw [biological warfare] research. But this falls well short of evidence that Allied POWs there were themselves the subjects of experiments. There is no firm evidence that they were so treated.

It is significant that the American scholar and researcher Sheldon Harris came to the same conclusion, singling out the same document, in his book on Unit 731, first published in 2002.[12] He would not have had access to the British government investigation's findings.

Chapter 11

Anniversary of Defeat

Shortly before the first anniversary of their capture, a small group of Loyals was interviewed by journalists who were researching a story to commemorate the Japanese triumph. As the war turned against Japan, reminders of past victories assumed ever-growing importance as propaganda. Alan Toze made a brief mention of the event in his diary, recording that the reporters were confused by the expression 'All's fair in love and war', and were disappointed that there had been no bayonet charges.

The 'round table discussion' that appeared in *Keijo Nippo* is reproduced below.

> It has been a year since Singapore, the proud bastion of the British invasion of East Asia, fell on that significant day in history. On 15 February,1942, at 7 pm, our General Yamashita met with the enemy General Percival. With decisive words from General Yamashita demanding a 'Yes or No' answer, Percival signed the unconditional surrender at 7:50pm with his trembling hand.
>
> **Q**: When did you start preparing for defence on the Malay Peninsula? And how long did you think Singapore would hold out?
>
> **Colonel Elrington**: My battalion was transferred from Shanghai to Singapore on 6 April, 1938. We thought Singapore would hold out forever.
>
> **Q**: Can a non-commissioned officer become a platoon leader in the British Army?
>
> **Sergeant Strange**: Normally, it is an officer's position, but when my unit moved to Malaya, our platoon leader was injured, so I took over.

Q: Where were you captured during battle?
Captain Paque: We were not captured. We were told by Commander Percival to lay down our arms.

Q: Where were you at that time?
Captain Paque: I was in the Gillman Barracks in the Alexander area.

Q: How was the battle against the Japanese forces?
Colonel Elrington: On 8 February and 9th, the Japanese attacked from the northeast and northwest, but we didn't know where the attack would come from. There were no defence facilities on the west coast before the war. The Australian and Indian troops confronted the Japanese here, and after two days, we were pushed back to Bukit Timah. Our battalion was ordered to move from our barracks to Bukit Timah on the 10th, and we held our position near Bukit Timah until the night of the 12th. On the 12th,we saw Japanese troops breaking through the jungle and moving behind us. These Japanese troops were excellent soldiers.

On the 13th, we received orders to retreat and that night we fell back to Alexander Road. At that time, the Japanese army was advancing rapidly along the roads of Bukit Timah with tanks and infantry. On the 14th and 15th, our battalion defended the Gillman Barracks while being attacked by Japanese artillery and from the air. This battle was the closest we had fought.

We were astonished by the fierce attack of the Japanese. There were bayonet charges by Major Leighton (2nd Company) and Warrant Officer Moffat (attached to the 3rd Company) until the evening of the 14th, but against the Japanese charging with bayonets, our team could only counter with machine guns. No matter how much we shot, the Japanese soldiers kept coming like little demons. It felt like they were not human. In this fierce battle, only a few members of our 2nd and 3rd companies survived.

Our battalion's left wing had a Malay battalion. The Japanese broke through there and took control of the sea near the left wing. I had to order the next line of defence to be set up on Washington Hill as the battalion commander. This was between 2 and 3 pm on the 15th. At 8 pm, we received an order from General Percival for everyone to surrender. The next day, a Japanese officer came and praised the Loyal Regiment for its bravery.

Captain Paque: Our first encounter with the Japanese army was on 14 January in Segamat. We were bombed, but it was not a battle, we retreated. The Japanese Army we were facing at that time had beautifully broken through the rubber plantations and the jungle, coming around the sea to our rear.

Colonel Elrington: In the battle at Payong, between Muar and Yong Peng, seven Japanese tanks appeared, and the infantry advanced.

Major Leighton: The Japanese tanks broke through the normal barbed wire and anti-tank mine obstacles, but there was no engagement, and we retreated on that day.

Warrant Officer Moffat: We could never predict the actions of the Japanese army; they always came around from behind, forcing us to retreat. The Japanese Army was very good at mobile operations.

Colonel Elrington: We had lost 40 per cent of our soldiers by the time we retreated to Singapore. We arrived in Singapore by truck on the 26th and were re-equipped as a reinforcement unit.

Warrant Officer Moffat: When crossing Johore, we had not yet seen the Japanese army.

Q: How did you feel when Singapore fell?

Colonel Elrington: I was surprised when I received the order to surrender. We did not anticipate this. We had fought with all our might, but there was no choice once the order was received.

Q: How did you feel when you heard that the Japanese army had landed in Singapore?

Colonel Elrington: I expected it at that time.

Captain Paque: We were prepared to fight until we were all killed, but there was no choice once the order was received.

Q: What do you think was the cause of the fall of Singapore?

Colonel Elrington: The facilities for defence against attacks from the north were not sufficient. Singapore was defended facing the southern sea. Also, the air force was very weak. The direct cause of the surrender was 'to avoid civilian casualties and destruction of the city, as the Japanese army had taken control of the water supply,' as General Percival said.

Lance Corporal Ankers:[1] The Japanese army was numerically superior, and their air bombing was skilled; we were just defending our position.

Sergeant Strange: I was injured in the hand by a rifle bullet during the battle at the Gillman Barracks. I still have that bullet as a souvenir.

Colonel Elrington: The Japanese army was good at mobile operations like breaking through the jungle and attacking unexpectedly.

Q: So, are you saying that the Japanese Army's attack through the jungle and mud, striking from unexpected places, was ungentlemanly?

Colonel Elrington: No, no, that is not the case. In our army, the motto is 'All is fair in love and war.' The Japanese Army's attack was excellent.

Q: Colonel Elrington, what was the last order that you gave to your subordinates?

Colonel Elrington: I ordered each company to pile up their weapons and wait for orders from the Japanese Army, and I gave the following message to everyone: 'I am pleased that you have fought very well. We surrender not because of your mistakes, but because of orders. Remember your comrades who showed duty and discipline in death and defeat. Do not disgrace the honour of the Loyal Regiment, even as Prisoners of War.' Currently, we do not harbour any hostility towards Japan as soldiers.

Warrant Officer Moffat: All of us are grateful for our fair treatment by the Japanese Army.

We see in the article the reiteration of the usual propaganda themes: the enemy provides a description of Japanese might in battle and expresses gratitude for the fair treatment it has received since capture. But it displays a necessary change in the depiction of the prisoners, imposed on the Japanese by defeats. By now, it was useless to pretend that the enemy was ready to throw down his weapons at the first opportunity. 'Jiminy' Paque's assertion that they were prepared to fight until they were killed represents a new perspective on the enemy, as is Elrington's comment that the enemy congratulated him on how well his men had fought.

Historians have noted a hardening in attitude towards the Japanese after the American bombing raids began. The enemy was now seen as a devil, a figure of pure evil who deliberately targeted hospitals and children with his bombs. But here there is no hatred, and Stan Strange's inconsequential remark that he has kept a bullet as a souvenir serves to humanise him. The men are allowed to retain some of their dignity as fighters.

There are numerous inventions in the article, such as the lavish praise for the Japanese forces and the fictitious bayonet charges in place of the real ones the reporters were seeking. But a great deal of fact appears. Dates and places are correctly reproduced, although these may have had little significance to Korean readers. Some of the broad outlines of the Loyals' experience in action are given, and the men's frustration at the lack of opportunity to attack the enemy rather than fight rearguard actions comes across. The men freely admit some of the key weaknesses – inadequate defences and lack of air support – as well as Japanese strengths: their superior mobility and relentlessness in attack. We also get a sense of Paque's powerful personality and his combative attitude towards his captors in the camp, described by various diarists. The manner in which he contradicts his interlocutor when he says 'We were not captured. We were told by Commander Percival to lay down our arms.' captures something of his personality. Elrington's final message to his men after the surrender, as reproduced in the article, is a rough approximation of what he actually said. However, his final exhortation, 'Remember the lads who have fought and died, and show the same spirit of duty and discipline in defeat;' is reproduced as the rather deflating injunction: 'Do not disgrace the honour of the Loyal Regiment, even as Prisoners of War.'

The article is not a superlative example of the art of propaganda. Although the main propaganda themes are present, the article as a whole is cluttered with too much detail, some of it inconsequential, and it lacks a simple guiding narrative for the reader to follow. But it is interesting to note that the gloating, derisive tone of the earlier propaganda has now disappeared.

Chapter 12

Writing at Keijo

As we have seen, on their arrival in Korea the prisoners were made to write essays. From time to time over the ensuing years, they would also be required to answer questionnaires. Most men regarded this as just another example of weird Japanese behaviour, along with activities such as the racial comparison tests. In his memoirs, Arthur Cramsie refers to the 'strange' questionnaires they were given, but also conjectures that they may have served a research or propaganda purpose.

In fact there was nothing weird about the questionnaires. Allied intelligence officers gave questionnaires to enemy prisoners as a means of intelligence gathering, psychological analysis and propaganda development. By understanding what frightened, motivated or confused enemy troops, propaganda could be targeted more effectively. Seemingly innocuous questions could also be used to assess the enemy's combat motivation, morale and loyalty to the regime. It is reasonable to assume that the Japanese questionnaires served the same purpose. The Korean camps would be particularly suitable for such research as a less brutal environment meant that the men would be more likely to give an honest response without the fear of reprisal. As well as questionnaires, the essays, with open questions such as 'Your Opinion of the Japanese', or 'Your opinion of the voyage to Korea', gave plenty of scope for obtaining insights into the enemy's mind.

My father transcribed a questionnaire issued in April 1944 with its accompanying introduction:

> The purpose of this questionnaire is to find out about your present state of mind, your experiences, and your opinion about the war. Your answers may have a large bearing upon our policy to you in future. You often complained that we don't understand you. Well, here is an opportunity for you to express your honest to goodness opinion. We wish you

to take this opportunity to convey your opinions to us. With regard to 'D' part, you need not be afraid of being truthful. We advise you that no punishment or similar measures will follow upon examination of your opinions, and furthermore, we have no intention of causing you any trouble in future, both here and on your return. The Konan and Jinsen POWs have already given their sincere opinions, and we appreciate their cooperation. Hope you do likewise.

A. Experiences on the battlefield (conditions and situations of battle under which one fought, battle conditions immediately prior to capitulation, things admired about the Japanese forces etc).
B. Confessions from the battlefield (tragedies, from the standpoint of both the individual and unit, things that were sad, dreadful, frightful, suffering, happy etc).
C. Your opinion, or impression about the Japanese forces before, during battle and after capitulation.
D. Is it profitable, or advisable, for Britain to fight against Japan?
E. Your opinion concerning the establishment of the Greater East Asian Co-Prosperity Sphere.
F. How long do you think the war will last? When do you think you will return to your country?

As well as eliciting propaganda material about Japanese superiority in the battlefield, the questionnaire is also looking for the same sorts of things as the Allied questionnaires: combat motivation, morale and fears and vulnerabilities that might be targeted.

John Lever recorded that most of the men gave straightforward replies to the questionnaire, and proclaimed their complete confidence in an Allied victory: 'We were told to write what we thought, as the idea was not to punish anyone for stating their opinions. The replies were quite direct, no effort was made to be complimentary. Comparisons were made of Japan's attitude two years ago with what it must be now. Prophecies of Japan's capitulation were made and a lot said without necessarily using foul language. They must have found it very enlightening.'[1]

My father's answers were brief and misleading. He wrote that he had never heard of a 'Greater East Asian Co-Prosperity Sphere', although he would have come across the term whenever he read a Japanese newspaper. In response to question C, he wrote that the Japanese tended to give away their night positions by the noise they made, contradicting what he had recorded in his diaries earlier. (One diary entry describes sitting in the darkness of the Malayan jungle and vainly listening out for sounds of the Japanese, at the same time wondering 'what devilment they might be up to').

The Japanese could not be certain that the prisoners' responses to a questionnaire were genuine, but their diaries, written over a period of years under the assurance that they had complete freedom of expression, would have been a more reliable resource for getting inside the prisoner's mind. In May 1944, they were collected to be read by the camp authorities, necessitating many hasty excisions. My father wrote: 'We are permitted to be as abusive as we like, expressing ourselves completely with no fear of punishment for they say (!) they recognise the fact that these are private, personal diaries but we must be prepared to have them perused from time to time.'[2]

Most of the prisoners had been circumspect when writing about their 'hosts'. There are few references to the Japanese before the capitulation in Major Rigby's diary other than a brief reference to his fellow medic, Dr Uchida, who struck him as a 'very nice man'. There is an abrupt change of tone after the capitulation, with Rigby admitting to his diary that he had previously been cautious in what he had written about the Japanese, 'the little bastards'.[3] He now hoped that they would face long sentences and execution as war criminals.

Others had shown no such reticence. My father's diaries give various abusive vignettes of the guards, identified by nickname: 'Smoko' is described as 'conceited, arrogant and stupid, heartily disliked by all the men'; another, 'Smiles', is an 'ill-mannered slobber-guts'. Corporal Takuma is 'an evil-visaged, short-arsed runt of an individual'. These remarks were read by the camp authorities and his diary was duly returned, with the censor's stamp on various pages, without comment. That my father could express himself in these terms with impunity illustrates the value the Japanese set upon reading their captives' unrestrained thoughts.

Writing in Secret

At all the Far Eastern camps, prisoners were desperate for news of the outside world. Many risked their lives in constructing and operating secret camp radios. At the Party B camps the principal sources of news were two men who had mastered the Japanese language. At Mukden, the New Zealander Lieutenant Greig was able to translate newspapers supplied by friendly guards. Until D Day in June 1944, the prisoners at Keijo were supplied with newspapers, although the camp censor took a pair of scissors to them to remove information deemed unsuitable for the prisoners. (One edition had been reduced almost to ribbons. My father impetuously asked a Japanese guard the reason for this and received the reply that they had removed reports of recent bombing raids wreaking devastation on British cities. Colonel Noguchi did not want his prisoners to be upset by reading them.) Thanks to the language lessons at Keijo, my father was eventually able to gain a reading knowledge of Japanese and translate the scraps of newspapers that the prisoners found for him. He talked about this to me a couple of times, as if it was an amusing prank on his part, although he added that some of the pages of newsprint brought to him had been previously used for wrapping fish, and that the smell of them made him feel sick. In fact, as Colonel Elrington wrote, he did translation work under the constant risk of detection.[4] After D-Day, newspapers were no longer allowed, and my father became the sole conduit of information about the outside world. Alex James recorded how newspapers got into the camp:

> Early in May, the garden assumed a new importance. Until that time, our sources of news and newspapers had been restricted and had nearly all been within the camp, but one day a successful contact was made with a Korean youth who lived near to the garden. He rapidly proved to be the most significant contact we had ever had. Almost every day, in exchange for a packet of American cigarettes, he delivered, right under the noses of the guards, a Japanese newspaper. The daily supply was so regular (also for security reasons – Japanese interpreters were always snooping) that it was referred to as 'the milk' and the Korean boy was known

> as the milkman. Two sentries who had previously been contacts within the camp, but were now dropped, were naturally very suspicious, but although they knew the transaction took place in the garden, their effort to detect the new source was unsuccessful.
>
> It made a tremendous difference to our lives to be up to date with the news. The daily bulletins gave us something to look forward to, and provided ample scope for discussion. We owe a great debt of gratitude to George Baker, an officer with a remarkable ability for languages, who did the translating. Had anyone in the chain of delivery slipped up, everyone concerned, especially George, would have received very severe punishment.[5]

The 'milkman' made his delivery through a sliding panel at the back of a shed in the garden and the newspaper was then brought back into camp in a false sleeve that had been sewn on the inside of an officer's web belt. My father produced a written summary of news which was circulated among the prisoners and then destroyed. His last edition, produced after the Japanese capitulation, is held in the Lancashire Infantry museum.

A further significant boost to morale was another clandestine operation, the Officers' magazine, *Nor Iron Bars*.[6] The first edition appeared at Changi, and in all there were fourteen, spanning the entire period of their captivity. It included crosswords and bridge puzzles, short stories, skits, parodies, caricatures and sketches contributed by a variety of anonymous officers. It was edited with considerable skill and also courage by lieutenants Henling Wade, Paddy Given-Wilson and John Turner.

A great deal of its content was devoted to ridiculing the Japanese. The *Nippon Times* had its counterpart, or rather its antithesis, in *Nipoff at Times*, whose reports were a feature of the various editions. The exaggerations and hyperbole of Japanese war reporting are reproduced in an interview with kamikaze pilot Naka Arimasen, who has single-handedly destroyed an entire American fleet and returned home safely.[7] 'With boiling blood, I dived to the attack, I was flying one of our new rubber planes so when I body-crashed the first battleship I bounced across to the next one, and so on, down the line…'

The increasingly ludicrous optimism of Japanese war reporting was also parodied:

> Over the last two years we see our glorious empire advancing irresistibly to complete and glorious victory. True, there have been one or two incidents of a grave nature on one or two fronts but these have merely served to allow our glorious armed forces to swing into action in other spheres, and after all, the Solomons, New Guinea, The Gilbert and Caroline groups of islands, Attu, the Philippines and Burma are not much if you say the words quickly…

Nipoff at Times also carried reports of prisoners being well-treated:

Eden's Lies Blasted

Interview with our Special Tame Prisoners clears fair name of Japan

'The sprat shows which way the whale blows'.[8]

> Field Marshall O U Lyre, a British Prisoner, who was captured during our recent brilliant victories on the mountains of the moon said, 'I love the Japanese. They are so nice to me. They give me all I can eat. I have eggs and bacon for breakfast, rump steak and cauliflower for lunch and then pork pies for dinner'.

One of the most ingenious parodies, 'A Visit to a Modern Cigarette Factory', has several targets. It mocks the propaganda that stressed Japan's technological achievements and the modern infrastructure and technology Japan brought to the Co-Prosperity Sphere. Also targeted are the inferior quality of Japanese cigarettes, and the florid, grandiloquent prose of the newspapers. The cigarette factory is located in an imaginary suburb of Keijo and as the reporter approaches it he is overwhelmed by its immensity and magnificence, with chimneys that were visible 'several furlongs away'. It boasted an 'awe-inspiring façade of corrugated iron, which rose almost thirty feet into the air'.

> Inside the factory a thunder of machinery smote my ears: before us lay row upon row of huge shiny engines – sleek, efficient and thrumming with activity, while silent and quick-fingered operatives nimbly handled the controls and supervised the smooth working of these mechanical monsters.

The factory's design took its inspiration from Heath Robinson, possessing bizarre but intricate machinery connected by snaking conveyor belts. There was an 'adhesivicator' which glued the cigarette papers together, fed by a rice paste which an operator poured into a funnel. At the factory, the manager assured visitors that the safety precautions were second-to-none. But the 'deadly revolving knives' which divided the long rolls of cigarettes into shorter lengths also had a tendency to cut off the workers' fingers.

However comic the intention of the authors and artists in their work for the magazine, there is nevertheless a darker edge to a great deal of the content, whether intentional or not. As well as the Korean labourers who had their limbs mangled at Konan, several of the Keijo prisoners had serious accidents resulting in a lost finger or toe, or in Harry Kingsley's case, a leg.

The short stories indirectly explore themes relevant to their current circumstances: isolation, stagnation, misplaced loyalty, a wasted life, violence. Locations include remote parts of Norway and Brazil. In Shanghai, a group of White Russians remain faithful to their Tsar after the revolution, but they are a forgotten group and after twenty years of waiting for support, they realise their lives have been wasted. 'The Stranger' is a surrealist, intentionally obscure narrative, which tells of the narrator's quest to come to an understanding and rapprochement with a mysterious Japanese man and his wife. He first meets the man on a beach and is fascinated by him, but the stranger, never named, is almost entirely silent, although he communicates with brief gestures and occasional monosyllabic responses. The narrator, a solitary and confused Westerner, devotes long years of his life to his quest. At last, he is invited to dine with the couple, where they discuss suicide and death. The protagonists are obviously intended to be symbolic, but its interest lies rather in what it reveals of the author's mental state.

A narrative device shared by several of the stories is to begin by presenting an everyday scene which is subverted by the sudden unexpected incursion of death, violence, or evil. There is of course a correspondence with what the prisoners wrote in their diaries. For example, we have seen how John Lever describes his bridge partner, Jackie Whiting, catching a cold. Two days later, the young man has died of diphtheria. As Alex James and his friends make their way to the beach for a pleasant morning swim, they are surprised by the sound of Chinese civilians being machine-gunned.

In one short story an officer returns to his squad room after breakfast to find a man, in good health just moments earlier, lying dead on his bed; in another, a man goes to his barber, but instead of receiving his usual haircut, the previously amiable barber threatens to slit his throat. In 'The Stranger', a grand dinner party is gate-crashed by a distinguished-looking man who offers to play the piano for the guests. They are literally entranced by his music, and fall into a deep sleep, filled with terrifying nightmares. When they wake the following morning, the man has vanished, and they realise that they have been visited by the devil.

Another short story is set at the Café Royale. (Fine food, wine and cigarettes were popular subjects). A young man and woman meet for lunch and during their meal make a pledge to give up smoking. They agree to meet in a year's time. At the second meeting, the woman has lost her beauty and is now morbidly obese. She has substituted cakes for cigarettes. The man has also undergone a horrible metamorphosis: his physical appearance reflects the ill effects of the morphine addiction that has replaced his previous addiction to nicotine.

As well as the unexpected translation of the mundane into the horrific, the short story also shares a theme – physical deterioration – that recurs not just in the men's writings, but in the sketches, caricatures and cartoons the men drew at the camp. It takes an extreme form in the short story 'That Man Again'. It opens with the narrator looking at a man he once loved, but now hates. The face, once attractive, is now repellent; it bears the marks of ageing and ill-health, and the narrator is disturbed by the various expressions the man pulls. There were few visions that aroused in me a more profound feeling of repulsion than that man. Again I saw him standing before me. I could never decide if his expression was not an insulting grimace directed deliberately at me. To begin with I used to admire him inordinately. But lately a deep loathing has overcome me. In a fit of uncontrollable hatred I struck at him with all my might.

The blow breaks the narrator's shaving mirror.

The dehumanising effect of captivity is obliquely expressed in the many sketches produced at Keijo where the men depict themselves as animals and insects. One of the most talented artists, Private Harry Kingsley, included himself in several sketches as a monkey with a cigarette hanging from his lips, and a bandage around his leg to indicate the work accident that had crippled him. Other cartoons depict the men bathing and waiting in line to be weighed, their bodies grotesquely distorted. Similarly grotesque distortions occurred in real life. Men became crippled and bloated from beriberi, 'tottering around like infants learning to walk', as John Lever described it.

After the war, the fourteen editions of *Nor Iron Bars* were bound together and deposited at the regimental headquarters in Preston. Colonel Elrington wrote an introduction, explaining how NIB was a great 'fillip to morale'. The magazine certainly illustrates the men's resilience and ability to retain a sense of humour. But it is laughter in the dark. Whether consciously or not, the writings also convey a sense of horror at the life they were living.

Chapter 13

Radio Propaganda from Mukden and the Bunka Camp

Messages from POWs had formed an important element of Japanese radio broadcasts to the enemy from the beginning of the war. The first message, from an Australian prisoner, was read out by an announcer in December 1941 on Radio Batavia (Jakarta), which broadcast to Australasia. Japan quickly established radio stations in its newly conquered territories, and soon prisoner messages could also be broadcast from Singapore, Shanghai and Saigon. By withholding prisoner lists, the Japanese could be sure of a large audience. Using the same technique as the Russians, messages from the prisoners were interspersed unannounced between programmes, thereby ensuring the audience had to listen to a great deal of propaganda in the form of news and commentary.

The Japanese also targeted American servicemen in the Pacific and civilian listeners on the west coast of America. Aware that they would benefit from the services of prisoners who would be able to correct the sometimes faulty English of the Japanese broadcasters, three prisoners with previous broadcasting experience, Americans Norman Reyes and Walter Ince, and an Australian, Major Charles Cousens, were coerced into working for Radio NHK in Tokyo. Cousens had at first refused, but at his second interview he was beaten to the ground and kicked in the stomach until he vomited. After that, he agreed. Having to perform this work left him at times suicidally depressed. He suffered a heart attack and a nervous breakdown during captivity.

The Japanese also became conscious that a diet of news, opinion pieces and prisoner letters was unlikely to appeal to the average American GI. In April 1943, *Zero Hour* was launched, based on an American DJ format that had hitherto been unknown to the Japanese. Prisoner letters were also an integral part of the shows. Having initially been chosen simply as proofreaders, the men were soon deployed as scriptwriters and announcers. *Zero Hour* was presented by Norman Reyes, a big jazz fan. As well as swing and big band numbers, he played nostalgic tunes like *Home on the Range*, intended to induce homesickness among the servicemen. The show was regarded as a great success by the Japanese and they decided to increase its length. They also followed Charles Cousens' suggestion that they should use female presenters. Although there were several different women who worked as DJs on the show at various times, they were given the generic name 'Tokyo Rose' by the listeners. The woman most associated with the role, Iva Toguri, was a *nisei*, a second generation American who had the bad luck to be visiting relatives in Japan when war broke out. Music was interspersed with prisoner letters read out by her in what has been described as a sultry, smoky voice, along with teasing comments. She would ask her listeners, for example, to imagine what their girlfriends and wives back home might be getting up to during their long absences. By 1943, the Japanese had developed technology capable of monitoring American medium-wave transmissions, and the programme's news reports could also include factual but disheartening news from the homeland, such as a train crash, flood or other natural disaster. It was regarded by the Japanese as a potent mixture. Certainly, Tokyo Rose was a great favourite of the GIs.

Mukden, along with Zentsuji, provided many hundreds of messages for broadcast. (The prisoners either recorded their messages at the camp, or had them read out by the broadcasters. In the latter case, the messages were often doctored or were sometimes completely invented). After the Memorial service in July 1943, Peaty wrote: 'one hundred two-and-a-half-minute recordings were made of messages for relatives'.[1] There were numerous visits from the propaganda corps and each time similar quantities of messages were harvested.

The senior British officer at Zentsuji had forbidden his men to write or record messages for broadcast on the grounds that they would be used as propaganda. At Mukden, there was also considerable suspicion about how the messages might be used, and according to Private Jack Roberts, men were only allowed to send messages after they had been approved by senior officers. Each message contained their name and army number.[2] To prove their authenticity, the messages also identified family members, friends or neighbours by name. It is no surprise then, that the longer messages that exist came mainly from Americans. They share common themes: although well-treated, the prisoner is homesick; if he has children or grandchildren, he addresses them individually and regrets that he is unable to be with them as they grow up.[3] They are intended both to convey and to arouse the pain of separation.

Members of Party B at Mukden were obviously keen to send out messages that they were alive and well. Jack Roberts recalled how his message reached his mother by a very circuitous route. It was picked up by a neutral ship in the Pacific and then passed on to the Red Cross. Months later it reached his mother in a 'very garbled' form. But it was enough to let her know that her son was alive.[4]

A consequence of the perceived success of *Zero Hour* was the decision to recruit more prisoners and increase the range of programmes. The prisoner lists held by the *Huryo* meant that suitable candidates could be identified from camps across the Japanese territories. An assortment of newsmen, radio broadcasters, artists and musicians, numbering forty in total, were brought for interview at Omori camp in Tokyo late in 1943. Nine of them were from Korea, suggesting that the show and music recorded during the first Christmas at Keijo had impressed at the highest levels. For obvious reasons, there is little reliable evidence concerning the activities of prisoners who were involved in creating propaganda for the Japanese. It exists mainly in the form of court testimony and other attempts to apportion blame or at self-exculpation. It is therefore worth recording Party B's experiences, as they add to the exiguous sum of knowledge.

In November 1943 Eric Wallwork's diary recalls records his band's summons to Japan:

> We were told that the band was being sent to Tokyo on a special mission and that it was no use trying to get off the party as the order had come from Tokyo itself. We were told that we need not worry as we would have a good time and that we had finished with work, but we would be able to play music for the benefit of others all the time. So, although it meant leaving all our friends behind, we felt more contented and more or less welcomed the change.[5]

Jack McNaughton, a professional actor and the director of various shows at Changi, and of *Chosen Calling* at Keijo, was also selected, along with Henling Wade, who had worked as a journalist in Shanghai before the war. From the moment their move was announced until their arrival at Omori camp in Tokyo, the party received surprisingly good treatment. Wallwork wrote:

> The move was to take place on 5 November. On the 4th we had to be issued with good kit. On the morning of the 5th we were inspected by the Japanese clothing officer to see that our kit was in good condition (most unusual) ... On arrival at the railway station our kit was taken to the train on a luggage cart to save us the trouble of carrying it... Our seats were even marked reserved for us (later we understood why we were being treated so differently).

It was only on their arrival at Omori camp that the men realised that they had received better treatment throughout their time in Korea, not just during preparations for their journey. Wallwork was shocked:

> We used to grumble at the camp we left in Korea, but that was like a holiday camp in comparison with this one, the Tokyo headquarters camp in the Omori district. We were given a piece or lump of stale bread and a drink, and then we were told about the happenings and daily life of the camp, which more or less shocked us and speaking truthfully frightened us ... After what appeared to have been a lifetime, morning came, all of us not being able to move for a few minutes owing to cramp in our legs etc. The first thing we heard was the ringing of a bell. This was the call for everyone to parade for roll-call, this also being the first glance of the other POWs. What a shock. I never thought I would see English men in such a state, pale and frail looking, saying nothing of the bootless feet and clothing that was only fit for burning. Their morale seemed to be rock bottom. I think the same thought was running through all our minds, wishing we were getting out of this camp at the earliest possible moment.

The men received another shock when the real reason for their journey was revealed. None of them wished to help the Japanese war effort, still less be tried for treason after the war. There followed an anxious wait of several weeks before they were interviewed. The initial interview took a soft approach, but if any reluctance to participate was perceived, the interviewers became threatening and aggressive at the subsequent one. Henling Wade and an American, Mark Streeter, have both described their surprise at the courtesy of their interviewers.[6] Each records encountering three well-dressed civilians who stood up and bowed when they entered the room. Streeter was offered a cigarette by a distinguished-looking man, Count Norizone Ikeda, who also took the trouble to light it for him. Ikeda was an alumnus of Balliol College, Oxford, and was to be one of the supervisors at the Bunka camp, where he used to surprise the prisoners by singing snatches of opera to himself. He impressed the interviewees both by his detailed knowledge of world affairs, and, more worryingly, by his knowledge of their pre-war careers. At the first interview the prisoners were asked what they thought of the Japanese and of their attitude towards the war. Then came more specific questions about their careers. Henling Wade progressed to a second interview:

> On this occasion the main interrogator was a tall, American-educated Japanese with shiny black hair plastered close to his scalp and suspicious, snaky eyes. His hatred of America was obviously that of one who owes a debt to another nation and probably feels some inferiority. He shouted, threatening immediate execution to prisoners who said they did not wish to go to Bunka.[7]

Thirteen men were eventually selected from the forty, with two members of Party B being chosen. There were two other British prisoners: Donald Carswell Bruce, a lance bombardier in the 155th Field regiment, whose role at the Bunka camp was restricted to typing scripts, and civil servant, George Williams. From Keijo came Jack McNaughton, and bandsman Harry Pearson. A close friend of Alan Toze, he had worked as a proofreader on *The Times.* He was also a singer and pianist who did impersonations of Noel Coward and ‘Hutch’, a cabaret pianist and singer popular at the time. Wade and Eric Wallwork had escaped selection, to their great relief. Wade remained at Omori camp and suffered under the particularly brutal regime of Sergeant Watanabe, nicknamed 'The Bird', a man notorious for his cruelty. (At the camp, Wade was a witness to the brutal treatment of Louis Zamperini, an American Olympian whose experiences in captivity there were later recreated on film. Wade lived long enough to be able to complain to the *Daily Mail* that his offer to work as an adviser to the film had been ignored.)

On 1 December 1943, the group of thirteen was taken to the Bunka camp in the Kanda district of Tokyo. Formerly a girls' school, the Suragadai Cultural Institute, it was a two-storey building constructed around a courtyard. There were at most twenty-five prisoners held there at one time, made up of a mix of nationalities. It has been suggested that conditions at the camp were significantly better than elsewhere. That may have been the case, but their living quarters were infested with rats; and, as in Korea, their bedding and clothing were inadequate for the colder months of the year. They were allowed one bath a week but had to use the same bath water the Japanese guards had already washed themselves and their clothes in. Discipline was strict, and beatings were frequent.

On the morning after their arrival the prisoners were assembled on the courtyard and addressed by the chief of the propaganda unit, Major Tsuneishi, who reminded them of what refusal to cooperate would entail. At the end of his speech, he commanded anyone present who was not willing to broadcast over Japanese radio to step forward. The young English civil servant George Williams, who had been captured on the Gilbert Islands, duly took a step forward. Tsuneishi exploded with rage, drawing his sword and advancing on Williams as if intending to kill him. At the very last moment he lowered his weapon, and signalled for Williams to be dragged away by guards. The men were told that they would never see him again. This proved to be correct, and the men naturally assumed that he had been executed. The message was clear: the alternative to cooperation was death. After rough interrogation by the *Kempeitai* Williams was sent to a mining camp, Mitsushimi, on the suggestion of Ikeda. Conditions were so bad there that it was reasonable to believe that he would be dead within a few months. It is pleasing to write that Williams survived and was later decorated by the British government for his bravery.

Relations between the men were always uneasy. Not unreasonably, they were suspicious of each other's motives. Mark Streeter was a construction worker in his forties from Ogden, Utah, who had been working on Wake Island at the time of his capture. He nursed a virulent antipathy towards Roosevelt. One of his early contributions to the propaganda broadcasts was an 'Ode to Roosevelt', describing its subject as an 'oily, double-crossing politician'. His fellow prisoners came to the conclusion that he was mentally unstable. At Omori camp, Henling Wade had met Sergeant Provoo, describing him as 'a blond, good-looking young American, who had become a Buddhist priest and studied Japanese culture before the war'.[8] It was his genuinely pro-Japanese views rather than his good looks which struck his fellow captives. After the war, he was tried for treason, but was found not guilty on a technicality. The FBI showed a considerable post-war interest in all the prisoners at the camp. A 1948 report from their California office states that Harry Pearson had at first co-written news scripts but later took part in broadcasts as a musician. His main occupation was as the camp cook. It also recorded that Pearson had emigrated to South Africa and was working as a journalist in Cape Town. Jack McNaughton's address is also recorded as 26 Elvaston Place, London SW7, but no attempt appears to have been made to contact either man.[9]

Letters continued to play a large part in the broadcasting schedule – a programme by the name of *The Postman Calls* was entirely devoted to prisoners' letters – but the POW experience was also presented in a light-hearted weekly show, *Three Missing Men,* which both McNaughton and Pearson worked on. *Jamboree* was a similarly light-hearted mixture of sketches, improvisations and sing-songs, broadcast on a Saturday evening, showcasing the talents of Harry Pearson.

Count Ikeda commissioned radio adaptations of books which contained strong anti-war sentiments or were critical of American society. McNaughton was to play a significant part in their creation and production. The first adaptation, John Steinbeck's *Of Mice and Men*, was criticised by some of Ikeda's Japanese colleagues on the grounds that McNaughton and others appeared to enjoy working on it too much, and because it lacked strong propaganda messages. Ikeda countered by citing research done by British propagandists in the First World War which argued that the propagandist should aim first to create a 'favourable atmosphere' for the reception of later propaganda. Its impact would thereby be much stronger. Later productions included R.C. Sherriff's First World War play *Journey's End*, which ends with the death of the three protagonists as they go over the top, and Irwin Shaw's 1936 one act anti-war play *Bury the Dead.* It depicts six dead American servicemen, representing a cross-section of American society. They refuse to be buried and decry the futility of war.

The prisoners tried to sabotage the intention of these broadcasts in as many ways as they could think of, without falling foul of the ever-suspicious Japanese. They chose music that the Japanese would not realise would be unpopular with listeners, such as an accordion version of *In a Persian Market*, a tune popular in Britain before the First World War. They also played recordings of British dance bands in preference to the more popular, and indeed superior, American bands. Certain inflections of the voice, indiscernible to the Japanese, could be used to hint that the speaker was being ironic. The Japanese did not see the scripts before the live broadcasts, and the performers introduced deliberate ambiguities into their speeches. They spoke quickly and used a lot of slang, hoping that the censor, who was seated next to the 'cut' button, would not understand. Iva Toguri tried to subvert her broadcasts by reproducing the awkward sentence constructions commonly used by Japanese when they spoke English, such as her frequently repeated comment 'you are liking please'. She was regarded as a comedy act by the American servicemen.

The broadcasts continued uninterrupted until the Japanese surrender. At the camp, the men suffered from the food shortages that afflicted the general population. Mark Streeter described the last eighteen months at the camp:

> About this time men in Bunka were beginning to crack up. Major Cousens cracked up with a nervous breakdown and spent several months in a nearby Japanese hospital. Sgt. John Provoo broke down, Stephen Shattles had become a great problem, he was slipping badly mentally and physically, and some of the other POWs were on the very verge of mental breakdowns; the food situation had gotten so bad that cats were trapped and eaten, as were snails, old bones, leaves, bark, anything that looked like it might contain a little energy. The food ration now consisted only of boiled millet. The situation got so bad that the Japanese, sensing that they were apt to lose their entire POW broadcasting group from

> starvation, as a final resort gave the worst prisoners vitamin shots.[10]

After the war, the ordeal continued for some of them. The American government reacted strongly against those it suspected of collaboration. Mark Streeter was held in Tokyo's Sugamo prison alongside Japanese camp commandants and officials awaiting trial for war crimes. Sergeant Provoo was charged with treason and found guilty, but on appeal his verdict was rescinded on a technicality. Charles Cousens, who had been tortured by the Japanese for refusing to cooperate, found himself on trial in Australia, apparently due to the insistence of General MacArthur. The case was dropped, but he was dishonourably discharged from the Australian army. Fortunately, his old employers at a Sydney radio station took him back. Iva Toguri, 'Tokyo Rose', was not so lucky and was sentenced to ten years, of which she served six. She was eventually pardoned in 1976 by President Gerald Ford.

Chapter 14

Konan Camp and the Working Life

We have seen how the initial propaganda showing the prisoners enjoying leisured lives was soon replaced by accounts of the men working for their keep. The new propaganda message was introduced to the public by newspaper articles throughout the Japanese territories announcing that prisoners were to be 'mobilised for industrial purposes on the homeland [...] The present measure has a three-fold purpose, namely, to reduce the cost of upkeep, to make the prisoners contribute to Nippon's productive activities, and at the same time to contribute toward the betterment of the individual prisoner's health'.[1] As corroboration of this, reports of prisoners at work appeared at the same time. The *Huryo* chief, General Uemura, allowed his name to appear in the articles, suggesting his close involvement in this new deception. *The Tribune*, published in Manila, offered the following:

> TOKYO, Nov. 8 1942 (*Domei*). — Cheerfully performing their assigned jobs, British, American and Dutch war prisoners employed in various factories in Tokyo and its vicinity were found to be in the best health following a visit to these plants yesterday by a *Domei* reporter. Before inspecting the factories, the reporter made a surprise call on certain workers in the Tokyo war prisoners camp. He was pleasantly surprised when fourteen or thirteen workers suddenly popped their heads from the windows, their faces smiling. All of them were cleanly shaved and neatly dressed in clean uniforms, feeling happy that they are able to forget their bitter experiences listening to the heavy gunfire and the crackle of machine guns and crawling about the menacing jungles, their bodies covered with mud and flies and hotly pursued by the Japanese forces. Lieutenant-General Mikio Uemura, Director of the war prisoners intelligence bureau,

> arrived to make his regular inspection of the camp … The officer in charge said that all the inmates in the camp are given work according to their interest and talents, being particularly careful of their welfare while those taken ill are given special care in hospital wards. They are employed as stevedores and factory workers in Tokyo and Kanagawa districts. The officer in charge revealed that at first their efficiency was chiefly hampered by language difficulty; however, at present they are able to display about 60 to 70 per cent the average efficiency of Japanese workers. Working hours have been set from seven in the morning to four in the afternoon with ample intervals for meals and recess. The officer said: 'They are obedient, follow instructions and go about their assigned tasks cheerfully.' Following his visit to the prisoners' camp, your reporter proceeded to the wharf station of the Japan Transport company. Here he found a number of war prisoners busy pushing bales of rice and wheat on hand carts. The superintendent in charge said although their long legs are rather weak they have strong hands and are capable of performing their tasks.[2] Substantiating the statement, your reporter watched these workers go about their jobs whistling the merry tune 'Whistle while you work' as they moved a huge pile of rice and wheat bales in no time.

As the war continued, Keijo and Jinsen increasingly became officers' camps. and other ranks were dispatched to provide labour to support the Japanese war effort. In March 1943, two hundred of the fittest men were sent to a newly constructed camp, Konan, in the northeast of Korea. As happened when some of the party had left for Mukden, men cried openly at being separated from their friends.

The prisoners were led from Konan's train station along a causeway to reach the camp, which had been built on reclaimed land in the middle of a swamp. Its location meant that the men were tormented by mosquitoes during the warmer months. But Arthur Kerr's first impressions were of the immensity of the sprawling industrial complex at Konan seen from the causeway, evidence of the industrial revolution wrought by the Japanese. Later, this liminal area marking the boundary between

North and South Korea would become the site of various conspiracy theories. It is still claimed that a nuclear bomb was manufactured in the complex and tested off the coast near Konan. But Kerr's diary, as well as the testimony of other prisoners, suggest that the complex lacked the infrastructure, manpower and technology to make such a claim remotely feasible. Rather than engaging in fission-related activities, the prisoners' labour was confined to the production of carbide.

On entering the camp, the men were all pleasantly surprised. It was of similar construction to Jinsen, but at Konan the floor was bricked over and the walls were plastered, which meant that hygiene was considerably better than at Jinsen and that the rooms retained more warmth during the winter. Kerr wrote:

> It is not necessary to get out from under a roof to go to any of the seven squad rooms, the cookhouse, bathrooms, latrines, or in fact any place you want to go. There is a well equipped hospital: in fact, providing things go right it looks like being a good camp.[3]

There were only five officers among the 300 men, and to their delight they found they had been allocated a spacious private room which contained a table, an item of furniture that Jinsen lacked. On the first two evenings at the camp, the prisoners were served fresh bread that had been baked in the camp kitchen, and generous portions of fresh fish. The prisoners were also allowed a hot bath every night. These were all luxuries by FEPOW (Far Eastern Prisoners of War) standards and it can be suggested that at this stage at least, the conditions had been influenced by an intended propaganda function.

Their food soon deteriorated in size and quality, and fish disappeared from the menu. Three months later, Kerr was to write: 'Meals are light, bloody light in fact. Sundays off are starvation days. They save three days' rations when we are off as all meal issues are about half-weight.'[4] The size of a prisoner's meal was calculated by how much energy he expended, although the calorific value was always insufficient. 'Hard work, more rations; light work, lighter rations; holidays, smaller rations. If you are ill you do not need food, as you neither work nor move about.'

The hospital, superficially impressive, also proved to be a disappointment. Arthur Kerr gave many details about the camp's medical facilities: 'Medicine is limited to a few staple items. Aspirin is the mainstay for all complaints, and a little zinc cream as an antiseptic.' But the men could obtain treatment for cuts, sprains and fractures, Kerr describes it as 'rough and inclined to butchery'. As was the case at Keijo, once the prisoners had got the measure of the hospital and its Japanese medical assistants, they preferred not to be treated there if at all possible. In his memoirs, Lieutenant Arthur Cramsie makes the claim that the camp dentist preferred to have his appendix removed without anaesthetic by the Canadian doctor, Harry Morris, rather than go into the hospital: 'He was strapped to a table and opened up with a razor blade, without anaesthetic. Mercifully, the patient passed out almost immediately. The operation was entirely successful, and they sewed him up with a needle and thread.'[5]

As at the other Korean camps, the environment was one where individual Japanese could display their humanity without risk of retribution. Lieutenant Yosotaki, the oldest Japanese officer, had lived for some years in Manchester and spoke excellent English. An amiable man, he spent a lot of time in the officers' squad room, reminiscing about his days in England. Overall, however, the regime was more brutal than at Keijo or Jinsen. Daniel Fraser remembered that you could be slapped just for looking at a guard and that, for fun, the guards might dip you into the open sewer that served as a latrine.[6] Men often had to be carried back from work after a beating. As a punishment for minor offences, the guilty party was made to stand outside the guardroom in freezing weather, partially clothed. Like all the Japanese camps, Konan had its bullies and sadists. Corporal Shito was particularly feared. Like Terada at Keijo, he would engineer excuses to inflict suffering on his prisoners. Athur Cramsie remembered how the corporal unexpectedly entered the bath house, not allowing the men sufficient time to stand to attention or salute. As a punishment for not saluting, six of them were prodded with rifle butts and made to stand outside for an hour in freezing weather, naked and wet. Cramsie was surprised that there were no deaths. One man who did die after such ill-treatment was an Australian, Corporal Reg Hayter, one of the most popular men at the camp. Shito had accused him of shirking at the factory and he was taken outside, still damp with sweat from his work at the furnace, and made to stand for two hours wearing only a loin cloth, with snow on the ground. He developed double pneumonia and died six weeks later from lack of medical attention.

Initially, the men's job was to provide maintenance and cleaning for the carbide factory, but before long they were told they would take over from the group Korean labourers who stoked the furnaces at the factory. Every few days the furnaces used to overheat and there were explosions, showering the workers with molten carbide and causing terrible casualties. The men threatened to strike. Harry Morris wrote:

> An ugly situation was averted when the Japanese promised to introduce various safety measures. We finally mastered the secret of the furnaces and could tell when an explosion was pending. At this time the men absolutely refused to work until the danger was past. Many did suffer from burns but no one died.

At other camps, refusing to work would have met with terrible retribution, suggesting again that a propaganda function had worked in the men's favour.

The furnaces were large open constructions which rose 30 feet in the air, and the prisoners had to walk up a metal staircase and along a gantry to reach their workstations. The guards stayed at ground level to avoid the intense heat. Three-man teams would feed the electric furnaces with coal balls and limestone. The furnaces operated at a temperature of 3,000°F and had to be fed at high speed, otherwise the surface contents of the furnace became white hot, and conditions of work became 'even more akin to Dante's Inferno', as one prisoner put it. Each man stoked for twenty minutes, then took a forty-minute break, when the other two men on the team took turns at their shifts. In an eight-hour shift each POW would therefore stoke the furnace eight times, bringing his total time at the heat face to two hours and twenty minutes. Comparatively speaking, this was a relatively humane work schedule. The furnaces generated enough heat to melt the coal balls and limestone into liquid, and this was collected at the bottom of the furnace by Korean civilians, whose number included women and children. They poured the liquid into large moulds and once it had cooled, took it to a crusher. In its final form, calcium carbide, it was then loaded into sealed containers and onto railway trucks.

Although the prisoners had negotiated successfully for safety measures, the Japanese were unwilling to allow the Korean civilians more than the most basic protection. Arthur Kerr recorded the horrendous result:

> Safety precautions are very lax and accidents occur daily. On Sunday for instance, two killed, three injured. On Monday, a boy had his arm taken off, and every day somebody either has legs, feet, arms or fingers jammed or mangled. Last week a car ran into a passenger train: three killed, no.1 of works included.

This was the reality of the Greater East Asian Co-Prosperity sphere for the Korean population.

Any account of the prisoners' working life under the Japanese must mention that sabotage took place everywhere that they were put to work. The Australians were particularly known for their ability as saboteurs and none was more skilled or daring than Reg Hayter at Konan. He had been an engineer in civilian life, and was able to apply his knowledge to commit significant acts of destruction at the factory.

The furnaces in the carbide factory were dependant on a water-cooling system which ran on a single pipe. If the pipe could be blocked, Hayter calculated, the furnaces would eventually overheat and explode. He located an inspection point on the pipe which was secured by just three bolts. They could easily be unscrewed. Waste material could then be stuffed into the pipe to cause a catastrophic blockage. He discussed this with his two co-workers and they agreed to put his plan into action immediately. On their next shift, Hayter unscrewed the bolts, and his mates blocked the pipe with the rubbish they had smuggled in. At first, nothing happened, and as the minutes passed they began to have fears that their scheme had failed. But an hour or so later, steam started to belch out from the water cooler, provoking terror among the guards on the ground. As the prisoners bolted along the gantry and down the staircase, there was an air-splitting explosion. The furnaces were out of action for a week while a gang of Korean plumbers repaired the water cooler.

The additional burden of hard labour meant that the sickness rate at Mukden was higher than at the other Korean camps. An analysis of Arthur Kerr's diary over the period of a sample month, July 1944, gives an idea of general health at the camp and of the less serious ailments that were a regular part of prisoners' lives. At the beginning of July, he wrote that he was suffering from a hernia and an injury to his right arm. The intense heat of the furnace meant that he was drinking excessive amounts of liquid:

> It's bloody warm one way or the other working, and I lose buckets of sweat daily. To compensate I who never drink fluids normally, consume about 15 to 20 mugs while on the job.
> 5 July: Dysentery is on the rise in the camp, bacillic and amoebic, but they are being caught fairly early, thank goodness.
>
> 17 July: During this period a stool sample was taken and I, among others, was found to be harbouring worms … Treated and maybe I am shot of them. Don't know, although plenty saw their castoffs, some were at least 8 inches long. Had a checkover by the MO. No comments, so apparently OK. Only remark was to the effect that the hernia was enlarging.
>
> 21 July: Talk of the plagues of Egypt, we have two: innumerable small flies that positively swarm on one during the day and hordes of mosquitoes at night, making life an utter misery.
>
> Juy 29: I have developed a sweat or heat rash that is causing me considerable bother. Treated every night, but it still seems to be spreading. Right armpit is absolutely full.

Over the next twelve months Kerr would also suffer from bronchitis and malaria. The men at Konan got progressively weaker, and in 1945 started to die at the rate of one man a month. In comparison to other camps this was a low mortality rate, but had the Japanese not surrendered in August 1945, the trend would have continued and accelerated. Dr Morris estimated that every man at the camp would have been dead within twelve months.

Can we say that conditions at Konan were affected by its propaganda role? Lieutenant Arthur Cramsie reckoned that if you were an officer, there was no better place to be held prisoner by the Japanese. His only job was to organise the manpower for the various shifts, and he was able to stay out of the way of the most sadistic guards, receiving just one serious beating during his whole time at the camp. But the regime for all the men, other ranks as well as officers, was less horrendous than at other camps. The death total of five men was remarkably low. It can be said that the men at Konan were 'fortunate' in comparison to the suffering of others. Of the roughly 50,000 British servicemen captured by the Japanese, 30,000 were sent to work on the Burma–Thailand railway. They worked up to eighteen hours a day with inadequate tools, suffering not just from malnutrition, disease and beatings, but torture. One of the most important sources for the history of the 'Death railway' is the diary of 'Weary' Dunlop. His diary entry for March 1943 is just one of hundreds of possible examples that could be given to illustrate the conditions the men worked under:

> Obviously the N [Nipponese] have a great reserve of manpower at Changi and they are showing every intention of breaking men on the job with not the slightest consideration for either life or health. This can only be regarded as a cold-blooded merciless crime against mankind, obviously premeditated. Ration position: no vegetables, meat or fish for 5 days, just rice. Five hundred and sixty-six men of whom two hundred and twenty-four have no boots.[7]

The lack of boots led to leg ulcers and then amputations.

Those prisoners who survived the Burma Railway and were sent to the northern areas such as the Japanese mainland and Taiwan often found that conditions were actually worse.[8] Many POWs worked in mines, where they dug, hauled and transported heavy loads in dark, airless tunnels. Equipment was primitive or defective, and POWs worked barefoot and in rags. Cave-ins, accidents and gas poisoning were frequent occurrences.

Among the worst were the mines in the Fukuoka district in Japan and the copper and tin mines in Taiwan. At Kinkaseki in Taiwan, prisoners worked seven days a week, with one rest day allowed after fifty consecutive days of work had been completed. During the day they were permitted just one single thirty minute break, and if they failed to reach their work quota they were punished with up to twenty blows from the shaft of a mining hammer. One prisoner recalled that there was on average a minor accident at work every day, and a major one every week. Injury from falling rocks was a constant danger. The men worked naked apart from improvised loin cloths in temperatures of up to 130°F, and in some parts of the mine they were drenched by the acid water which dripped down on them.

None of the Korean camps witnessed the most extreme forms of punishment. Elsewhere, prisoners were burned with cigarettes and hot irons. They endured various forms of water torture and electric shocks administered through wires attached to the body, mainly to the genitals. Methods of execution included public beheading by sword or being buried or burned alive. Indian prisoners were used for bayonet practice, and there is evidence that a group of them were also the victims of cannibalism. Although it can be said that Party B received less severe treatment, we are measuring their experiences against the furthest extremes of human cruelty.

Chapter 15
Letters To and From Home

'Do you know that I am alive and well, Mum? Are you alive and well too? It's rotten not knowing.'

Alan Toze Diaries, January 1943.[1]

A simple but effective form of propaganda was to allow prisoners at the Party B camps to write letters home. At most camps, prisoners were at best allowed to complete pre-printed postcards allowing the prisoner to choose options such as 'I am in good health/I am in hospital, I am not working/I am working for pay'. But at Keijo the officers were allowed to write eight letters per year with a length of up to 400 words, although my father complained that the Japanese were 'infernally touchy' about the letters' contents. The occasions when permission to write was given usually coincided with positive events, such as the distribution of relief supplies. At the beginning of January 1944, letter paper was issued 'so that we could mention what a wonderful time we'd been given at Christmas,' he wrote.[2] But some of the prisoners' letters proved unacceptable.

> Last Monday six of us were summoned to the office and had letters returned. Ushihara gave some advisory asides in which he counselled avoidance of being too detailed in statement – a harmless vagueness was preferable. Then Terada appeared and the letters were returned with the offensive passages bracketed in red. Terada said: 'Colonel Noguchi does not want you to paint life here in glowing terms (!!!) but does not want the bad side of it to be stressed', which seemed to me to be fair. Clean paper issued and given until one to rewrite. They were exceedingly annoyed that many had not mentioned Christmas with sufficient enthusiasm, or indeed had ignored it all together. Peter Cazalet spent an hour being arraigned in the office for

> writing 'we had a quite a good Christmas eked out with Red Cross parcels'.[3]

Any hint that the prisoners were not getting enough to eat was utterly forbidden. The phrases that my father had to remove included 'we received a slice of white bread – a unique treat', and 'we were given a dollop of stew' had to be amended to, 'we were given stew'.

The letters that left the camp corroborated the ICRC reports. Prisoners could also enclose photos in the letters to strengthen the message of good treatment still further. Christmas festivities, Red Cross parcels and the camp garden were the staple news items. If a prisoner needed to paint an unrealistically bright picture of life at the camp to get past the censor, he might do so just to let his family know that he was still alive. There was also the natural desire to reassure families at home. Even a prisoner who had just had his leg amputated at Changi wrote home saying he was in good health. But there were various ingenious attempts to give hints of the reality as well. Captain Jesson managed to write a somewhat ambiguous postcard which escaped censorship and was later published in a Red Cross magazine: 'Still well and happy, nearly eleven stone on an oriental diet. With many old friends, chief events, meals, sleep, reading, talk, smoking, enough of each. Always freezing now but warm enough. Cheery Christmas: carols, stew (Irish) saki, show (self-stage manager) made usual greeting cards.'[4] 'Nearly eleven stone on an oriental diet' indicates he had lost weight; 'always freezing but warm enough' is a somewhat contradictory statement, and his very mundane list of chief events qualified by the phrase 'enough of each' may hint at the profound boredom and stagnation of which his journals occasionally complain.

One of the entirely justified complaints made by the Allies was that the Japanese did not respect the prisoners' right to receive letters, as required by the Geneva Convention. As part of its counter-propaganda, Dr Paravicini was invited to a Tokyo sorting office where POW mail was supposedly processed. He was able to observe prisoners who had been brought into the office for the day to play the part of mail sorters. In a photograph in *Nippon Times*, Dr Paravicini is seen 'casting an approving eye' over the efforts of the men as they worked through the backlog. The report explained:

> There are many other post offices which handle as large quantity of mail but probably no other which receives so

> many letters to persons whose address is not known. Up to this writing [*sic*] more than 700,000 letters have been placed in the dead letter file after untiring efforts were made to locate the addressees. In view of the fact that the post office has been functioning for only a few weeks, this is a phenomenal record.
>
> One reason why 700,000 dead letters have piled up during so brief a period lies in the fact that the addresses are not specific and cannot be specific. Many of the senders, for one thing, are not certain whether the persons to whom they have written are dead, missing or in war prisoners' camp. There are more than a hundred thousand American and British war prisoners and it is almost as difficult to find a given prisoner by having his name alone, as it is to find the proverbial needle in the haystack.[5]

In reality, the reason why the addresses could not be specific was because the Japanese had deliberately withheld prisoner information from the Allies. The POW Management Office kept up-to-date records of all the prisoners' locations, as well as their next of kin and home addresses. In a later stage of imprisonment, at Omori camp, Henling Wade spent some of his time working as a mail sorter. His first impressions contrast with the suggestions of modernity and efficiency given by the newspaper:

> I now looked in at the post office for the first time … five officers wearing mitts to keep their hands warm and with blankets round their legs were seated at different tables with rudimentary home-made pigeonhole racks in front of them, sorting letters.[6] The entire team consisted of no more than half a dozen men under the leadership of a Major Frankcom. The Japanese were reluctant to waste resources on this activity. Letters for prisoners of war, which had been very slowly sorted by Japanese students working at the Propaganda Bureau, [presumably *Huryojohokyoku*] now came to Omori. Major Frankcom asked for and received lists of prisoners in every camp in Japan. These lists were

> always out of date, so the information on the envelopes was all we had to guide us. We would then send it to, say, Changi (Malaya) or Cabanatuan (Luzon); if it returned in a few months it might say 'moved to Thailand' (or Borneo or Manchuria) and a date. We would then redirect it accordingly and hope ... Every couple of months, after much begging by Frankcom, the Japanese post office would collect the 70 to 100 mailbags we had filled since their last visit.[7]

Wade claims that things got so bad that in May 1944 the team was temporarily reduced to just a single man, a Norwegian sailor.

Only a very small percentage of the contents of the mailbags ever reached the prisoners, even if they reached the camps. As was the case with Red Cross supplies, the *Huryo* ensured that the Party B and other show camps received mail, but it was of no concern to the Japanese whether prisoners in other camps received mail or not. Before being issued to prisoners, all letters had to be read and censored, a task which could be avoided by destroying the mail or leaving it unopened in the mail bags. On average, a Far Eastern Prisoner of War received three letters during the three-and-a-half years of captivity. Many received none at all. The Indian prisoners were particularly unfortunate. Japan steadfastly maintained the fiction that there were no Indian prisoners to write to. In November 1944 at Jinsen, Captain Stacey Sinclair, who had grown up in India, wrote to his family in Darjeeling: 'I have received no mail so far and I almost feel like God has forgotten me. However, I hope to see you all again.'[8]

Although there was a long wait before the first batches of mail arrived in Korea, thereafter an irregular flow of letters to and from the camps was maintained. The emotional impact of letters from home can hardly be overstated. It was not until July 1943 that the first mail from Australia reached Jinsen, and it consisted of just two letters. One of these was for Alex Johnstone, from his wife. They had been married for just three months before he had been despatched to Singapore. He poured his emotions out into his diary: 'O mine own beloved, nothing could possibly have given me greater pleasure than your letter, it being five hundred and twenty days since I heard from you and only God knows how I have longed, yearned and prayed for news of you.'[9] Alan

Toze had experienced similar emotions when he received his first letter on 12 February 1943:

> With greater feelings of joy than I have experienced for two years, I record with humble and heartfelt thanks the receipt of no less than 19 letters, 18 of which are from Mum and Bet, from which I learn that up to the 25th January last year, one year and three weeks ago, they were alive and well and had had unofficial news of my safety. They are an answer to my despairing prayers, the terrible two years' silence from my loved ones has been broken. I trust that I shall never have to endure such another period. I trust too that they have not been so long without a word from me. What a marvellous change in things it has made for me. The loving phrases, the messages, the old friends, the news of family and friends – and greatest joy the snap of my dear Mum with Sally. It has combined to give me – literally – a new lease of life, new hope, new courage.

In the latter part of 1943, the permitted length of the letters to prisoners was reduced to twenty-five words, either typed or written in capital letters, for the convenience of Japanese censors. This appears to have increased the flow of correspondence, although my father thought it ironic that the prisoners, who had so little to report about their monotonous lives, were allowed to write 800 words, while their families and friends could only write a couple of sentences. But they received, comparatively speaking, a huge amount of mail. John Jesson recorded that in all he had received fifty letters and cards during captivity. The contents of each batch of letters were eagerly shared at the camps. Pieces of news such as the ringing of church bells to celebrate British victory in Northern Africa helped raise morale. At Keijo, Captain Frank Beattie learned that his brother, a POW in Germany, had been awarded the Victoria Cross, and that the commandant of the camp had taken him out to dinner to celebrate.

The letters, of course, also brought bad news. During this period the jocular but sad expression 'Dear John letter' came into existence among American servicemen. Some of the prisoners in Korea received these letters. Many POWs shrugged off this news as insignificant in contrast to their present circumstances, but others were also deeply affected. Prisoners also learned of the death of parents or friends and relatives who were killed in action. 'Black market' Muir-Harding was to learn that his mother, a nurse who had been working with an ambulance brigade in Egypt, had been killed. John Lever received news of the death of his father. Like Alex Johnstone's, his diary was written in the form of a letter to his wife. Its entry for 11 July 1944 offers a glimpse of his calm personality and also of his mental strength and dignity:

> I received four letters. One was your twenty-five word letter of 15 October telling me the sad news of father's death. The letters come in any sort of order and I had already received two of your later letters (both twenty-five words). Although neither of these mentioned father, from these and your previous letters, I had sensed what had happened so it was not altogether a shock.

At Keijo, prisoners even received letters from complete strangers. In Britain, a 'write to a chum' scheme had been dreamt up with the idea that members of the public could write to random prisoners as a means of ensuring that every prisoner received at least one letter and did not feel forgotten. John Lever was a beneficiary of this scheme:

> I went out with a working party on Thursday and came back to find I had received nineteen letters. Two were from yourself, your letters are the 'meatiest' I get, they are full of vital news and give me the best picture of things at home that I want to know about. One was a typewritten one from the Cromptons signed Tommy, so obviously dictated by him. Two were from Tommy and Wrekin. I was tickled to death to hear from Tommy and it seems apparent that he writes quite often. Practically all the others were from a girl in Birkenhead who, out of the kindness of her heart, writes to me every week or two. There is very little in her letters and if I received them every week or two they would be very acceptable but a dozen or so arriving in one batch ruins this effect. This particular batch of letters covered a period of about 6 months ... By no means all were written to me.[10]

Receipt of Letters in Britain and Australia

After the fall of Singapore families at home heard nothing for several months, and then received official letters reporting their son or husband as 'missing', or 'missing, believed dead'. The word 'missing' would have had a horrible resonance for those with memories of the 1914–18 war. As soon as she heard that her only son was on the missing list, Captain Jesson's mother wrote him a letter, unsure if she was 'writing to a ghost'; 'I have of course been down to the very utmost depths, which is only natural, and still dip pretty deep if I let my imagination go out of control.'[11] But Jesson's mother was relatively fortunate. She finally heard that her son was alive on 4 November 1942. Most families had to wait until 1943 or even later before they knew whether their son was dead or alive. Some had still heard no news whatsoever months after the Japanese surrender.

According to British Red Cross statistics, as late as August 1942 only a few hundred names of prisoners had been released. By January 1943 the total stood at only 10,000 British and Dominion prisoners. Matters were made worse by the British government's bureaucratic failures. When Sir Harold Satow, head of the Foreign Office Prisoner of War department, came to publish a report on his department's activities during the war he admitted that even at the end of 1943 'arrangements for information and publicity about the Far East were little short of chaotic'.[12] As has been observed elsewhere, Satow was not a man given to self-criticism, to put it no stronger, so his admission is significant. The two most important bodies for analysing POW information were the Directorate of Prisoners of War at the War Office, and the Prisoners of War Department at the Foreign Office, but other departments at the War Office also held an interest in POW issues, and the Navy and Air Force both wished to maintain responsibility for their own men in captivity. Responsibility for publicity and organising relief supplies had been devolved to the British Red Cross, an independent organisation which was not trusted enough to be given any knowledge of Japanese atrocities. Family members seeking news were passed from one department to another, often receiving coldly unsympathetic official responses to their desperate enquiries.

Some men were reported dead when they were in fact alive; others were reported to be alive and well many months after they had perished through maltreatment. There were several cases of women being told that their husband was dead and then remarrying, only to find out that they had unwittingly committed bigamy.[13] One family had been told that their son was dead, but found out that he was alive when he turned up on their doorstep in November 1945. Their emotions can be imagined.[14]

Such was the paucity of information that Party B letters and cards became news items, useful for boosting morale. On 28 May 1943, for example, the *Chelmsford Chronicle* reported that a Keijo prisoner, Private Saye, 'wished to be remembered to all Essex people', and that 'there was plenty of food and clothing, he was in excellent health and the climate was good'. In Australia, prisoner families had received even less information than British families. A letter written by Elrington to his wife in South Africa was of sufficient news interest to be published in the regional newspaper, *The Western Australian*:

> Friends in Perth have received a copy of a letter to his wife. 'It is dry cold here, like Switzerland. We had a snowy, cheery Christmas with extra food, Communion, carols, and a concert. I am senior officer here and my dealings with the camp staff are amicable. We want warm vests and underpants for winter, razor blades, shaving soap and books. Don't be anxious. Roll on 1944.'

There were also encouraging letters from the Australian prisoners, containing much the same content as the letters that appeared in British newspapers. Even by the summer of 1944, information about the camps was so scarce that letters were newsworthy. On 22nd July *The Western Australian* reported:

> Mrs C.H. Gray, a member of the 1/4th Machine Gun Battalion Women's circle, has received a letter from her son Charles William Gray, who is a prisoner of war at Keijo, Chosen. This letter, which her relatives say is in the same style of writing as those he sent before the fall of Singapore, has been encouraging to other members of the circle: 'We are living under pretty good conditions. The quarters themselves are clean and comfortable, having coal stoves to heat the rooms in winter. There are also ample

> washrooms and bathrooms and we get two hot baths a week. Now, Mum, don't worry about us, things are going to come right soon.'

When letters first started to appear in British newspapers, there was a flood of enquiries to the Post Office and government departments from families desperate to know whether more post was on its way. A formal response was published in all local and national newspapers:

> In view of the number of enquiries on the subject, the Post Office announces that some 7,000 letters and postcards have been received in the last few weeks from camps in Japan, Korea, Formosa, Shanghai and Hong Kong.[15] The Japanese authorities announced recently that mail had been despatched from all camps except three, at which the necessary arrangements had not been completed. It is, therefore, probable that more letters are on the way, but it cannot be stated when they are likely to arrive. Prisoners in Mukden (Manchuria) and Jinsen (Korea) have been allowed to give some information regarding conditions in the camp. From the other camps the information is very brief, consisting of a type-written card informing the next-of-kin that the prisoner's health is excellent, good or poor, that he is either working or not working, as the case may be, and ending with a request to look after the welfare of certain near relatives. These cards, have in most cases, taken about six months in transit, and it is anticipated that mail from the camps in Japanese-occupied territory such as Malaya, Java etc will take a considerably longer time to reach this country.[16]

The statement that more letters were on their way from the other camps was of course misinformation from the *Huryo*. But although they offered false comfort to FEPOW families, the letters were, paradoxically, useful propaganda for the British in their attempts to sustain morale and keep public concern about the Pacific War low. The press also offered upbeat summaries of the ICRC reports as their contents were released. In its edition for 8 August 1943 a Scottish newspaper gave readers positive news from the show camps: 'Conditions in camps in Japan, Korea and Hong Kong were pretty good generally. Not Ritzy, but bearable.'[17] Although the diet was monotonous, it said, the prisoners had sufficient food, and at one camp the men were allowed to keep hens and rabbits. At another, the prisoners were let out for recreational walks of the sort Colonel Noguchi had mooted with Dr Paravicini. Keijo is the only camp mentioned by name: 'a one-time mill, surrounded by a wooden fence. Prisoners sleep sixty to a room on folding Japanese mattresses. They have sufficient blankets.'[18]

The announcement also carried government disinformation, stating that 'nothing definite was known about camps in Sumatra, Thailand, Borneo and Malaya'. In fact, by August 1943 a great deal was known for certain about atrocities in Thailand and Sumatra.

Chapter 16
Animosities

> Colonel Nakao Yahagi, Chief of the Army Press Section of Imperial Headquarters, declared that Anglo-Americans interned in Japan are on extremely bad terms with each other and find every chance to quarrel among themselves. He said that if Americans and British prisoners are made to cook together, the latter invariably raise objections and ask the authorities to make separate arrangements so that they may be able to cook independently. Facts such as these, Col. Yahagi pointed out, reveal how flimsy are the ties which bind the British and Americans.
>
> *The Tribune* (Filipino newspaper)

Animosity between the different nationalities at the prison camps was a recurring theme of Japanese POW propaganda, employed to mirror reports of the dissensions that marred relationships between the Allies at the level of high politics. This form of propaganda began as soon as the prisoners at Singapore were marched off to Changi. The news agency *Domei* reported: 'Anzac, Indian and British prisoners form own cliques, displaying mutual contempt and calling each other names.' According to the report, Australians complained that during the fighting the British had taken great care to remain well to the rear, while ordering Australian troops to go to the most exposed positions. For their part, the British complained to the reporter that the Australians were 'uneducated' and were 'always repeating the same mistakes' on the battlefield. As for the Indians, they were 'nothing more than an army of coolies'. The Indians were offended by the racist arrogance of the British, saying that 'they never treated us as humans', nor were they impressed by the Australians: 'They are all drunkards who are only seeking a good time.'

All mention of Indian prisoners disappeared after this early report. Their existence would have harmed Japan's pose of being India's friend and sponsor of Indian independence. But the animosity between the Australian and British members of Party B was reported as soon as they arrived in Korea.

On the dockside, the naval officer in command of the *Fukkai Maru* spoke to reporter Kim Jung Won, telling him of the Australians' gratitude and respect for the Japanese, which contrasted with their feelings towards the British.

> In comparing British and Australian POWs, the Australians worked harder and had better physiques than the British. Also, Australians don't have good feelings about the British. This is because during the Greater East Asian War there have been many times they have been deceived by Britain. Meanwhile, their feelings towards Japan are that the Japanese are very kind and they are very thankful. As well, they expressed how brave the Japanese army is, calling them 'fierce tigers of the jungle'.

On board the train making its way to Keijo, reporter Kim Jung Won also spoke to the senior Australian officer, Captain Wilf Fawcett:

> Captain Fawcett, who had put on a clean suit and gave the appearance of having come to Chosen from Malaya to do some sightseeing, looked like he'd had no experience of war and his face hadn't even avoided the sunshine. The Australian captain said the UK was his mother country, but the deceitful British, being pursued by the Imperial army's fierce attacks, did not aid his country, and he was discontented by this.

What was the reality of the relationship between Australian and British prisoners in Korea and Manchuria? The picture that emerges from Party B is that the two nationalities got on well. However, the first encounter between the nations in Hold Four of the *Fukkai Maru* was not a happy one. Colonel Elrington describes how he was pushed at the point of a bayonet down steep steps and along a narrow gangway, with 300 men behind him: 'The hold was piled in the centre with bags of rice and barley, and from its walls ran two shelves covered with straw matting and Australians.' His opening words to the Australians, a request for them to make room for his men, received the reply 'Why don't you get your bloody Percival to sort it out?', to which he replied: 'If you're so bloody clever why don't you tell me how to get a quart into a pint pot you lousy ------------?'. 'This had the desired effect of raising a laugh against the noisy "old sweat" who had first spoken and of ceding some half space.'[1]

Crammed together in their dark, hot and vermin-infested hold, it is unsurprising that at first there were arguments, which on a couple of occasions led to punch-ups. But Elrington described how the men gradually bonded over a shared hatred of their captors, and how 'mutual respect and the beginnings of real friendship' developed. 'The Aussies, for all their vast continent, were far more insular in outlook and conscious of the superiority of all things Australian, at the same time proving themselves good talkers, good givers and easy in fellowship.' In another hold, Lieutenant Arthur Cramsie was disgusted by the behaviour of some of the other ranks, but they were his own people. 'I am ashamed to say that the Australians behaved themselves much better than the British.' The Australians were better at companionship than his own men, he decided. He attributed their ability to live together as a unit to their better education and greater maturity.[2]

Throughout captivity there was always a minority of men who caused trouble. According to Cramsie, most of them were regular private soldiers. His estimate that they constituted about 20 per cent of other ranks is corroborated by other testimony. They complained continually and initiated quarrels and fights. Their number included thieves, and, most despised of all, 'white rats'. At each camp there was at least one man who informed on their fellow prisoners to the Japanese in return for food and better treatment. As Arthur Kerr wrote, captivity brought out the best and worst in men. Both he and Cramsie also observed that the behaviour of men in captivity was often a revelation. In Cramsie's words, 'Frequently and strangely those who were expected to behave badly were towers of strength and those whom one expected to behave well went to pieces and were quite useless.'[3]

Despite the quarrelling, nationality was never a cause of conflict. Australian prisoners also recalled that they got along well with the British. But Colonel Des Brennan added the qualification that a language barrier had to be overcome first. The thick Lancastrian accent of the Loyals was at first almost unintelligible to him and his fellow Australians. A light-hearted Christmas message from the Australians to the British teased them on this. One of the great challenges of captivity it said had been to come to terms with two unknown languages, Japanese and Lancastrian. Of the two, Lancastrian created the most 'cacophonous' sound.

The diaries also provide evidence of real friendship between the two nationalities. Alex Johnstone, an Australian, records how he discovered presents from an Englishman who had left Jinsen for Mukden:

> An Englishman whom I'd chummed up with and helped with cigs and money etc left me a note and two presents, including a crucifix. I opened it after he'd gone and it gave me a shock, believe me. It's nice to know that one's efforts are appreciated.[4]

His closest friend at Jinsen appears to have been an Anglo-Indian officer, Lieutenant Sinclair. He spent countless hours 'yarning' with Sinclair in the evenings. In his diary, he seriously contemplates emigrating to England after the war.

Captain Lever's diary records him making plans to emigrate in the other direction. Before the war he had been a manager in a cloth manufacturing business, and he seriously discussed starting a similar business in Australia after the war with his friend, Herb Geldard:

> I had a talk with Herb. Geldard about producing Rayon in Australia after the war. This would be a good job for me. Herb is an Australian rather over 50 who went through the last war and acted ADC to General Gordon Bennett in Malaya. Gordon Bennett got away but Herb is here with us.[5] Herb has some money he could put up and has one or two friends he could rope in. My idea is that the business could be started on a smallish scale on a profitable basis and the scale increased. Herb will make the necessary investigations re new materials and protective tariffs and the attitude of the government while I root around the machinery end of the business about producing Rayon in Australia after the war. This would be a good job for me.[6]

Nevertheless, there are hints that the relationship between the nations was not without friction. The camp magazine *Nor Iron Bars*, produced in secret by three English officers at Keijo, consisted mainly of light-hearted contributions, but one of its editions contained a serious piece by Wilf Fawcett, contrasting the Australians with the British. He implies that the term 'bushwhacker', frequently used by the British in a jocular way, was in fact unconsciously condescending. The piece argues that the Australian bushwhacker was a far more resourceful human being, equipped with a far greater array of practical skills, than the average Briton. A bushwhacker had to learn how to live off the land and fend for himself, whereas the average British 'chap' faced no greater challenge than choosing which tie or shirt to wear to the office. Given that John Jesson had criticised his own men for 'lacking the practical skills of a ten year old boy scout', there was no doubt that Fawcett had seen evidence to support his view It can also be added that one or two of the officers' diaries implicitly display a world outlook based on the premise that the most evolved form of the species homo sapiens was the 'English gentleman', as manufactured at the nation's public schools. All other members of the human race were judged against the codes and prejudices instilled in them at boarding school or Sandhurst. The practical skills that a bushwhacker possessed would have been utterly irrelevant to them in estimating a man's worth.[7]

A disparaging reference to the British is found in only one diary, Arthur Kerr's. But at the same time he complained that his own countrymen were even worse than the 'Bines'. Writing at Konan on 1 January 1945, he describes an atmosphere of intense irritation at the camp:

> A big percentage are ready to fly off the handle at any moment, and a few are decidedly childish and irritable with anyone near them. Myself, I don't worry much but even so there are a great number if I never see them again that will be too soon, and strange to say the majority are our own. As for the English troops, the larger portion well, the less said the better. But judging the ones I have mixed with as an average sample, never try and tell me about who are the salt of the earth and who are sportsmen.[8]

Above: Konan camp, PW painted on roof for benefit of B29s delivering relief supplies.

Right: Open-air service at Keijo with Padre Peter Cazalet, October 1942.

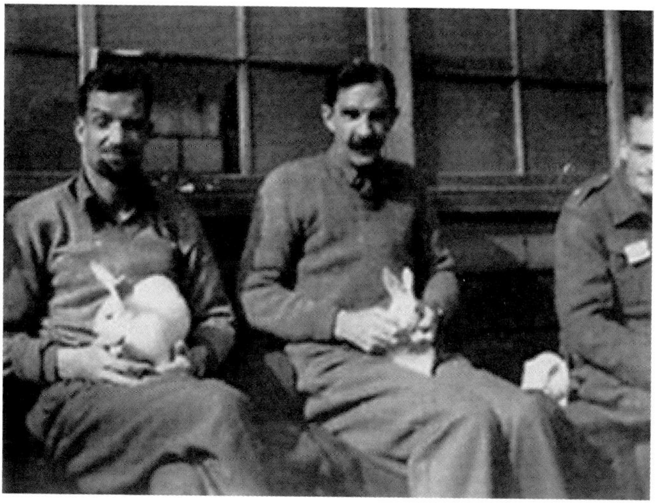

Left to right: Captain Beattie, Colonel Elrington and Major Holohan with the Keijo rabbits.

PRISONNIERS DE GUERRE BRITANNIQUES AU JAPON

Camp de Keijo

3. Hommage de l'armée japonaise aux défunts

4. Service divin britannique

Above: Officers' garden, August 1943, Peter Cazalet in foreground, wearing vest.

Left: Photographs of memorial service reproduced in ICRC magazine.

Above: Bunka Camp, unwilling propagandists. Jack McNaughton back row, second from left; Harry Pearson front row, second from right.

Right: Lance-Bombardier Arthur Butler in his stage persona, Gloria D'Earie.

Below: Christmas lunch, Keijo 1943.
My father looks at the camera, Peter Cazalet to his right.

Fukkai Maru.

Above left: Fusan victory parade.

Above right: Caricature of Japanese bugler in *Nor Iron bars.*

Cemetery at Mukden.

In the officers' garden.

Liberated Australian POWs hold 'the Milkman' aloft at Keijo.

Officers at Jinsen, Alex James standing far left.

Major Leighton transformed into a fly, one of many drawings depicting the prisoners as insects and animals.

Members of Loyal Regiment at Changi.

Photograph published in ICRC magazine with the caption 'Cuisine de camp', in reality a staged photographed taken in the kitchen of *Hotel des Indes*, the Japanese military's headquarters in Batavia.

Making bread at Keijo.

Above left: Alan Toze, portrait by Donald Teale.

Above right: Lieutenant George Baker, taken on his return home in November 1945.

Elsewhere he records his pride in his nationality. His remark should perhaps be placed in the context of his circumstances when he wrote them.

According to Japanese propaganda, Americans and British were no more able to live in harmony than the British and Australians. The national types are more clearly delineated than the Australians, although both British and Americans shared an effeminate concern with personal appearance. An early report from Zentsuji carries the headline: 'American and British Prisoners at Zentsuji forget shame: only interested in dress up.' The reporter decried the frequency with which both nationalities 'washed their shirts and underwears [*sic*] in an attempt to keep up their dandyism'.

But despite a shared interest in 'dress up', the national arrogance of the British alienated them from the Americans. A *Domei* report from an unnamed camp in February 1943 informed readers:

> One strange and unexpected thing is that in most of the prisoners' camps there is no love lost between the American and British POWs. What makes the Americans see red is the manner in which the British regard themselves as having given assistance to the Americans, whereas the Americans see it as the opposite. The American and British prisoners are hardly on speaking terms. The Americans keep to their side of the grounds, and the British to theirs. From the way in which the two groups scowl at each other, anyone can see that there is a feud. Fundamentally, the reason seems to be that the Britishers look down on Americans in general.[9]

The superior wages of the American serviceman was also a bone of contention, as described in another article from 1943: 'Yankees because of their wages, disliked by Britishers, Australians.'[10] Americans are depicted as being the most materialistic of the enemy races, with an excessive love of money. If the British at first were more interested in playing than fighting, the Americans viewed life from a financial perspective. An American prisoner captured at Guam is reported as saying: 'We, as war prisoners, are given a family allowance of $200 at home, and are safely looked after by the Japanese.'

The *Domei* report also found that the Americans possessed other national failings: they were sentimental, voluble and egotistic, and lacked any sense of dignity or reserve.

> As soon as they saw me, the American officers sprang forward and began bowing and scraping before me. Although I did not ask them any questions, they vied with each other in telling all about their past records and life histories. I was disgusted with them.
>
> I picked out a young officer and asked him: are you a bachelor? Jabbering something excitedly he pulled out a picture of his sweetheart and started weeping. Not to be outdone, the other officers similarly pulled out similar photographs of their sweethearts and began to weep, too.

By contrast, 'The British were made of much sterner stuff….' For once the British are portrayed in a more positive light, but only to highlight the failings of the Americans.

The evidence from Mukden is that the Americans and British got on well, although, like the encounter between Australians and British in Hold Four of the *Fukkai Maru*, the first contacts between the two nationalities were not frictionless. One British officer remembered that just after their arrival an American came into the British officers' squad room and asked: 'Say guys, anyone want to buy a shirt?' A particularly pompous individual drew himself up and replied: 'We are not "guys", we are British officers.' […] That got us off to a good start.' He suggests that an awareness that they were in the minority may have tempered the behaviour of some of the more self-important British officers. There was a quarrel early on over the distribution of a bulk supply of cigarettes, with the British believing the Americans had taken more than their fair share. But this was a minor incident, soon forgotten, and not the harbinger of lasting conflict.

According to Arthur Christie, friendships between the other ranks and the American enlisted men started as soon as they met, and in his case lasted for the rest of his life. 'From the start we seemed to hit it off, squabbles over nationality and status were just something we joked about and kidded one another... We shared what little we had with one another.'[11] On one occasion, British and Americans worked together to fool the Japanese and gain a holiday for the British on 4th July, as Major Peaty's diary explains:

> The Japanese were greatly puzzled about this Independence Day. The first year, the Americans asked for permission to celebrate one of their great national holidays, and the Japs asked what it was; 'Independence Day' they were told. 'What is that?', they asked. 'The anniversary of the day we cut ourselves free from British rule' was the answer. Immediately the Japanese seized on it as a good idea, for they were always trying to play off the British against the Americans, So we went along and asked for permission to celebrate too (by pre-arrangement with the Yanks). The Japs said 'What is it that you want to celebrate?' and we said Independence Day. 'But that is an American festival, the day they were liberated from the British yoke'. 'Ah yes, but we celebrate the same day to commemorate having got rid of the Americans.' This left them completely bewildered, and we had our holiday too. The Americans always played up well on this sort of thing, and we got on very well together.[12]

Living together in such circumstances it was inevitable that conflict, sometimes significant conflict, would arise, but nationality was not a cause. Interestingly, several of the prisoners independently pinpoint the first anniversary of the capitulation as the nadir of prisoner relationships, both at Jinsen and Keijo. Arthur Kerr wrote:

> End of the first 12 months as POW and the same faces are beginning to pall. Conversations are boring. We have just about talked ourselves dry and any untoward noise, voice or sound, sets up an irritation and causes someone to fly at someone else's throat. Complaints and moans arise from the slightest irregularity especially food, and the hawk-eyed hungry-gutted ones are ever on the watch to see that no one gets a larger portion than the other.

Disputes between the men often turned into what the Lancastrians among them termed 'a shouting'. It also led to fights; Toze records several, and gives the impression that they were an accepted, even welcome, part of camp life, offering entertainment and excitement. On one occasion, he writes:

> The day was ushered in by a fight between Mick Pledge and that incorrigible troublemaker, Bill Lee, immediately after breakfast. Blood was smeared all over the place when they'd finished, with Mick having perhaps the advantage. They had to be separated as it was not a clean fight. During the fight Mick broke his left hand.

He also saw a fight between two officers, Captains Muir-Hardinge and Proctor: 'Both got in some good punches, with perhaps Proctor having the better of it.'[13] Sometimes, whole groups of men were involved:

> As I am writing the whole building is in uproar. Chesty Kirke and another tough, Bill Lee, are going round beating up the squad leaders. Have just witnessed beating up of Jim Gatley. Jim had been tipped off and quietly removed his glasses and tunic. Chesty asked Jim for an apology, and got a good answer, a clout. (He is a tough, big ex-seaman, splendid physique, about forty, broken nose, cauliflower ears, but maybe a bit brutal to those whom he dislikes). The gang then sat on him.

In the ensuing struggle Gatley had his nose and four of his ribs broken. Despite this, 'Gatley was not one whit upset, barking defiantly at them as they trailed away slowly…'

Both Alex James at Jinsen and John Jesson at Keijo wrote that the men consciously made the effort to learn to live together. After a year of imprisonment, James wrote, they realised that they had to develop tolerance of one another's ways, Both men wrote that they were successful in this. Considering their circumstances, James thought, there was remarkably little conflict. His view, however, was that of an officer.

As we have seen earlier, the greatest divisions at Changi, unnoticed by the Japanese, were between British officers and the men under their command. Resentment did not vanish on arrival in Korea and it appears to have reached its peak on the anniversary of their imprisonment in

February 1943. Following the arrival of the first Red Cross parcels, the men became aggrieved at what seemed to them to be the unequal distribution of bully beef by the Japanese messing officer in favour of the officers. Bypassing the officers, a group of NCOs went to the camp office to deliver a letter of complaint to the Japanese. Elrington makes no record of the incident, but his response may be imagined. Arthur Kerr recorded that the men responsible were in danger of being charged with mutiny.

Eric Wallwork provides an account of the official response:

> On 4 March we had a very surprising talk given to us by the 2nd in command Major HK Watkins. It was a very straightforward talk, he told us he was disgusted in the way we were talking about the officers over such things as the bully etc. He also asked had we ever stopped to think what the officers had done for us such as the comforts fund, the collections that they had had to buy people spectacles who were being troubled with bad eyes. This amounted to hundreds of Yen; he said this was just one thing, saying nothing of how they were asking the Japanese for things that were to our advantage more than to the officers and how they were trying to look after our small complaints, and so he went on. He finally finished by saying that the cause of all this was put down to about twenty per cent of the fellows in camp and that they were leading the whole camp anyway. He said if we were fed up with the officers, it was just the same as they were, fed up with the other ranks. A point worth noting is that the officers should not be in the same camp as other ranks as they are entitled to better living conditions and better food. The only fault about this speech was it was given about six months too late, but it certainly went home to those concerned.

Earlier, Wallwork had complained about the selfishness of the officers at Changi, but thereafter he makes no criticisms of the officers, and indeed records his great respect for Elrington. The 'comforts fund' he refers to consisted of money pooled from the officers' wages to purchase items for the other ranks. Arthur Christie, a private, certainly had no love of the British officer class, but in his memoirs he records his lasting respect for the senior officer at Mukden, Robert Peaty, and other officers such as the two New Zealanders, Captain John Horner, and Lieutenant A Greig.

Prisoners lived at a high emotional pitch, cold, hungry, unwell, deprived of news of the outside world. The uncertainty about their fate added to the pressure; as John Jesson was to write, it was 'the most trying suspense that a man can endure'. All of the prisoners suffered from beriberi at some stage of their imprisonment. One of its symptoms is irritability. It is little wonder, then, that living under these conditions the men should have fights or confrontations.

Animosities should be set against the deep bonds of supportive friendship that formed between the men. Interestingly, a pattern can again be seen at all the Party B camps. Men formed their own friendship circles, numbering at most about half-a-dozen individuals. Arthur Kerr, for example, was one of a group of six men who shared everything. John Jesson was proud to be part of a small group of officers who called themselves 'Cads' Corner'. Arthur Toze was to write that in captivity he had never been so sick of his fellow men, but at the same time had formed the 'staunchest friendships imaginable'. He records how his small group of close friends put up with his moods and didn't take offence when he fell silent; tried to cheer him up when he was despairing and looked after him when he fell ill.

Chapter 17

Death of Dr Paravicini

At a dinner given in his honour by the Korean Red Cross to mark the end of his visit to their country in November 1942, Paravicini had fainted. This was both an indication of the stress of his work and also the first sign of an illness which he neglected in favour of his work and would eventually kill him, fourteen months later. His death was respectfully noted with regret in the Japanese media. The Japanese Red Cross Society, which had played an active part in duping him, sent a translation of the obituary notice which appeared in their journal. It lavished praise on the deceased, tempered by the affectation of candour: 'This 'Para-San' contracted pneumonia arising from an influenza and has died ... The 'Para-san' who was diligent in his work and was loved by each with whom he came into contact, or at least provoked no ill-feelings, has died.'[1] Later, in an official account of its wartime work, the British Red Cross reasonably suggested that his death was the consequence of over-work and frustration.[2]

Paravicini, who had married a Japanese woman and lived and worked in Tokyo for nearly forty years, had known the best of Japanese society and culture. Although he was profoundly shocked by the change in attitude towards him when he took up his work again as a delegate, he had been unable to comprehend the full extent of the radical changes in society wrought by the militaristic governments of the 1930s. He still believed that the Japanese were sincere in their dealings with him, in spite of all the difficulties and obstacles he faced. He advised Geneva that the Japanese were totally focused on the prosecution of the war and everything else had to wait. Nevertheless, he remained optimistic that patience and perseverance would yield results. He saw procrastination as a typically Japanese characteristic. On 15 January 1943 he wrote to Geneva assuring them that 'although the Rising Sun only lets fruit ripen very slowly, progress was being made'. On 12 March he reiterated his point: 'Affairs ripen with a desperate slowness under the rising sun and one often feels that one is floundering. One makes progress, nevertheless'. The slow, incremental approach he was willing to adopt was entirely in keeping with his organisation's modus operandi at that time.

In the spring of 1943, he received fresh hope when his plans for a trip to Formosa came to fruition. There, he was taken to the senior officers' camps where members of Party A were imprisoned, while the very existence of the camps that served the tin and copper mines remained hidden from him. His pleasure at seeing what appeared to him to be satisfactory treatment in Formosa was widely reported in the Japanese media. But on his return, his friends were worried by his gaunt, pale appearance. He had lost a lot of weight. Within weeks, he was bedridden, but continued his correspondence with the *Huryo*, gradually getting weaker, and dying in January 1944.

During 1943, Paravicini had become aware that the positive sides of his reports were being exaggerated in local newspapers to the extent that, in his words, they described 'terrestrial paradises'. He wrote to Geneva about this: 'I stress the good side of things in my reports, as I believe it helps the prisoners.' He also added, 'but at Geneva you know how to read between the lines and that consoles me'.[3] This may have been the case with the first Head of the Far East Section in Geneva, Mouravieff, but his successor, Ducommun, was perplexed by Paravicini's communications, which struck him as highly unsatisfactory. Despite repeated requests for written reports in the form of letters, Geneva received instead lengthy telegrams offering irrelevant information. Ducommun was also dissatisfied with the excuses Paravicini gave for the lack of prisoner lists; for example, that the prisoners were in transit from north to south, or that the civilian internment camps in the southern areas were being reorganised. They were weak excuses, but they were Japanese excuses, not Paravicini's. The Japanese had promised Paravicini that in the fullness of time complete prisoner rolls would be supplied. He hung on to that hope. Ducommun was obviously unaware that the Japanese were tampering with communications, but it is impossible to be certain that this was the sole cause of his discontent. The archives contain a considerable amount of correspondence that had been received from Paravicini at the time of his complaint. Historians have noted that there were severe administrative failings at the headquarters, the result of its rapid expansion. It may be that some of the correspondence simply did not arrive at his desk.

In January 1944 Ducommun wrote a confidential memorandum to his superiors, voicing his suspicion that the head of their delegation in Japan had turned into a '*boîte aux lettres*'[4]:

> Paravicini's telegrams are barely comprehensible and the telegrams we send, which we have done our very best to make crystal clear, are sometimes misunderstood by him. His telegraphic reports about visits have a tendency to ramble and to misjudge the importance of different questions … Whatever … It is undeniable that the figure of forty camp visits in three years is not very high. It is also remarkable that it is invariably in summer when the visits are made, and that since last October only three camps, admittedly situated a long way from Tokyo, have been visited. He lacks initiative and seems content to play the part of a letter box. I have a thick file of letters sent to M Paravicini which have received no response. I will end by noting M Paravicini has never sent us the quarterly reports on his activities that we have requested from all our delegates, and we are very ill-informed on the technical side of his work. Finally, in the approximately six months I have worked with the Far Eastern delegates, I can't remember receiving more than one single letter from M Paravicini.

At the time Ducommun wrote his memorandum, Paravicini had in fact only a few days to live; he died on 24 January 1944.

As well as attracting the criticism of the Head of the Far East Section in Geneva, prisoners at the camps he had visited were also frustrated by the seeming lack of positive results from his inspection visits, unaware of the constraints he was operating under. Henling Wade, by that time a prisoner at Omori camp, wrote that,

> news of his death was posted on our noticeboard… The prisoners cheered—and cheered It was a sincerely welcome piece of news. As far as any of us could see, he achieved nothing during his appointment as senior International Red Cross delegate in Japan. What sort of a man, we wondered, was this Dr Paravicini, who could be satisfied

> with a fourteen-minute visit to a camp he had travelled over 400 miles to see, and where he had not spoken to a single prisoner or heard one single complaint or request? We were bitterly disappointed in him and in the International Red Cross. When I moved to Tokyo in November 1943 I heard that Dr Paravicini had behaved much the same in every camp he visited in Japan and that no improvements had followed his visits. I learnt that he had lived 30 years in Japan, was married to a Japanese and that his business depended upon Japanese goodwill. How could such a man negotiate with the Japanese with any degree of integrity?[5]

This is inaccurate both in its detail and what it implies. Paravicini had sacrificed his business to work without a salary for the Red Cross, and only permitted the organisation to cover his expenses. The suggestion that the visit to Keijo lasted only fourteen minutes is wrong. Paravicini could also claim one very substantial achievement, in that his continual pleas and suggestions for getting Red Cross aid into Japanese territories eventually paid off. It was his idea that the transfer ships used to exchange civilian internees in 1943 might also carry Red Cross supplies.

Criticism of Paravicini and his supposed lack of initiative has continued. But the ICRC had no legal right to a presence in Japanese territories and it is difficult to see what success a more combative or assertive approach would have achieved. The evidence of the large quantity of correspondence from Paravicini to Geneva is of a man who tried unremittingly to help the prisoners, even as his health failed. In his letters, he expressed himself with immense courtesy whether writing in French or elegant, grammatically perfect English. His occasionally self-deprecatory remarks are evidence not just of his disappointment, but of his courteous, old-world manner of expression.

Can we criticise Paravicini for emphasising the good points of what he saw in his reports, and for acquiescing in Japanese exploitation? In fact, Paravicini's actions were typical of his organisation at that period. He was a pragmatist: his job was to get aid to men who were desperately in need of it, and he was willing to compromise the principles of impartiality and neutrality to achieve this, whether through dwelling on the positive side of what he had seen, or by remaining silent in the face of exploitation by a belligerent party. It can be said that although the three foundational principles of the ICRC are impartiality, neutrality and humanity, the first two can, in some circumstances, be regarded as instrumental values in service of the fulfilment of the third.

History has been unkind to Paravicini. Perhaps the most fitting memorial to him is a letter of condolence from an unnamed Swiss diplomat based in Tokyo. Addressed to the President of the ICRC, Max Huber, it is an expression of genuine grief for the loss of a valued friend: 'You know what an admirable worker he was for the organisation you preside over. He encountered huge and incessant difficulties but I never saw him discouraged … Our dear friend Paravicini is dead. The loss is great: for you, for me, for our colony in Japan and for the entire country.'

Chapter 18

The British Government, the ICRC and Japanese POW Propaganda

Official news of Far Eastern Prisoners of War (FEPOWs) came to the British government through the ICRC and the Protecting Power, Switzerland. But there was no single line of communication. Although the Prisoner of War department at the Foreign office was the official point of contact with the ICRC and Switzerland, the War Office had independently established contacts with the ICRC at both its London office as well as the Geneva Headquarters. The British Red Cross also communicated directly with the ICRC, as well as relying on unofficial sources such as letters received by prisoners' families, which the organisation requested in its journals. It also contacted the ICRC on occasions to request photographs as publicity material. This led to confusion and, as we shall see, severe criticism of the Red Cross organisations.[1]

Government departments at last began to receive ICRC reports via Geneva in the first months of 1943. At the same time, the first POW letters, almost all coming from the show camps, began to arrive. News from unofficial sources had been received much earlier, however. In February 1942, the British government had begun to receive reports from escapees and intelligence sources of Japanese atrocities against its servicemen in Hong Kong. From then onwards, reports of appalling conditions intermittently escaped from Japanese territories, although not the northern areas, and in early 1943 the first reports of the terrible conditions in Thailand were received.

The departments at the War Office and Foreign Office were thus faced with the difficulty of obtaining an accurate picture of conditions from relatively little data, with unofficial reports contradicting the more reassuring impressions given in ICRC reports, photographs and prisoners' letters. The evidence suggests that although the most obvious propaganda was recognised and discounted, most of the reports and correspondence from the show camps were taken at face value as offering a realistic, albeit incomplete, picture of actual conditions.

One of the first reports to arrive in Britain was Egle's inspection of a civilian internment camp, Port Stanley in Hong Kong. It suggests an almost holiday camp existence and concludes with the words: 'I believe that ninety nine per cent of the inmates, once the time comes for their liberation, will leave the camp with a profound feeling of thankfulness and respect for the Japanese people.' The Foreign Office response was to note that this was 'too good to be true' and should be taken with 'pounds of salt'.[2] A cloud of suspicion thereafter hung over Egle in official circles until 1945, when the constraints he was operating under at last became fully known.

But the reports from the delegation in Japan contained nothing of Egle's effusiveness. They were written in sober, measured prose and contained criticisms of conditions at some of the camps; in particular they recorded the inadequacy of the prisoners' diet. Even the Keijo reports indicate dietary deficiencies, with the 1944 report noting that the prisoners felt their diet as 'greatly lacking in fat'. Summaries of them were presented at monthly meetings at the War Office.[3] Their minutes record that the first telegraphic reports of Red Cross inspections were received in February 1943, and came from Zentsuji, Keijo, Jinsen and an unidentified location in Shanghai. There is nothing in these or subsequent minutes to suggest that the veracity of the information given was ever called into question. Writing in 1950, Satow cites the reports from Japan, Manchuria, Formosa and Korea as evidence of the 'incomparably better conditions' in the northern areas.[4]

Prisoner correspondence was analysed at both the War Office and Foreign Office. The brevity and formulaic nature of the messages from most camps, often on pre-printed cards, coupled with knowledge of actual conditions in some of the areas the communications came from, led the government to suspect, rightly, that they were, in Eden's words, 'written in terms dictated by the Japanese'.[5] But government records indicate that the longer, freer letters from the show camps, bearing the imprint of the writer's personality, were regarded as valuable evidence of actual conditions. The Foreign Office sent analyses of the letters to ICRC headquarters. In a covering note sent to Geneva with an analysis of mail received over the Christmas period in 1943 the author states:

'The details are of necessity of a sketchy nature, owing to the limited facilities granted to the prisoners, but an attempt has been made to draw as complete a picture as possible.'[6] The implication is that these letters were reliable sources. It also notes that most of the letters came from Korea, but does not offer the suggestion that Jinsen, Konan and Keijo might be untypical of conditions generally.

Another document sent to the ICRC, 'Information regarding Prisoners of War in the Far East, secured from a study of the Mail received from them in June and July 1944', again focuses on Keijo and Jinsen.[7] The key points from the Keijo letters were summarised as follows:

> Mail from UK: First arrived in the camp on 22 August, 1943.
>
> Up to ten letters have been received by individual prisoners.
>
> Health: 'very fit', 'Best health and regaining lost weight', 'keeping remarkably fit'.
>
> Medical: Prison doctors and dentists
>
> Pay: Officer states that he does not need money. Another rank says that he is being paid for work done.
>
> Food: Bake own bread, eating brinjals, dehydrated turnips and other vegetables.
>
> Clothing: said to be adequate but one mentions that his socks are in a bad condition.
>
> Relief supplies: many references to Red Cross parcels being distributed monthly.

From its analysis, the government formed two misconceptions: first, that the propaganda from camps like Keijo, Jinsen and Zentsuji gave an accurate picture of conditions; second, and more significantly, that these camps were representative of the FEPOW experience in 'northern areas', a designation which included Korea, Taiwan, Shanghai, Hong Kong and Japan itself. Both misconceptions are illustrated in a speech by Eden to the House of Commons on 28 January 1944, reversing the government's policy of censorship and disclosing information regarding Japanese atrocities. Eden drew a distinction between northern and southern areas and told the House that the government was 'reasonably satisfied that conditions generally are tolerable' in the northern areas.[8] Although Eden's carefully worded speech was far from a candid disclosure of all the government knew, or of how long it had been in possession of this knowledge, the geographical distinction he made was an accurate reflection of government perceptions.

From these misconceptions arose another; the government deduced that the abuses that occurred in the southern areas were due to rogue elements acting under their own initiative, unconstrained by central control. In the summer of 1943 the government acted on this belief and made a series of broadcasts to Tokyo to reveal the maltreatment of prisoners in the southern areas, at the same time taking great pains to ensure that the contents of the broadcasts were kept secret from the British public.[9] The hope was that these broadcasts would stir the 'more responsible authorities' in the north to stem the abuses in outlying areas. Unsurprisingly, there is no evidence that these broadcasts had any effect whatsoever.

The idea persisted. In January 1945, the British Foreign Office Political Warfare (Japan) Committee minuted:

> There was evidence that prisoners of war in Japan itself and in the more accessible regions are treated reasonably well, according to Japanese standards, and that the reports of serious ill-treatment come from outlying areas where the Japanese government has little control over local military officers in charge of camps.[10]

Although Japanese propaganda did not cast doubt over intelligence of atrocities, it confused the British government as to the pervasiveness of maltreatment and led it to formulate and enact a futile strategy in broadcasting to the Japanese people.

The policy of silence over Japanese atrocities and the publication of ICRC summaries of manipulated camp reports meant that prisoner families received false comfort. The problem was compounded by the government failing to pass on its knowledge of atrocities to the Britsh Red Cross. As we have seen, responsibility for dealing with public enquires had been devolved to the British Red Cross, an independent non-governmental organisation. Following the fall of Singapore, a

Far Eastern Correspondence and Enquiry Section of the British Red Cross was opened in central London. Family members could contact the office by letter or telephone, or visit in person. It also published a magazine, *Prisoner of War*, free to MPs and POW families, which gave news about the prisoners and the efforts of the Red Cross and other organisations to supply aid and establish channels for correspondence. First published in 1942, *Prisoner of War* contained little information about Far Eastern camps, and what information it carried, such as the photograph of Keijo in its January 1944 edition, was Japanese propaganda.

The Red Cross also gave talks across the country to the families of the prisoners. It has been said that the Red Cross had to tread a fine line between maintaining morale and offering false comfort.[11] Japanese propaganda, and the government decision to withhold what it knew about atrocities from the Red Cross, meant that the line was sometimes crossed. One notorious example was a speech given in November 1943 to an audience in Liverpool by the Controller of the Far East Section of the Red Cross, Sydney King. The *Liverpool Echo* reported his assurance that 'there is not a single authenticated case of atrocities in POW camps in Japan'. Summarising his words the report stated: 'Treatment was considerate, but food could be improved. Morale was tremendously high'.[12] In his report on the activities of the Foreign Office's Prisoner of War section, its head, Sir Harold Satow, later criticised the Red Cross for being 'over-anxious to provide reassurance without strict regard to accuracy'.[13] But his statement that his own organisation could not 'of course' share its knowledge of atrocities with those responsible for informing the public is questionable, to say the least. The British Red Cross was used as a scapegoat for the administrative and policy failings of government bureaucracy on more than one occasion during the war years.

King's speech was picked up by national newspapers. It also appeared in a Reuter's report which was read by the Commander-in-Chief, India, General Claude Auchinleck. He sent an angry telegram to the War Office:

> 'While realising remarks were confined to Japan itself and did not refer to camps outside Japan I consider general impression conveyed is very far from truth and misleading, especially as only very small proportion of Allied prisoners

> held in Japan itself. Representative Indians, including princes and Indian officers, have expressed to me their bewilderment at our silence on Jap beastliness. They press for robust propaganda exposing Japs and do not anticipate any adverse effects from such publicity on public or military morale. Leader in Indian newspaper recently remarked that Japs could not be so bad after all, as there was no information about ill-treatment of population in occupied territories such as was published about Germans.[14]

Shortly after this, a memorandum from the Foreign Officer was circulated to the War Cabinet, offering arguments for disclosure. At this stage, it suggested, the Japanese must surely recognise that they could not win the war, and consequently its military and politicians would now be fearful of the repercussions arising from maltreatment of prisoners. Another argument for disclosure was that soldiers home on leave from Burma had complained that the public seemed unaware of their campaign against the Japanese, and that they were 'a forgotten army'. By revealing atrocities, it would bring home to the British public the true nature of the Japanese, create greater support for the troops and arouse a greater animosity and determination to defeat Japan.

Having weighed up the arguments, the government decided on disclosure, with synchronised announcements in Britain and America. Anthony Eden, the British Foreign Secretary, addressed the House of Commons on 15 January 1944. What he told the House about conditions on the Burma–Thai railway was enough to horrify the entire nation:

> It becomes my painful duty to tell the House that in Siam there are many thousands of prisoners from the British Commonwealth, including India, who are being compelled by the Japanese military to live in tropical jungle conditions without adequate shelter, clothing, food, or medical attention: and these men are forced to work on building a railway and making roads. Our information is that their health is rapidly deteriorating, that a high percentage are

> seriously ill, and that there have been some thousands of deaths. Here, may I add that the number of such deaths reported by the Japanese to us is just over 100. The railway and roads concerned lead into Burma, and the conditions I have described apply throughout their whole length. One eyewitness reports of a camp in Siam that 'I saw many prisoners clearly. They were skin-and bone, unshaven and with long matted hair. They were half-naked.' The same witness reported that they wore no hats or shoes: and this, may I remind the House, in a tropical climate, where the neighbouring country is virtually uninhabited, and that there are practically no local resources which could provide medical or other material relief.

Eden included the crumb of comfort offered by Japanese propaganda, saying that he was 'reasonably satisfied that conditions generally are tolerable in the northern areas'. Once the truth was known, anger at the overly reassuring statements previously given by the Red Cross was considerable. In the House of Commons, Conservative MP Captain John Gammans asked Secretary of State for War John Grigg 'whether he was aware of what Sidney King had said earlier about prisoners held "by the Japanese", and whether this was based on all the information the Foreign Office possessed.'[15] When Grigg admitted that the organisation 'might not have been in possession of all the facts', the member for Witney, Sir Alfred Knox, added: 'Would it not be better for the Red Cross to keep their mouths shut?'

The low level of public interest in the Japanese outside FEPOW families was temporarily replaced by widespread shock at Eden's revelations. The horrified response from the press was to denounce the Japanese as barbarians and to call for retribution on the whole of Japan after it had been defeated. In an article seething with anger the *Daily Express* declared: 'The bestiality of our other enemy commands the full hatred of all Englishmen. We shall avenge their deeds.' The *Daily Mail* told its readers: 'The Japanese have proved themselves a sub-human race. It is in that regard that they must in future be treated.'

Days after the announcement, Japanese propaganda photographs served as British propaganda to settle the public's nerves. A photograph of an outdoor religious service in Keijo camp's yard, taken in October

1942, appeared in newspapers for the first time, published in the *Daily Mail* with a caption proclaiming it to be the first photograph of imprisonment in the Far East ever to be published in the country. Days later, the Red Cross announced the launch of a new magazine, *Far East*, entirely devoted to news of FEPOWs. In its first edition the editor stated that its aim was to pass on 'every scrap of information' it received about the Far Eastern prisoners, but there was a lot of available information that did not appear in its nine editions. Although it did not entirely ignore reports of maltreatment and atrocities, there is nevertheless a strong slant towards more positive news; its editorial tone is calm and, wherever possible, optimistic. It is hard to believe that its pages could have been filled without Japanese propaganda. Each of the magazine's nine editions contains staged photographs, summaries of doctored camp reports and misleading letters. The first edition carries summaries of five camp reports, all of them 'show' camps: Keijo, Jinsen, Mukden, Kiangwan (formerly Woosun) and Zentsuji.

The editor informed readers that when choosing prisoner letters for publication their main criterion was the apparent freedom of expression and spontaneity with which it was written. This meant that at least one letter from Party B appeared in every edition. In all, there were ten letters from Keijo, with only Zentsuji being more fully represented with twelve.

The Japanese defence against these accusations was constructed from recently published ICRC summaries of inspections made by Paravicini's assistant, Max Pestalozzi. Under the heading 'Kind treatment given to Prisoners', the *Nippon Tines* rebutted the accusations:

> Speaking of the war prisoners' camps in Chosen [Korea] which he visited on 15 November, Mr Pestalozzi testified that 'the general condition is quite pleasant, that the camp prisoners are carrying on well, and that all facilities are efficiently organised ... These unbiased reports are attracting keen interest as a powerful refutation of the unfounded charges the British and American governments have been heaping on Japan regarding treatment of POWs.

A few days later, Pestalozzi's 1943 report was referenced again, this time to refute accusations made by Senator Breckinbridge Long in the

US House of Representatives. Under the headline 'Red Cross backs Japan, readers were told:

> At a press conference for foreign correspondents, Sadao Iguchi, a spokesman for the Board of Information states that Long's claims appear to be a continuation of the enemy's atrocity campaign which is wilfully fabricated propaganda. At a recent visit to Keijo camp, Max Pestalozzi found about one hundred Americans and British POW's and 10 Australians, all of them in good physical condition. The buildings in which they are housed are well-heated, the supply of clothing excellent and the quality of food satisfactory. The camp has facilities for out-door exercise, a library and necessary medical and dental equipment and services. The prisoners here keep their own truck gardens [sic] and raise poultry and rabbits. Officers are at liberty to work or not, but to the rank and file work is obligatory although they are given preferences for their labour.

Censored copies of the *Nippon Times* were supplied to Keijo, and the article was later read by my father, prompting a salvo of exclamation marks in his diary:

> There are no Americans in the camp. Good physical conditions cannot apply to any. Supply of clothing grossly overrated. What facilities have we for outdoor exercise on that miserably small yard? What are the indoor recreations? A library gives a very false picture. A limited number of books are fortnightly circulated through squad rooms. One man keeps rabbits! There are no poultry kept by any! Officers are compelled to go out on working parties! This is the grossly deliberate deception the J.'s delight in!

Although the British Red Cross continued to publish Japanese propaganda in its magazine *Far East* until its final edition in December 1945, a set of photographs that appeared in the ICRC's monthly journal in 1944 caused considerable anger at the Foreign Office, as Harold Satow was to write later:

> The Japanese attempt to refute the serious and entirely true charges against them regarding their treatment of prisoners of war was to provide, in January 1944, the ICRC delegate at Tokyo with photographs, alleged to have been taken in prisoner of war camps in Netherlands East Indies. The International Committee of the Red Cross at Geneva very foolishly published some of these in their periodical, to our great annoyance and embarrassment. As we pointed out to them, this action was all the more dangerous because the photographs had not been taken by ICRC representatives themselves. The result was an assurance that there would be no repetition of the offence.[16]

The offending photographs were in fact stills from *Calling Australia*, including one of the kitchen of the luxury establishment *Hotel des Indes*, taken by the Japanese as their Batavia headquarters. The kitchen workers are dressed in crisply starched aprons and chef's hats, standing amid gleaming white cauldrons within a spotlessly clean space, suggestive of ample resources and even of luxury. There are other photographs of healthy and well-clothed prisoners working in a camp garden, attending a religious service and enjoying an outdoor concert.

Why did the ICRC publish these photographs? There was no need to do so and the photographs suggest conditions that were greatly superior to those described in the reports that arrived at Geneva, however much they had been tampered with. We have seen how Paravicini had already informed them of the exaggerations that appeared in the Japanese newspapers describing his camp visits. In 1943, the British government had also sent Geneva, at their request, details of atrocities on the Burma–Thailand railway.

Inspector Pestalozi had been able to read the summary of his inspections that the ICRC had published. In February 1944 a telegram from him was received at headquarters spelling out his concern: 'Perturbed at finding *primo* considerable discrepancies some instances complete reversal facts *tertio* omission significant points quarto generally too favourable and not always accurate interpretation when comparing our original camp reports with your monthly review.'[17]

At a meeting on 14 March 1944. a decision was taken at Geneva to ask the Japanese government 'to ensure that when its delegates' reports were published in Japanese newspapers, they were quoted accurately'.[18] But the question of the reports being altered by the Japanese before their despatch to Geneva was not raised. Shortly afterwards, the organisation rescinded its decision on the grounds that it might be harmful to the fulfilment of more important schemes that were currently under negotiation with the Japanese. It was a choice perhaps guided by pragmatism, illustrating that the highest levels of the organisation shared Paravicini's belief that progress could be made through patience and perseverance. But it was one that weakened the government's hand in complaining of abuses against the international laws of which the ICRC was guardian.

Although the ICRC henceforward followed its own guidelines and only published photographs that had been taken in the presence of their inspectors, this simply meant that the organisation published photographs of scenes that had been faked for the benefit of the inspectors. *Far East* unknowingly continued to publish propaganda photographs until the end of the war. A particularly elaborate deception occurred at a Party A camp in Formosa in 1944, when the Japanese mocked up a prison 'farm' for the inspectors. Various animals were herded into an area adjacent to the camp before the inspection and herded out again immediately afterwards. As well as cattle and pigs, the 'farm' boasted ducks and a flock of geese, indicative of considerable planning. Photographs of the visit took up a page of an issue of *Far East.*

Japan was neither the first nor the last to exploit the organisation's cooperative and neutral approach. The greatest deception committed on the organisation was perpetrated by the Nazis at Theresienstadt, a ghetto in what is now the Czech Republic. This served as a transit point for Jews on their way to the extermination camps. The level of preparation and deception, and sheer evil, was incomparably greater than the entire Japanese POW manipulation strategy. Streets were swept, flower beds were planted and buildings were whitewashed or repainted. The Nazis set up staged shops, a bank, a post office and even a school to simulate normal life. The overcrowding in the ghetto was eased by by deporting thousands of its inhabitants to Auschwitz in advance of the visit. The activities on the day included children playing sport and appearing in musical and theatrical events. The ICRC inspector, Marc Rossel, was successfully deceived. Although neither his report nor the photographs he took were published, his confidential internal report echoed Nazi propaganda. The episode remains an element of the greatest controversy in the ICRC's history, its decision to remain silent about the Holocaust.

In Japan's case, it is hard to imagine that the ICRC would have achieved more had they made public denunciations of Japanese atrocities or challenged the Japanese authorities. Their presence was permitted for propaganda purposes, and there was no legal basis to sustain it. If the ICRC ceased to play Japan's game, then from the Japanese point of view, there was no point in continuing it. A by-product of the deception was that a limited supply of aid did reach the prisoners, which would in all likelihood have dried up completely had the ICRC criticised Japan. To that extent, the ICRC's pragmatism and cautiousness paid off. Against this must be set the damage to the organisation's reputation for neutrality, by allowing its name to be exploited for counter propaganda, and the confusion caused to the Allied governments. But its decisions must be placed within the context of the values of the time. In the post-war world the tendency has been to equate silence with complicity, with little allowance for pragmatism or utility. The post-war ICRC has itself become less cautious in denouncing atrocities. But it should be emphasised that its intentions were entirely good, and the delegates in the Far East all followed them with great tenacity and courage.

Chapter 19
Last Months at Mukden

Bombing Raid

The only members of Party B to die at Mukden were killed by an American bomb. By the summer of 1944, American B29 bombers were wreaking devastation on Japan and its territories. As the bombing intensified, prisoners of war became casualties. There were many camps whose location or very existence were unknown to the Allies, and the Japanese had ignored the provision of the Geneva Convention which forbids the siting of prison camps within two miles of a military installation. As a result, prisoners in camps near significant targets were killed or wounded by stray bombs and machine-gun fire. For the home audience, the bombings were represented as evidence of the callous disregard the Americans held for their own men. As a last desperate act of propaganda the Japanese also coerced the prisoners into writing letters of protest to the ICRC. One such letter came from a camp in Hong Kong:

> Sir,
> I have the honour to refer to the very regrettable incident of the air-attack on this camp by the Anti-Axis (American) Air force in China on Monday 16th October 1944 at about 1600 hours. I regret, however, to say that during the air attack on Monday, the camp was under heavy machine-gun fire from very low-flying planes … resulting in a total of thirteen Anti-Axis POW (including patients in the camp hospital) receiving injuries.
>
> I have further to say that as representative of this camp, I am caused to express regret and condemnation towards this recklessness which exposed the Prisoners of War here to extreme dangers.
>
> Signed, Boon Cecil Major,
> Liaison Staff Officer.

Mukden camp was situated close to an ammunition factory, an aircraft factory, and a major railway yard. On 7 December 1944, these became targets for an American attack. Peaty's diary records what happened:

> At 9.10 am there was an air raid 'Yellow alert' and at 9.50 a 'red alert', followed almost immediately by a salvo of bombs which fell nearby, dealing very effectively with a small-arms ammunition factory about 1km to the north of the camp. (I believe twelve bombs hit the factory: at any rate, it never functioned again). Following this salvo, we dispersed as wide as possible and lay flat on the parade ground. A second wave of B.29s came over, and two bombs fell in the camp, one of which hit No.2 Barracks' latrine and set it afire, although it did not explode. The other, which did explode, dropped right among us on the parade ground, causing fifty-four casualties.

Private 'Dingle' Bell an Australian from Party B, also recorded the bombing:

> Heard the engines of the bombers overhead. A great gush of flame as a bomber exploded on a collision with a Japanese fighter. Pieces fell from it, turning over and over in the air. Sounds of bombs falling some distance away from us. The delighted Americans saluting the waves of bombers as they flew over, then change to horror when one plane left the formation and 'shook' itself to release two stick bombs that had become stuck in the bomb gulley dispenser.
>
> Huge explosion, I slowly opened my eyes. It was dark. I closed my eyes again, waited for a few minutes and tried again. It was light again. I looked around and saw chaos. Piles of clothing all over the place, even a pair of trousers draped over the barbed wire nearby, but with shoes hanging from the cuffs, a great hole in the brick fence with a Jap guard looking through it, then panic as people realised that others had been killed by their sides or at their feet or mortally wounded; men screaming for stretcher bearers at the sight of a dear friend torn to pieces by bomb fragments.

> I was still shocked by the explosion and still not comprehending. In front of me I saw a hat peak and thought: 'that looks like an old hat, yet those hats were only issued in June or July'. I turned it over. It had brain tissue spread all over it, then it dawned on me, somebody had died in that explosion. I looked around me again. That pile of clothes was a pile of dead bodies. Those trousers were the last half of a body. That coat did not have a head coming out of the top.[1]

Robert Peaty recorded how the Japanese attempted to distort the event for propaganda:

> The commandant made a speech about the bombing, in which he said that the Japanese intelligence had proved it was all a deliberate attack on us, by the fact that the bomb that hit the building was a demolition bomb, and the one that fell in the parade-ground was an anti-personnel bomb. He did not explain why it was that if they could place these two so nicely, they should have been so careless as to let most of the others hit an ammunition factory … On 16 December, Lt. Murata assembled the prisoner officers and told them they must write an objection to the bombings of the prison camp … When these objections were written, many of them told of the lack of air raid shelters for the prisoners and that the Japanese had refused requests by the prisoners to construct trenches and fox holes previous to the time of bombing. Other letters described the nearness of military objectives. When Lt Murata read these letters he became so angry he tore them all up and reassembled the officers, telling them specifically the things they could mention. Some officers declined to write, but those who did tried to put as much information as possible in them with the location of the camp so that on future raids it would not be hit. But they were again angered on reading some of the letters turned in by hospital patients, some of whom had written such things us 'we don't care what happens to us, hit them with all you got'.[2]

Final ICRC Inspection, August 1945

Following the death of Paravicini, there was inevitably a long delay before a successor was found who was acceptable to the Japanese. Heinrich Angst, the Swiss diplomat who had unexpectedly arrived at Keijo when Paravicini was making his visit, took over as acting head. Eventually the Japanese agreed to the appointment of Dr Marcel Junod. He was an experienced employee who had been the organisation's representative in Abyssinia, but it was not until June 1945 that all the bureaucratic obstacles had been cleared and Junod, with his wife acting as his assistant, were able to set out for Japan. Here again the Japanese set obstacles in his path: he was not allowed to enter Allied territory on his journey from Europe to Tokyo, and as a result the journey took two whole months, passing through Egypt, Persia, China and the USSR. His agreed destination was Tokyo, but the journey also took him through Manchuria. He decided to make an impromptu visit to Mukden camp, although this had not been prearranged and no permission had been granted beforehand.

He arrived in Mukden at the beginning of August 1945, just days before the Japanese surrender. The imminent Japanese defeat was almost certainly the only reason Matsuda accepted the request, which was without precedent.

Junod's detailed account of his visit confirms the types of manipulation that routinely occurred. But it also offers something that is not captured in the diaries or later memoirs: the extent of the fear and subjugation that were part of the prisoners' existence. Junod makes no attempt to preserve a professional detachment and expresses his own emotions of anger and horror at what he saw. His account is therefore worth quoting from at some length, beginning with the interview with the colonel, given in the presence of his staff:

> 'When the prisoners arrived from the tropics,' he recalled, in a tone which suggested that he was greatly moved, 'they were in a pitiful state. Dressed only in shirts and shorts, they had not withstood the icy winter of Manchuria very well. Many of them died of pneumonia and recurrent malaria, despite the excellent attention that was showered on them.' At the end of each sentence, as though lost in admiration at

the cogency of his demonstration, he paused for a moment. Raising his right foot in a broad gesture and stamping on the ground with the other foot he tapped himself on the neck two or three times, accompanying the strange gesture with a sharp and audible inspiration of breath and ending with a sonorous exclamation: 'Na!'

And all his officers responded immediately with an obedient chorus of 'na!'

Margerita [his Japanese speaking assistant] and I looked at each other in a state of consternation. We were both thinking that the time limit for our visit was two hours and that one of them had already been wasted by this vain babbling. … I interrupted the colonel's flow to express our desire to see them.

'Certainly, just a moment though. There are very important things that I still have to tell you.' And he continued his paean of praise for Japanese magnanimity.

… Another half hour passed and I dared to interrupt the colonel again.

'I am growing more and more impatient to see a camp.'

Matsuda found it impossible to do any more stalling and so with a great clanking of sabres the party rose and a procession was set in motion.

At such short notice there had been no time to prepare the prisoners for the visit. All the prisoners who were fit enough to go to work had been sent away out of sight to the factory.

'Where are the prisoners?'

'They're at work.' Matsuda replied with a great show of nonchalance.

'Can you please take us to where they are working?'

'Oh, that's quite impossible, that's too far.'

'Perhaps we can at least see their representatives?'

'Na. Na. An unforeseen hindrance.'

Not for the first time in my career as a delegate of the International Committee of the Red Cross I felt anger rising hot in my breast. An incident on this very first 'visit' might create difficulties better avoided. And incidentally the

> colonel was taking us towards a building which appeared occupied.
>
> 'And here is our magnificent hospital,' he announced, with one foot on its step. At the top of the stairs stood four men in shirts and shorts at attention. They were the first prisoners of war I had seen in Manchuria.
>
> As our procession mounted the steps after him the four men bowed low, their arms kept tightly to their sides, until their heads were almost on a level with their knees.
>
> In a low voice, and making an effort not to show the indignation which was boiling up in me, I said:
>
> 'That's not the manner in which soldiers of an occidental army salute.'
>
> 'No, it's the Japanese manner,' replied Colonel Matsuda with his eternal and impenetrable smile…
>
> 'Would it be possible to speak to the prisoners?'
>
> 'Last year and the year before it was possible, but this year the central authority has not given any prepared form for the conversation.'

Inside the hospital, they went into one of the wards:

> Those prisoners who were unable to stand sat cross-legged on their beds, their arms crossed on their chests, and they too bowed as low as their bandages, wounds and mutilations would allow. When the last Japanese officer had passed they resumed the upright position, their eyes raised to the ceiling. Never once did their eyes meet ours. This was indescribably horrible. Matsuda tried to lead us on but I stopped in front of a group of four prisoners, three British and an American.
>
> 'Is there a doctor among you?' I asked, trying to keep my voice firm and not betray the emotion I felt. I stood in front of a big fellow who towered above me. I could see only his chin and his stretched neck as he stretched up to the ceiling. Not a muscle stirred and I repeated the question. There was still no reply and I turned grimly to Matsuda.
>
> 'Why doesn't he reply?' I asked. 'Isn't he allowed to?'

> The Japanese were stupefied by my audacity, but Matsuda was evidently unwilling to risk an unpleasant incident and he indicated one of the men standing against the wall with the others.
>
> 'This Australian is a doctor.'[3]
>
> I went towards the Australian colleague with outstretched hand. I had to overcome a lump in my throat to get out the banal words 'How do you do?'
>
> The man lowered his eyes, but not to me. It was colonel Matsuda's permission he sought. After several seconds which seemed incredibly long his hand rose slowly to mine......
>
> I took it and shook it warmly, trying to convey to him all the emotion and sympathy I felt and hoping that he would afterwards communicate them to his comrades.
>
> I told him briefly who I was and why I had come and I tried to get into conversation with him. He replied slowly and in monosyllables and each time before he spoke I could see that he silently sought the approval of Matsuda over my head.
>
> 'Will you accompany me on a tour of the wards? I asked finally.
>
> This time Matsuda intervened.
>
> 'No,' he said. 'A Japanese doctor will accompany you.'
>
> I felt it was impossible to insist any further and I let go the man's trembling hand which stiffened back to the attention against his side.[4]

Looking through the open door of a warehouse, Junod spotted piles of unopened Red Cross parcels. Matsuda explained that the prisoners had no need of the supplies, so he was saving them for Christmas. Later, about thirty thousand letters for the prisoners would also be found stored away. By that stage, the propaganda function of the camps had ceased. At the time of Junod's visit, Matsuda was in fact making preparations for the execution of the prisoners. Mass graves were being dug for them outside the camp.

Chapter 20

Release

The diary entries for the first months of 1945 convey a sense of diminishing energy and lowered morale. The men were now having to survive on rations that amounted to as little as 1500 calories a day. Entries are less frequent and briefer. 'Nothing seems exciting enough to write about', in the words of John Lever. The prisoners had stopped playing their occasional games of volleyball to conserve calories. Working in the garden had lost its appeal. My father wrote almost nothing during these months, apart from recording his progressively decreasing weight and an accident. He had blacked out one morning in the washroom and cut his head open. The dry humour which had seasoned Lever's earlier diary entries has now disappeared and some of his entries convey a sense of profound weariness: 'I don't hate the Japanese and I don't think the other fellows do. You couldn't say that you hated a lot of irritating insects or a mean-natured cur. Detest and despise are better words. They are too small to be favoured with the word 'hate'….'

But as spring came, the men were buoyed by news of victory in Europe. Air raids became ever more frequent both in Manchuria and Korea. On 6 August, Russia opportunistically declared war on Japan and invaded Manchuria, advancing at breakneck speed towards Korea. Elrington wrote:

> We were becoming excited as the Russians neared the capital, and on enquiring what arrangements were being made for our safety when the clash came, the CO [ie Elrington] was coldly informed that the men would be set free. But the Officers? Oh, since the Japanese were to die at their posts, they had taken steps to ensure that all the POW Officers would be shot first.

By that stage, Keijo's occupants were nearly all officers. Many years later my father described this moment to me: 'We were all very worried,' he said, seemingly amused at his recollection. But he believed the Japanese would carry out their threat. Plans were also in hand to kill all the men at Mukden and Konan, including the other ranks. At Mukden, deep pits were being dug outside the camp, and a friendly Korean sentry explained their intended purpose to one of Party B. At Konan, another sentry passed on the news that the guards had rehearsed the execution of the prisoners.

A plan of resistance was hastily devised at Konan, but it was assumed that if the Japanese used automatic fire, at most 30 per cent of them might survive. A twenty-four hour watch was organised to detect signs of impending execution and the prisoners secretly collected pieces of wood that could be used as weapons against the guards. If signs were detected, the watchman would clang plates together as a warning. It was decided that they would not die without putting up some sort of fight. Understandably, many of the men found it difficult to sleep at night at this period.[1]

Alan Toze was an eyewitness to the event that saved the men's lives. He had been transferred to a camp on the Japanese mainland, but still kept a diary in secret. On the morning of 9 August 1945 he was surprised to see 'a huge cauliflower of cloud above where an enormous fire is raging to northwards'. He had been looking towards Nagasaki. On 15 August, the Japanese surrendered.

As at many other FEPOW camps, the Japanese did not pass on the news of their surrender immediately. On 16 August a work party went out as usual to the officers' garden. Lever recorded:

> But during the day Koreans kept rushing up to the garden fence shouting 'tomadachi' (friends) and giving the thumbs up. On the way back to the camp under the usual armed escort, Koreans tried to get close to us but were pushed away by the guards. As we progressed into the more populated parts of town things got more and more out of hand, the sentries were mopping their brows and finally had to cave in in … Trams had been commandeered and were packed tight and oozing over with wildly cheering Koreans waving flags. They were getting in the way with their hands flying up and shouting 'Banzai', 'Japanese koto' (surrendered) and all sorts of things, rushing among our fellows, shaking

> hands with them and generally flowing over with bonhomie. They are deliciously happy Japan is beaten. Nobody loves a Japanese.

So much for Japanese propaganda. Neither Lever nor Jesson could sleep that night. Lever explained: 'It's the excitement of waiting to be reborn. We shall be out in the wild wicked world with all its temptations. Hold us back! Our resistance is low.' All the Korean guards at the camp deserted during the night. At Konan, the prisoners wept for joy. Elrington was able to pay Colonel Noguchi another visit. Compliments were paid on both sides and Elrington stressed that he held no personal animosity towards Noguchi. It was agreed that until the arrival of either American or Russian troops, the Japanese would remain officially in charge. Elrington ordered his men to treat the Japanese courteously.

There was a formal ceremony on the prison yard to acknowledge the end of hostilities. Noguchi and Elrington exchanged speeches. The prisoners gave the guards three cheers and the Japanese banzied them in return, although they were visibly upset, 'like a miserable little row of perplexed children', Jesson thought.

The question of revenge was on many prisoners' minds. As Jesson wrote, 'to have been insulted, humiliated, struck, starved, robbed, taunted and deprived of every reasonable amenity for over forty months is almost unforgettable for any normal man.' But to seek revenge, he decided, would be to descend to their level.

Others felt some sympathy. 'Sentries very dispirited: cannot look one in the eye, poor devils,' wrote my father. He had become friendly with one of his Japanese teachers, the civilian Mr Sato, and had recorded earlier the man's terrible worries about his family back in Tokyo and whether they were still alive. He did, however, permit himself to enjoy the change in attitude seen in Adjutant Terada. 'What a transmogrified, oleaginous Ted we have now, far from the jack-booted tyrant we used to know.' He also enjoyed the astonishment of various camp officials as they caught sight of him reading Japanese newspapers openly.

The diaries describe how the euphoria dissipated as the men waited and days turned into weeks with no news of when they would actually be liberated. It was not until 9 September that Americans arrived at the camp. An unending supply of saki entered the camps and some of the men spent their last days in the camp in a state of permanent drunkenness.

It was considered unsafe to leave the camps as there was still a Japanese military presence in the cities, but at Keijo the men had day trips organised for them in an attempt to curb their restlessness. My father went on an outing to the old Emperor's palace. Its grounds contained a zoo, and the visitors took the opportunity to tease its captives, as my father recorded:

> The men tried out Japanese words of command on an inoffensive parrot, but only when someone shouted *Kura* (Jap for' shut up') did he give a deep bow. Despondent monkeys returned our gazes, several fed with chewing gum which they dealt with expertly, a lit cigarette was also proffered and eagerly accepted and disposed of by slowly munching up to the lit end.

Harry Kingsley had drawn sketches of himself as a monkey holding a cigarette, and in his diary Lever had complained at a camp inspection that he felt like a monkey in a zoo. There was a weird symmetry in the men visiting animals behind bars and teasing them.

The futility and crassness of Japanese propaganda aimed at the Korean people is emphasised by their warmth towards the prisoners as they went out on their day trips: 'The Koreans are very demonstrative and very grateful for what we have done for them – and are feting us. One wonders what one has done for them,' my father wrote. Prisoners and locals celebrated together, as described by John Lever:

> Went to a house and had some shamshu. It's whitish like milk and tastes like a distant relative of champagne. Geoffrey [Barnes] and I then strolled along until we came to a small Korean cottage. Making ourselves welcome, we walked in and were invited to sit in the porch; admired the baby, and gave the boy, about 10, some chewing gum. Exchanging greetings with the locals until we came to a small village. We went into a small sort of butcher's shop and a pleasant young fellow there asked us to have a drink. He had a very friendly smile and a nice-looking daughter about 5 years old. I gave her a bar of chocolate. Our host

> produced a sort of teapot. I was afraid for a moment we were going to have a cup of tea, my fears were unfounded, it was sake. After a while we found it best to keep hold of the cup as he kept filling it every time we put it down. We handed round our American cigarettes and after a pleasant interlude said goodbye to most of the village who by that time were trying to congregate in the shop.[2]

The Russians were the first to arrive at Konan and Mukden, but it would appear that they did little to help the prisoners and left their welfare to the Americans. Now it was the Russians' turn to create propaganda. They had brought a film crew with them, and at Mukden the Japanese guards were paraded around the periphery of the camp. The Russians invited the prisoners to throw things at them, but the offer was refused. Prisoners and Russians united in wild celebration at Mukden when a lorry arrived laden with alcohol. The lorry also carried a band and women soldiers. The women, according to several accounts, were as unrestrained as the men in their celebrations. At Konan 'they went berserk', and when the alcohol dried up they got high on Avgas (aviation fuel).[3] They chose whichever prisoner they took a fancy to. Later, one of the men complained that he had been gang-raped raped in the back of a lorry.[4]

The prisoners' encounters with the Russians was very different from what the local population experienced. They brought chaos, disorder and violence to Manchuria and northern Korea. They looted and raped. They shot other looters and drunkenly ran over their own soldiers with their tanks. The first incident of the Cold War took place at Konan, where the Russians shot down a B29, the *Hog Wild*. The incident has given rise to various conspiracy theories, but the evidence suggests it was the result of the confusion and indiscipline that was endemic among the Russian troops. It was a harbinger of the barbarism that would characterise the regime of the soon-to-be-created nation of North Korea.

On 8 September 1945 the Americans finally arrived at Keijo. According to Elrington his liberator greeted him with the words, 'Say colonel, who d'ya want shot?'[5] Party B were among the last prisoners to be liberated. The men marched to the railway station to the accompaniment of cheering crowds waving American flags. They took a train to Jinsen and then boarded a ship to be taken to reception centres in Manila. Arthur Cramsie remembered:

> At Jinsen harbour we were received by the Americans in style with a military band and speech of welcome from a senior officer and then we embarked on the US hospital ship *Mercy*. No words can describe our appreciation of that hospital ship: it was shining and spotless and the cleanest and most comfortable thing we had seen for years and the nurses were fabulous, as was the food.
>
> If you have lived in discomfort, dirt and squalor for a long period, a sudden return to up-market civilisation can be dramatic and quite emotional. We spent almost a week in that floating hospital; the doctors, nurses and staff were the kindest, most caring human beings we had encountered for years.[6]

At Manila they received a similar welcome, this time from the Australian Red Cross staff at the reception centres. For the senior Australian officer Wilf Fawcett and his compatriots, it was good to be among their own people again after such a long time. Here they also met prisoners from other camps and became aware for the first time that in Korea they had been relatively fortunate, as my father's diary illustrates:

> Spoke to fellow who worked in Thailand in special officers work battalion. Cholera epidemic in July 1943. Many hundreds died. Some bad cases shot to death. 10 per cent quota allowed to go sick, MO had to send sick men out in stretchers to do stone cracking at side of road being built. The officer who told me this said he had been very lucky and very healthy, he had only had diphtheria, beriberi, pellagra and pneumonia.

He also heard about the fate of American prisoners on a voyage from the Philippines to Japan: 'Badly bombed, shot when attempting to get out of hold. 150 died of suffocation. More and more one realises now how lucky we Keijo prisoners were.'

Chapter 21

Afterlife

British and Australian prisoners of the Japanese were instructed not to speak of their ordeal. Two reasons were given: first, their families would not understand what they had been through, and second, if details of their experiences appeared in the press it would only serve to cause more distress for the families of those prisoners who had not returned. The point was not made by the British military with great sensitivity, and it is unsurprising that some of the men took offence at the tone of the written instructions on this matter, headed with the injunction 'Guard Your Tongue!'

The men themselves conformed to the prevailing attitude towards personal disaster and misfortune of that era: there was no point in looking back, and the best thing to do was to carry on regardless. This was easier said than done. My father returned intermittently to Keijo in his nightmares for the rest of his life. Prisoners also carried permanent reminders of their time in Korea and Manchuria through physical and mental ill-health. Alec Bourne recalled the difficulties of settling into life back in Australia. 'I had the most terrible nightmares and would call out in the night, disturbing my wife.'[1] During the first months it was a common experience to feel 'unsettled'. After a few days at home, Arthur Christie became, in his words, 'unbearably restless' and met up with a friend from Mukden. They spent a month drifting from town to town, getting drunk in the local pubs. Some were never able to settle back comfortably into civilian life. Among the Australians, Sergeant Stan de Groen's post-war life was blighted by depression and anxiety. His daughter, Professor Fran de Groen, has described how when she was growing up he seemed a distant, silent figure to her, 'otherwise engaged', 'drinking himself into a boozy stupor in front of the television almost every night'.[2] Post Traumatic Stress Syndrome had not yet been recognised as a medical condition.

Most British FEPOWs, including Party B members, were disappointed at their country's failure to recognise what they had endured. Sadly, this disappointment began as soon as they met their fellow nationals on the ships that took them home. Onboard his transport ship, my father wrote: 'Sgt Samuel told me of the disgust felt by the troops at their reception by their fellow countrymen on the *Queen Mary.*' The prisoners were enraged not simply by ignorance of what they had endured, but by an attitude that seemed contemptuous. The last leg of Arthur Christie's journey home was on board the *Isle de France*:

> It appeared as if we were an encumbrance, a disgrace to our country, it seemed that was the attitude of the British personnel aboard that ship. We'd sat out the last three years or more in a comfortable prison camp, while they had ridden the seas and fought the war.[3]

The senior officer onboard would not permit the ex-prisoners to remain idle while there were potatoes to be peeled in the galley, and officers to be waited on in their mess. Refusal met with a predictably explosive response. They would all face disciplinary action when they arrived home, and while they remained on the ship, food would be denied them. Such threats held little terror for men who had lived on the borderline of starvation for over three-and-a-half years. The impasse ended when other servicemen, not ex-prisoners, offered to take on the fatigues assigned to the Party B men. On arrival at Southampton, the men had another taste of British officialdom when they were ordered to go through Customs and have their kit bags searched. Again, the men refused. It was a great contrast to the reception that the Australians received: 'What a wonderful welcome Sydney put on,' Alec Bourne later remembered: 'The whole city seemed to be on the footpaths for some seventeen miles.'[4]

Their return prompted enquiries about the men who were still missing. Requests for information appeared in the personal columns of local newspapers across the country. Their understatement and – to modern ears – slightly stilted formality, make them all the more heart-rending to read.

The *Manchester Evening* News carried a message from a Mrs Hutchison: 'News would be welcomed from any returning prisoner' regarding her son, Leslie Hutchinson, last heard of in May 1943 in

Malaya. Mr and Mrs W Hole informed readers of the *Nottingham Journal* that 'they would be glad of any information about their only son, who was last heard of in Kuching, Borneo, about two years ago'. In Sunderland, a Mrs Parkinson of 71 Dock Street East, was 'desirous of contacting any ex-prisoners of the war from the Far East who could give information of her son, Pte Thomas Parkinson, missing in Malaya since 15 February, 1942'.

Soon after, announcements in the same newspapers showed that answers had been given to these queries: 'Gunner George Griffiths is reported to have died of dysentery in a Japanese POW camp. This is the first news of him since he was reported missing in February 1942'.

The Australians were automatically registered with the Veterans administration, entitling them to free medical and welfare care. The medical and welfare needs of the returning British were for the most part disregarded. Henling Wade, like many others, reported himself as A1 in health in order to speed up his demobilisation, and he was allowed to leave the army immediately without a medical examination: 'I never received one talk, one leaflet, one pamphlet, any guidance on how to return to civilian life in much-altered Britain after three years and seven months of prison camp and over five years of army service.'[5] The prisoners were generally left to fend for themselves. In 1952 the British government did, however, give them financial recompense for their ordeal in the form of compensation received from the Japanese government. This amounted to cash payments of £76.10s- each, (roughly £2,800 in 2025) with an additional £3 for those who had worked on the Burma–Thai railway. The survivors were not impressed. A young upper-class Labour politician, The Hon. Anthony Wedgewood-Benn, explained to the House of Commons that to ask for more would be wrong now that Japan was 'getting back on its feet' and that, in any case, the British had committed equally barbaric misdeeds on its imperial subjects over the last 300 years

Despite the long-term health consequences of their imprisonment, many of Party B were able to build fulfilling post-war lives. Colonel Elrington continued his military career, eventually reaching the rank of acting brigadier. But his lungs had been permanently damaged at Keijo and for health reasons he and his wife Jose emigrated to the warmer climate of Santa Fe, New Mexico, where he took up a new career at a private school. It goes without saying that he became its headmaster. His name is commemorated in the 'Elrington cup', which is awarded each year to outstanding students.

John Jesson's journals offer a continuous analysis of his mental states and their link to external events and stimuli. During his captivity he had even traced his moods against the courses of the moon. It is unsurprising then, that he decided to specialise in psychiatry after the war. He married a fellow psychiatrist and lived in a fine Georgian house with imposing gardens. He remained devoted to his mother, who moved in with them. Sadly, according to his daughter Alison's account, this led to the breakdown of the marriage. Alison has written a novel based on her father's writings at the camp.[6]

When war broke out, Major Rigby had just succeeded in establishing a successful private practice as a General Practitioner. Although he was in his mid-thirties and could have avoided conscription, he abandoned his practice to enlist, at considerable financial sacrifice to himself. But after the war he was able to return to his work and build up his practice a second time. I had the pleasure of meeting his granddaughter, Helen Sherpa. She told me that he seldom spoke of his time at Keijo, but he had retained his diaries along with a record of every single meal he ate at Keijo.

Alan Toze qualified as an architect and enjoyed a lifelong friendship with John Jesson. In later years his views on Keijo softened and he eventually came to enjoy discussing his time there. Comparing his experiences in Korea to the camps on the Burma–Thai railway, he wrote, fifty years after his release, that apart from the four-and-a-half winter months, life at Keijo was 'not so bad'.[7] In the early years of this century he found photographs of some of his former captors online. The memories they evoked were so distressing that he chose never to look at them again, an illustration of both the fallibility and the complexity of memory's processes.

Jack McNaughton resumed his career as an actor, and appeared as a bit part player in many of the best British films of the 1950s. His career in television included appearances in early episodes of *Coronation Street*.

Private Harry Kingsley had been a window cleaner before joining the army, but on returning home he was awarded a grant which enabled him to go to art college. His later paintings – mainly of city scenes – are entirely dissimilar to his drawings and sketches at Keijo. He also became a lecturer at an art college.

In Australia, Alex Johnstone returned to his career in accounting, but he bore the injuries to his legs from his accident at the docks in Jinsen. His daughter suggests that he post-war life was unsettled, with frequent house moves.[8] He died at the relatively early age of 56. Arthur Kerr married soon after his return to Australia and worked in construction. He lived on until his eighties, producing a large family.

On his return, my father passed exams for the diplomatic service. But Keijo was responsible for denying him this career path. The Foreign Office worried that he might have been 'turned' by the Japanese and he was rejected at the last hurdle as a potential security risk. He returned to University College London and completed his science degree. An old CV of his states that during his vacations he helped his father out on the Stock Exchange and also took work as a lumberjack in Finland. In 1949 he began a career as an industrial scientist. He later gained a degree in economics while working full-time in a research laboratory for a paper manufacturer, Bowaters. Having finished his economics degree he taught adult education classes in Spanish, French and Russian in the evenings. Like many former prisoners of war who had developed the discipline of self-study in the camps, he continued with it as a lifelong habit. Despite the unpleasant circumstances his diaries describe, it was a pleasure to read them and hear his voice again after so many years. At his funeral, his two surviving brothers blamed Keijo for the series of illnesses that had blighted the last ten years of his life.

Propaganda, Memory and Politics

The popular memory of the Far Eastern Prisoners of War has been shaped by books and films which are mainly fictional.[9] In some cases, fiction has been represented as the truth. It is perhaps surprising to note that in comparison to the experiences of prisoners held in Europe, the story of captivity in the Far East has received far less attention. This book illustrates the diversity of experience within just four camps. A comprehensive account of the varied conditions in the thousand or so camps which came into existence remains to be written.

Collective memory is, of course, shaped by politics. Although Churchill promised an official enquiry into the Fall of Singapore, and had the opportunity to initiate one when he returned as prime minister in 1951 none was ever held. Unlike Dunkirk, it was not a disaster that could be spun into something positive. Churchill's decisions with regard to the defence of the island were also ones which he may not have wished to revisit. Plans to include a separate volume on Far Eastern captivity in the government's official history of World War II were also abandoned and no official record has ever been published. When he returned home, General Percival was ignored by the military and political establishment. He was an honourable man, and devoted the rest of his life to the Far Eastern Prisoners of War Association. From the 1960s Japan became an increasingly important trading partner, so it was economically beneficial to let the past be forgotten. Memory of Far Eastern imprisonment remains far stronger in Australia and has been employed by politicians to shape the nation's identity. We can also contrast the collective memory with the experiences of Indian prisoners of the Japanese, which appear almost forgotten except in India.

Even if it failed in its primary intentions, Japanese prisoner of war propaganda has survived in intriguing ways. There is still a tendency to believe that the ICRC delegates were too friendly with the Japanese. We have seen how Henling Wade accused Paravicini of corruption, writing fifty years after the man's death. Wade had spent his entire professional career as a journalist and by the 1990s there were ample printed sources to explain Paravicini's predicament. One of the main online resources on Far Eastern captivity, Mansell.com, also states that one of the ICRC delegates, with an 'Italian name', was very friendly with the Japanese.

The misconception that maltreatment only occurred in areas outside the restraining influence of central control, an idea long dormant, has been revived by recent academic studies. It has been claimed that the case of Keijo shows us that when the central authorities concerned themselves with prisoners, their fate was not a cruel one. The propaganda function is downplayed, and it has been stated that it ceased entirely in 1943. The suggestion that Colonel Noguchi's 'bark was worse than his bite' sits awkwardly with his intention to kill the prisoners at the Korean camps, to offer just one example.[10]

A similar willingness to accept Japanese statements at face value, even those made by the news agency *Domei*, has also led to the argument that Colonel Suga, commandant of the Borneo camps, took up his role with the intention of it being a civilising and educative one.[11] Although he acted the part of a benign custodian at his home camp of Kuching, elsewhere he could indulge his taste for the extremes of cruelty. The prisoners at Sandakan, a notoriously barbaric camp, always feared his arrival, as it would inevitably lead to more gratuitous beatings and other punishments. The opinion of one of the few survivors from the camp – that Suga was a brutal thug and hypocrite – fits the evidence more comfortably.

Arguably, Allied propaganda against the Japanese also persisted. The Japanese were depicted in pre-war propaganda as a backward people, lacking the technological advantages of the West. The outbreak of war soon dispelled that notion. Nevertheless, the post-war conception of Japanese industrial success as the 'Japanese economic miracle' was based on this misperception of backwardness. There was nothing miraculous about Japanese economic success.

When the revelations of Japanese atrocities appeared, the media, as we have seen, when the revelations of atrocities appeared, the media portrayed the Japanese as subhumans. The idea that only the Japanese or Nazis could be capable of such barbarity against prisoners of war has also persisted. The higher death rate of both German and Russian prisoners in the eastern theatre of Europe during World War II refutes the perception. Sadly, there are many other more recent examples to draw on. The activities of British jihadists should disabuse us of any notions of moral superiority over Japan in the twenty-first century.

Although this is a study of prisoner of war propaganda, it is also a history of a group of men who endured hunger, humiliation, beatings, sickness, uncertainty and isolation for their country. They lived and worked in squalid conditions, suffering from the extremes of cold for months of the year. They bore the mental and physical scars of their imprisonment for the rest of their lives. Although a small minority of men illustrated normal human weaknesses, the great majority displayed the very best human qualities to an abnormal degree. There were many heroes among the Party[12]. Colonel Elrington best fits the military conception of a hero. He was a man of complete integrity who had been courageous on the battlefields of two world wars, and had proved an exceptional leader in captivity. One of his qualities, not evident in all British officers by any means, was that he felt a genuine affection for his men, or 'our lads', as he called them. For a great deal of the time at Keijo he was ill with bronchitis, but nevertheless he fought for his men with great wiliness and indefatigability in his negotiations with the camp officials.

There were other sorts of heroes. The padre, Captain Peter Cazalet, was awarded a Military Cross for going to the aid of the wounded and dying during the fighting 'without the least concern for his own safety', as his commendation states. In prison he was unceasingly cheerful and a generous supplier of cigarettes as well as spiritual comfort. Saboteurs like Reg Hayter were also true heroes in their ingenuity and daring. The medical officers Harry Morris, at Konan, and Des Brennan at Mukden, won the admiration and respect of all the men at their respective camps for their almost superhuman efforts on behalf of sick men. Although Arthur Christie was a severe critic of the officer class as a whole, he also singles out the senior officer at Mukden, Robert Peaty, for praise, writing nearly fifty years later that he would always think of him as 'sir'. Equally heroic, although not in the conventional military mould, was Albert Nuttall, the 'Pig Man of Mukden'. The amount of pork and bacon he produced for his fellow prisoners and the ingenuity and courage that it took to do so, mark him out as truly exceptional, as does the unconcern with which he recorded the beatings and other punishments inflicted on him. As a whole the men of Party B displayed a resilience and sustained support for one another that is surely heroic. The British members of Party B in particular received scant recognition on their return home. But the memory of all the men of the party, of whatever nationality, deserves to be honoured.

Endnotes

Introduction

1. Diaries of G.S. Baker, in author's possession.
2. At the Yokohama War Crimes trial it was claimed that the beating lasted two hours, but Lieutenant 'Chook' Frazer's statement that it lasted forty-five minutes, given in a postwar affidavit, seems more probable. p.189.
3. 'Report Regarding Plans for the Internment of POWs in Korea' from Commander in Chief of the Korean Army, Seishiro Itagaki to Minister of War, Hideki Tojo, 23 March 1942 in Pritchard and Sonia Magbanua Zaide (eds), *The Tokyo War Crimes Trial: The complete Transcripts of the Proceedings of the International Military Tribunal for the Far East in Twenty-Two Volumes* (New York: Garland, 1981). pp.14512–13.
4. Speech to House of Commons, March 1942.
5. The original typescript of Peaty's diary states ' better than any other camp'. However, this has been crossed out and replaced with a handwritten amendment , 'better than most camps'. Presumably the revision is Peaty's. (Imperial War Museum, Private Papers of Robert Peaty Documents 6377.)
6. Cited in *Report of the Activities of the International committee of the Red Cross during the Second World War,* (Geneva: ICRC, 1948) p.443.
7. I wish in particular to thank Matt Van Volkenburg for allowing me to quote from his translations of relevant articles in *Maeil Sinbo*.
8. These include the late Alison Jesson, daughter of Captain John Jesson, Helen Sherpa, granddaughter of Major Conrad Rigby, Mark Sullivan, grandson of Colonel Vincent Sullivan, Merrie Frazer Bott, daughter of Lieutenant 'Chook' Fraser, Johnny Howard, son of Captain Jack McNaughton, Christopher Given-Wilson, son of Lieutenant Paddy Given-Wilson.

9. G.S. Baker *Diaries*.
10. Ibid.
11. Imperial War Museum, Documents 1133, Private Papers of Alan V. Toze (Diary).

Chapter 1

1. Barak Kushner *The Thought War: Japanese Imperial Propaganda* (Honolulu: Hawaii University Press, 2007).
2. David C. Earhart *Certain Victory: Images of World War II in the Japanese Media* (Armonk, New York: M.E. Sharpe, 2008); Robbins, Jane M. J. (1998) Tokyo Calling: Japanese Overseas Broadcasting 1937–1945. PhD thesis, University of Sheffield.
3. Kushner, *Thought War*, p.1.
4. See Ben Ami Shillony, *Politics and Culture in Wartime Japan* (Oxford: Clarendon Press,1981).
5. Japanese films from this period are discussed by John Dower, 'Japanese Cinema Goes to War,' in *Japan in War and Peace:* (New York: New Press,1993). pp. 91-93
6. See Sharlyn Orbaugh, *Propaganda Performed: Kamishibai in Japan's Fifteen Year War* (Leiden-Boston: Brill, 2015).
7. 'Precautionary Matters Concerning Censorship of News of Prisoners of War', reproduced in R.J. Pritchard and Sonia Magbanua Zaide (eds), *The Tokyo War Crimes Trial: The Complete Transcripts of the Proceedings of the International Military Tribunal for the Far East in Twenty-Two Volumes* (hereafter *IMTFE*), vol. 6 (New York: Garland,1981) pp.1412–15.
8. Nitobe, Inazo, *Bushido, The Soul of Japan* (Philadelphia: Leeds & Biddle, 1900) pp. 21–24.
9. Speech to House of Commons, 10 March 1942.
10. Benesch, Oleg, *Inventing the Way of the Samurai* (Oxford: Oxford University Press, 2014).
11. Quoted by Yoichi Kibata in 'Japanese Treatment of British Prisoners of War: The Historical Context' in Philip Towle, Margaret Kosuge and Yoichi Kibata, (eds), *Japanese Prisoners of War* (London and New York: Hambledon and London, 2000).
12. R. Keith Mitchell *Forty-Two Months in Durance Vile* (London: Robert Hale, 1997) p.117.

13. John Fletcher-Cooke, *The Emperor's Guest* (London: Hutchinson, 1971) p.78.
14. See Aiko Utsumi, 'Japan's World War II POW Policy: Indifference and Irresponsibility', *Asia-Pacific Journal,* 3:5 (2005).
15. *Philippines Tribune* 10 April 1943.
16. See Paul Kratoska and Ken'ichi Goto 'Japanese Occupation of Southeast Asia, 1941–1945' in John W. Hall et al. (eds), *The Cambridge History of Japan*, vol.6, Peter Duus (ed.), *The Twentieth Century (*Cambridge: Cambridge University Press, 1988).
17. Susan C. Townsend, 'Culture, Race and Power in Japan's Wartime Empire,' in Philip Towle et al. (eds), *Japanese Prisoners of War* (London: Hambledon, 2000), p.186.
18. Satow, H, and M.J.Seé, *The Work of the Prisoners of War Department during the Second World War*, (London: Foreign Office, 1950).
19. *Osaka Mainichi*, 12 March 1942.
20. Diaries of John Lever, Lancashire Infantry Museum.

Chapter 2

1. The private account of the Malay campaign is held by Phil Karshis. Elrington's account of his battalion's experiences from 1941-1945 appear in various editions of the regimental magazine *The Lancashire Lad* over the period 1947-1952. Those relating to the period of captivity appear in editions for September 1947, January, March and June, 1950 and March 1952, under the heading 'With 2nd Loyals in Captivity'.
2. Cramsie, Arthur, *Guest of an Emperor* (Enniskillen: Trimble, 1987) p.12.
3. Toze *Diaries*.
4. Alex James, Diaries.
5. Journals of Captain John Jesson.
6. Diaries of Arthur Kerr.
7. Diaries, G.S. Baker

Chapter 3

1. *The War Diary of 3859081 Lance Corporal Eric Wallwork 2nd Battalion, The Loyal Regiment* reproduced on website boltonremembersthewar.org.uk.

2. John Jesson *Journals*.
3. Earhart, *Certain Victory*.
4. Alex James, *Diaries*.
5. Quoted in Canadian newspaper article 'Globe-trotting the Hard way', *Atlantic Guardian* Vol 2. No.5 May 1946.
6. Lancashire Infantry Museum, LIM, 846/2.2.165, Miscellaneous.

Chapter 4

1. Ibid.
2. Elrington, *Lancashire Lad*, June 1950.
3. Ibid.
4. IWM John Jesson papers.

Chapter 5

1. Toze, *Diaries*.
2. *Maeil Sinbo* September 24 1942.
3. AWM 54 1010/2/55 affidavit of Lieut. W.H. Frazer.
4. *Maeil Sinbo* 26 September.
5. IWM Sound Archive Captain Ivor Thomas.
6. In an early history of Far Eastern captivity, *Knights of Bushido,* its author, Lord Russell, tacitly accepts the validity of the document, and places the arrival to Party B in August 1942. This is incorrect.
7. Kuniaki Koiso was Governor-General of Korea from 1942 to 1944. He became prime minister of Japan at the end of 1944.
8. *Keijo Nippo,* September 25 1942.

Chapter 6

1. Elrington, 'With 2nd Loyals in Captivity'.
2. J. Norwood, E.Shek, *Camps in Areas other than the Four Principal Islands of Japan*, American Prisoner of War Informatioon Bureau, 1946.
3. IWM 4630, Thomas.
4. Lever, *Diaries*.

5. IWM 4630, Ivor Thomas.
6. Interview with Colonel Cardew, *Maeil Sinbo*, 25 September 1942.
7. Kerr, *Diaries*.
8. Toze, *Diaries*.
9. Ibid.
10. Ibid.
11. Kerr, *Diaries*.
12. *Keijo Nippo*.
13. Ibid.
14. Toze, *Diaries*.
15. Cramsie, *Guest of an Emperor*, p.81.
16. Elrington, *Lancashire Lad*.
17. Translated copy in author's possession.
18. James, *Diaries*.
19. Lever, *Diaries*.

Chapter 7

1. Ibid.
2. Ibid.
3. S. Strange and A. Toze, *In Defence of Singapore: A Series of Brief Sketches with Notes* (Preston: Snape & Co, 1947).
4. ACICRC Archives, Geneva V-P-HIST-E-02330, Letter of thanks to Colonel Noguchi.
5. Conrad Rigby *Diary*.
6. Toze, Diaries.
7. Rigby *Diary*.
8. Jesson, *Journals*.
9. Rigby, *Diary*.

Chapter 8

1. Wallwork, *Diaries*.
2. Linda Goetz Holmes, *Guests of the Emperor,* (Annapolis: Naval Institute Press, 2010).
3. Wallwork, *Diaries*.

4. Lever, *Diaries*.
5. Ibid.
6. James, *Diaries*.
7. Lever, *Diaries*.
8. Explanatory text on the reverse of a cartoon of rabbits at Keijo, LIM, Miscellaneous.
9. Arthur Christie, *Mission Scapula*, (privately published) p.120.

Chapter 9

1. See Sibylla Jane Flower, 'British Policy Makers and the Prisoner of War issue', Perceptions and Responses,' in Ian Gow, Yoichi Hirama and John Chapman (eds), *History of Anglo-Japanese Relations,* vol. 3, *The Military Dimension* (Basingstoke: Palgrave Macmillan, 2003) pp.232–241.
2. Ibid.
3. International Committee of the Red Cross, *Report of the International Committee of the Red Cross on its Activities during the Second World* War, 3 vols. (Geneva: ICRC, 1948), vol. 2, pp.1123–126.
4. ACICR G8/76 letter from Paravcini to Geneva, '*Mais le soleil levant ne laisse murir les fruits que tres lentement*'.
5. Quoted in Christophe Laurent, 'Les Obstacles Rencontrés par le C.I.C.R. dans son Activité en Extrême Orient (1941–1945)', Master's thesis, University of Lausanne, 2003, p.25.
6. ACICR G8/76 V, Paravicini letter to Geneva, December 1942.
7. Baker, *Diaries*.
8. Lever, *Diaries*.
9. John M Beebe (ed.), *Prisoner of the Rising Sun: The Lost Diary of Brig. Gen. Lewis Beebe* (College Station: Texas A&M University Press, 2006) p.54.
10. ACICR G8/7 V, Paravicini, letter to Geneva, December 1942.
11. Toze, *Diaries*.
12. Fletcher Cooke, *The Emperor's Guest* p.190.
13. HO/215/94 International Red Cross visits to Camps, Keijo, Korea.
14. Toze, *Diaries*.
15. Ibid. p.55.
16. Australian War Memorial AWM2019.22.192 Collection number PR01044: Documents relating to the service of Alexander Roland Campbell Johnstone.

17. Ibid.
18. Toze, *Diaries*.
19. Mordaunt Elrington 'Loyals in Captivity'.

Chapter 10

1. IWM 6377 Diaries of Robert Peaty.
2. Alex James, *Diaries*.
3. Ibid.
4. Christie, *Mission Scapula*.
5. WO/ 224/197N Manchuria Camp reports.
6. Major R Peaty *Papers*.
7. Ibid.
8. FCO 21/3529 Unit 731(Mukden): claims by former British prisoners of war (POWs); NA DEFE 68/1231 Experiments on Prisoners of War by Unit 731 of the Imperial Army.
9. Anecdotal evidence from American survivors is discussed at length by Linda Goetz Holmes in *Guests of the Emperor*.
10. NA DEFE 68/1231 Experiments on Prisoners of War.
11. Chris Given-Wilson *You Must Endure* (Lancashire: Palatine Press, 2021) p.126
12. Harris, Sheldon, *Factories of Death: Japanese Biological Warfare, 1932–45, and the American Cover-Up* (1994, revised 2002). Change first published in 2002 to first published in 1994.

Chapter 11

1. No one named Ankers was among the party. It is likely that the name has been distorted during the process of translation into katakana and back again.

Chapter 12

1. Lever *Diaries*.
2. G.S. Baker, *Diaries*.
3. Rigby, *Diary*.
4. Reference written for Baker by Elrington, in author's possession.

5. James, *Diaries*.
6. *Nor Iron Bars*, Copy held at Lancashire Infantry Museum.
7. The literal translation of *naka arimasen* is 'there is no back'.
8. The phrase appeared in *Nippon Times* and is one of several mixed metaphors recorded by my father.

Chapter 13

1. Peaty, *Diaries*.
2. IWM Sound Archives, 6058 Jack Roberts, Audio Recording.
3. One such example is reproduced in an article by Mark Streeter *They Called us Traitors* published online the blog *SAGACITY*.
4. Jack Roberts, IWM Sound Archives.
5. Wallwork, *War Diaries*.
6. Tom Henling Wade, *Prisoner of the Japanese* (Ipswich: Kall-Kwik Printing, 1994).
7. Ibid.
8. Ibid.
9. FBI report dated 4 February 1948, California. File reference has been redacted. The document is reproduced on the website Mansell.com.
10. Streeter *They Called us Traitors*.

Chapter 14

1. *Domei* report, November 1942.
2. Westerner's long legs were objects of amusement and ridicule for Japanese propagandists.
3. Kerr, *Diaries*.
4. Ibid.
5. Arthur Cramsie, *Guest of an Emperor* (Trimble 1987 Eniskillen,) p.73.
6. IWM Sound Archives 8302 Daniel Fraser.
7. Edward Dunlop, *The War Diaries of Weary Dunlop* (Australia: Random House, 1986).
8. See, for example, Brian MacArthur, *Surviving the Sword* (London: Time Warner Books, 2004) pp.344 et seq.

Chapter 15

1. Toze, *Diaries.*
2. Baker *Diaries.*
3. Ibid.
4. Letter published in *Far East* magazine, May 1944 edition.
5. *Nippon Times* April 1943.
6. Wade, *Prisoner of the Japanese.*
7. Ibid.
8. The letter is quoted in a brief biography of Sinclair on *Far Eastern Heroes* website
9. Alex Johnstone, *The Years Between.*
10. Lever, *Diaries.*
11. David Tett, *A Postal History of Prisoners of War and Civilian Internees in East Asia during the Second World War* vol 6 (Bristol: Stuart Rossiter Trust Fund, 2002), p.108. Jesson and his divorced mother had an unusually close relationship: She had even come to live with him when he took up a place as a medical student in London.
12. See,for example, Barbara Hately-Broad, Barbara, *War and Welfare, British Prisoner of War Families, 1939–1945* (Manchester: Manchester University Press, 2009) p.142.
13. These were known as 'Enoch Arden' cases, after the poem by Tennyson which dramatizes the same predicament.
14. Brian McArthur *Surviving the Sword.*
15. As well as the Party B camps, the announcement is referring to the show camps Zentsuji (Japan) and Woosun (Shanghai). There was also a civilian internment camp in Hong Kong, Port Stanley, which was used for propaganda.
16. *Lincolnshire Standard and Boston Guardian,* 24 July 1943.
17. 'Prisoners of the Japanese: what it means' *Sunday Post* 8 August 1943. As well as the Party B camps, the article is referring to a civilian internment camp in Hong Kong, Port Stanley, which was occasionally exploited for propaganda, and Zentsuji in Japan.
18. Harold Satow, M.J. Sée, *The Work of the Prisoners of War Department during the Second World War.*

Chapter 16

1. Elrington, *With Loyals in Captivity*.
2. Cramsie, *Guest of an Emperor* p.72.
3. *Ibid*, p.80.
4. Johnstone, *The Years Between*.
5. Gordon Bennett was the General Officer Commanding (GOC) the Australian 8th Division. He escaped from Singapore in controversial circumstances, leaving his men behind. Japanese propaganda applied the Homeric epithet 'fleet-footed' to his name.
6. Lever, *Diaries*.
7. *Nor Iron Bars* Lancashire Infantry Museum.
8. Kerr, *Diaries*.
9. *Japan Times*.
10. Ibid.
11. Christie, *Mission Scapula*.
12. Peaty, *Diaries*.
13. Toze, *Diaries* p.35.

Chapter 17

1. ACICR G/8/77a.
2. G. Cambray, G.B. Briggs, *Red Cross and St John: The Official Record of the War Organisation of the Humanitarian Services of the British Red Cross Society and Order of St. John of Jerusalem,1939–1947* (London: Sumfield & Day, 1949).
3. *Nos rapports accentuent en général plutôt les bonnes côtes et je crois cela aide plutôt aux prisonniers et internes en mains adverses, malgré qu'ils n'aiment pas lire dans la presse locale qui fait la propagande, que nous ayons décrites les camps comme des paradis terrestres.* ACICR G7/76 VI, Letter from Paravicini to ICRC, May 1943.
4. ACICR G8/Para: *Remarques complémentaires sur l'activité de M. Paravicini, 19/01/44*
5. Wade, *Prisoner of the Japanese*

Chapter 18

1. These figures are taken from the February 1944 edition of *Far East*, ('No.9, Park Place', *Far East*, February 1944) The figure of 44,000 is significantly lower than current estimates of approximately 50,000.
2. Cited in Caroline Moorehead, *Dunant's Dream: War, Switzerland and the History of the Red Cross* (London: Harper Collins, 1998), p. 231.
3. TNA WO/32/9890, Imperial Prisoner of War Sub Committee 'A','Summaries of actions taken in matters relating to Prisoners of War, 1941–45'.
4. Satow, *Work of the Prisoners of War Department*, p.32.
5. Eden, Speech to House of Commons, 28 January 1944.
6. ACICR 720/84, Prisoners of War Department, Foreign Office, 'Information regarding Prisoners of War'.
7. ACICR 720/84, Information regarding Prisoners, June–July 1943.
8. Speech to House of Commons January 1944.
9. Satow, *Work of the Prisoners of War Department,* pp.101–3.
10. TNA WO/203/5609, British Foreign Office Political Warfare (Japan) Committee, 'Minutes, January 1945.
11. Barbara Hately Broad.
12. *Liverpool Echo* October 28 1943.
13. Satow, *Work of the Prisoners of War Department.*
14. TNA, CAB/66/42/34. 'Publicity concerning Japanese Treatment of British Prisoners of War and Civilian Internees'.
15. Knox had been a concerned and critical voice on behalf of POWs and their families throughout the war.
16. Satow, *Work of the Prisoners of War Department.*
17. Quoted in Laurent, *Obstacles,* Annex 224.
18. '*Nous le prions de veiller à ce que les rapports de nos délégués, lorsqu'ils sont cités, soient reproduits de façon exacte.*' Later, the decision was reversed: '*Il ne faudrait pas, en effet, risquer de compromettre, par une telle démarche, le résultat favorable qui pourrait être donné à d'autres questions plus importantes*'. Quoted in Laurent, 'Les Obstacles', Annex 224.

Chapter 19

1. PDF file 'Prisoners of War of the Japanese 1942–1945' accessible at https://www.pows-of-japan.net/booksetc/HOTEN-CAMP-MUKDEN-MANCHURIA.pdf.
2. Peaty, *Diaries*.
3. Colonel Des Brennan.
4. Marcel Junod *Warrior Without Weapons* (London:Cape, 1951).

Chapter 20

1. Cramsie, Guest of an Emperor pp.113–115.
2. Lever, *Diaries*.
3. Suzanne Boddigton, 'The Other years Between,' in Newman,ed, *Legacies of Our Fathers* pp.72–85.
4. Gavan Daws *Prisoners of the Japanese* (London: Simon & Schuster, 1994) p.340.
5. Elrington, *Loyals in Captivity* March 1952.
6. Cramsie, *Guest of an Emperor* p.129.

Chapter 21

1. *Bourne2Learn*.
2. Fran de Groen 'Letter to my Father' in Caroline Newman ed. *Legacies of our Fathers: World War Two Prisoners of the Japanese* (Sydney, NSW: Hachette, 2006) pp.133–144.
3. Christie, *Mission Scapula* p.231.
4. *Bourne2Learn*.
5. Henling Wade, *Prisoner of the Japanese*.
6. Alison Jesson, *The Mind's Garden* (London: Troubadour Press, 2010).
7. Introduction to *Diaries,* IWM.
8. *Suzette Boddington* 'The Other Years Between' *in Legacies of our Fathers,* pp.72–85.

9. See Sibylla Jane Flower, 'Memory and The Prisoner of War Experience: United Kingdom', in Blackburn and Hack, *Forgotten Captives*, pp.120–155.
10. Sarah Kovner, 'Allied POWs in Korea', in Barak Kushner and Sherzod Muminov (eds), *The Dismantling of Japan's Empire in East Asia: Deimperialization, Postwar Legitimation and Imperial Afterlife* (Routledge: Abingdon, 2017).
11. Felicia Yap, 'Prisoners of War and Civilian Internees of the Japanese in British Asia: The Similarities and Contrasts of Experience,' in *Journal of Contemporary History*, 47:2, April 2012, pp.317–346.
12. See: Dawson, Christopher, *To Sandakan: The Diaries of Charlie Johnstone, Prisoner of War 1942–1945* (St Leonards, NSW, Australia: Allen and Unwin, 1995) p.68 et seq.

Bibliography

Balfour, M., *Propaganda in War, 1939–1945: Organisations, Policies and Publics in Britain and Germany* (London: Routledge & Kegan Paul, 1979)

Barker, A.J., *Behind Barbed Wire* (London: William Clowes & Sons, 1974)

Bayley, C., and Tim Harper, *Forgotten Armies: Britain's Asian Empire and War with Japan* (London: Penguin, 2004)

Beebe, John and M. Beebe (ed.), *Prisoner of the Rising Sun: The Lost Diary of Brig. Gen. Lewis Beebe* (College Station: Texas A&M University Press, 2006)hy

Benesch, Oleg, *Inventing the Way of the Samurai: Nationalism, Internationalism, and Bushido in Modern Japan* (Oxford: Oxford University Press, 2014)

Bergamini, David, *Japan's Imperial Conspiracy* (London: Panther, 1971)

Bourke, Roger, *Prisoners of the Japanese: Literary Imagination and the Prisoner-of-War Experience* (Queensland: Queensland University Press, 2006)

Braddon, Russell, *The Naked Island* (London: T. Werner Laurie Ltd, 1952)

Bugnon, Francois, *Le Comité International de la Croix-Rouge et la Protection des Victimes de la Guerre* (Geneva: International Committee of the Red Cross, 1994)

Bull, Stephen, *'Nor Iron Bars': Lancashire Artists in Captivity 1942–1945* (Lancashire: Lancashire County Council, 2005)

Cambray, G., G.B. Briggs, *Red Cross and St John: The Official Record of the War Organisation of the Humanitarian Services of the British Red Cross Society and Order of St.John of Jerusalem, 1939–1947* (London: Sumfield & Day, 1949)

Cardia, Isabelle Vonèche, *Neutralité et Engagement: Les Relations entre le Comité International de la Croix-Rouge et le Gouvernement Suisse, 1938–1945* (Lausanne: SH SR, 2012)

Chapman, Ivan, *Tokyo Calling: The Charles Cousens Case* (Sydney: Hale & Iremonger, 1990)

Chung, Young-Iob, *Korea Under Siege, 1876–1945: Capital Formation and Economic Transformation* (Oxford: Oxford University Press, 2006)

Christie, Arthur, *Mission 'Scapula': Special Operations in the Far East* (London: M Christie, 2004)

Cliff, Norman, *Captive in Formosa: A British P.O.W.'s Struggle for Survival, 1942–45* (Rochford: Rochford Press, 1993).

Coates, J., *Railroad of Death* (London: Hyperion Press, 1946)

Christie, Maurice (ed,) *Mission Scapula*

Cramsie, Arthur, *Guest of an Emperor* (Enniskillen: Trimble, 1987)

Crossland, James, *Britain and the International Committee of the Red Cross* (Basingstoke: Palgrave Macmillan, 2014) pp.86–103

Cunningham, Michelle, *Defying the Odds: Surviving Sandakan and Kuching* (Sydney: Hachette, 2007)

Cunningham, Michelle, *Hell on Earth: Sandakan – Australia's Greatest War Tragedy* (Sydney: Hachette, 2013)

Daws, Gavan, *Prisoners of the Japanese* (New York: Simon and Schuster, 1994)

Dawson, Christopher, *To Sandakan: The Diaries of Charlie Johnstone, Prisoner of War 1942 –1945* (St Leonards, NSW, Australia: Allen and Unwin, 1995) p.68.

Dean, C.G.T., *The Loyal Regiment (North Lancashire) 1919–1953* (The Loyal Regiment: Preston, 1955)

Dear, C.B. and M.R.D. Foot (eds), *The Oxford Companion to World War Two* (Oxford: Oxford University Press, 2001)

Dower, John W., *Japan in War and Peace: Selected Essays* (New York: New Press, 1993)

Dower, John W., *War Without Mercy: Race and Power in the Pacific War* (New York: Pantheon, 1986).

Dunlop, E.E., *The War Diaries of Weary Dunlop* (London: Harmondsworth Viking, 1989)

Durand, André, *From Sarajevo to Hiroshima: History of the International Committee of the Red Cross* (Geneva: Institut Henry Dunant, 1978)

Earhart, David C., *Certain Victory: Images of World War II in the Japanese Media* (Armonk, New York: M.E. Sharpe, 2008)

Felton, Mark, *The Devil's Doctors: Japanese Human Experiments on Allied Prisoners of War* (Barnsley, South Yorkshire: Pen & Sword Military, 2012)

Fletcher-Cooke, John, *The Emperor's Guest* (London: Hutchinson, 1971).

Ford, Douglas, *The Pacific War: Clash of Empires in World War II* (London: Continuum, 2012)

Forsythe, David P., *The Humanitarians: International Committee of the Red Cross* (Cambridge: Cambridge University Press 2005)

Forsythe, David P., Barbara Ann J. Reiffer-Flanagan, *The International Committee of the Red Cross: A Neutral Humanitarian Actor* (Abingdon: Routledge, 2007)

Garon, Sheldon, *Molding Japanese Minds* (Princeton: Princeton University Press, 1997)

Gibney, F. (ed.), Beth Cary (trans.), *Senso: The Japanese Remember the Pacific War: Letters to the Editor of the Asahi Shimbun* (Armonk, N.Y: M.E. Sharpe, 2001)

Given-Wilson, Chris. *The Lancashire Loyals in Japanese Captivity,* 1942–1945 (Lancaster: Palatine books, 2010)

Gluck, Carol, *Japan's Modern Myths: Ideology in the Late Meiji Period* (Princeton: Princeton University Press, 1985)

Goetz Holmes, Linda, *Guests of the Emperor* (Annapolis, Maryland: Naval Institute Press, 2010)

Hack, Karl and Kevin Blackburn, *Forgotten Captives in Japanese-Occupied Asia* (Abingdon: Routledge, 2008)

Harouel, Véronique, *Histoire de la Croix-Rouge* (Paris: Presses Universitaires de France, 1999)

Harris, Sheldon, *Factories of Death: Japanese Biological Warfare, 1932–45, and the American Cover-Up* (London: Routledge, Taylor & Francis Group, 1994)

Hately-Broad, Barbara, *War and Welfare: British Prisoner of War Families, 1939–1945* (Manchester: Manchester University Press, 2009)

Havens, Thomas R.H., *Valley of Darkness: The Japanese People and World War Two (*New York: Norton, 1978)

Havers, R.P.W., *Reassessing the Japanese Prisoner of War Experience: The Changi POW Camp,1942–1945* (London: Routledge Curzon, 2003)

International Committee of the Red Cross, *Report of the International Committee of the Red Cross on its Activities during the Second World* War *(1 September,1939 – 30 June, 1947)* 3 vols. (Geneva: ICRC, 1948)

Jackson, Ashley, *The British Empire and the Second World War* (London: Hambledon Continuum, 2005)

Jesson, Alison, *The Mind's Garden* (London: Troubadour Press, 2010)

Junod, Marcel, *Warrior Without Weapons* (London: Jonathan Cape, 1951)

Kasza, Gregory J., *The State and the Mass Media in Japan,1918–1945* (California: California University Press, 1993)

Keene, Judith, *Treason on the Airwaves: Three Allied Broadcasters on Axis Radio during World War II* (Westport, CT: Praeger, 2009)

Kushner, Barak, *The Thought War: Japanese Imperial Propaganda* (Honolulu: Hawaii University Press, 2007)

Lebra, Joyce C., (ed.), *Japan's Greater East Asia Co-Prosperity Sphere in World War II: Selected Readings and Documents* (Kuala Lumpur: Oxford University Press, 1975)

Lindsay, Oliver, *At the Going Down of the Sun: Hong Kong and South-East Asia 1941–45* (London: Hamish Hamilton, 1981)

MacArthur, Brian, *Surviving the Sword: Prisoners of the Japanese, 1942–45* (London: Time Warner, 2005)

Mackay, Robert, *Half the Battle: Civilian Morale in Britain during the Second World War* (Manchester: Manchester University Press, 2002)

Gavan McCormack and Hank Nelson, *The Burma-Thailand Railway* (Thailand: Silkworm Books, 1993)

Makepeace, Clare, *Captives of War: British Prisoners of War in Europe in the Second World War* (Cambridge: Cambridge University Press, 2017)

McLaine, Ian, *Ministry of Morale: Homefront Morale and the Ministry of Information in World War II* (London: George Allen & Unwin, 1979)

McEwen, John, *Out of the Depths of Hell: A Soldier's Story of Life and Death in Japanese Hands* (London: Leo Cooper, 1999)

Meo, Lucy D., *Japan's Radio War on Australia, 1941–1945* (Carlton, Victoria: Melbourne University Press, 1968)

Minear, Richard H., *Victors' Justice: The Tokyo War Crimes Trial* (Princeton: Princeton University Press, 1971)

Mitchell, R. Keith, *Forty-Two Months in Durance Vile: Prisoner of the Japanese* (London: Robert Hale, 1997)

Moore, Bob and Barbara Hately-Broad (eds), *Prisoners of War, Prisoners of Peace: Captivity, Homecoming and Memory in World War II* (Oxford: Berg, 2005)

Moore, Bob and Kent Fedorowich, *Prisoners of War and their Captors in World War Two* (Oxford: Berg, 1996)

Moorehead, Caroline, *Dunant's Dream*: *War, Switzerland and the History of the Red Cross* (London: Harper Collins, 1998)

Newman, Carolyn, *Legacies of our Fathers: World War Two Prisoners of the Japanese – their Sons and Daughters tell their Stories* (Sydney, NSW: Hachette, 2006)

Nitobé, Inazo, *Bushido: The Soul of Japan* (Philadelphia: Leeds & Biddle, 1900)

Orbaugh, Sharlyn, *Propaganda Performed: Kamishibai in Japan's Fifteen Year War* (Leiden-Boston: Brill, 2015)

Parkes, Meg and Geoff Gill, *Captive Memories: Starvation, Disease, Survival: Far East POWs & Liverpool School of Tropical Medicine* (Lancaster: Palatine, 2015)

Roland, C.G., *Long Night's Journey into Day: Prisoners of War in Hong Kong and Japan, 1941–1945* (Waterloo, Ontario: Wilfrid Laurier Universty Press, 2001)

Rollings, Charles, *Prisoners of War, Voices from Captivity During the Second World War* (London: Ebury Press, 2007)

Russell, Earl of Liverpool, *The Knights of Bushido* (London: Cassell, 1958)

Shillony, Ben-Ami, *Politics and Culture in Wartime Japan* (Oxford: Clarendon Press, 1981)

Smith, Colin, *Singapore Burning: Heroism and Surrender in World War II* (London: Penguin, 2006)

Smith, Donald, *And All the Trumpets* (Bles: London, 1954)

Snow, Philip, *Fall of Hong Kong: Britain, China and the Japanese Occupation* (New Haven: Yale University Press, 2003)

Steinacher, Gerald, *Humanitarians at War: The Red Cross in the Shadow of the Holocaust* (Oxford: Oxford University Press, 2017)

Taylor, P.M., *Munitions of the Mind: A History of Propaganda from the Ancient World to the Present Day* (Manchester: Manchester University Press, 1995)

Tett, David, *A Postal History of Prisoners of War and Civilian Internees in East Asia during the Second World War*, 6 vols. (Bristol: Stuart Rossiter Trust Fund, 2002)

Thorne, Christopher, *The Issue of War: States, Societies and the Far Eastern Conflict of 1941–1945* (London: Hamish Hamilton, 1985)

Towle, Philip, Margaret Kosuge and Yoichi Kibata (eds), *Japanese Prisoners of War* (London: Hambledon & Co, 2000)

Wade, Tom Henling, *Prisoner of the Japanese* (Ipswich: Kall-Kwik Printing, 1994)

Waswo, Ann, *Modern Japanese Society, 1868–1994* (Oxford: Oxford University Press, 1996)

Waterford, Van, *Prisoners of the Japanese in World War II: Statistical History, Personal Narratives and Memorials Concerning POWs in Camps and Hellships, Civilian Internees, Asian Slave Labourers and Others Captured in the Pacific Theater* (North Carolina: McFarland & Co, 1994)

Welch, David, *Propaganda, Power and Persuasion: From World War 1 to Wikileaks* (London and New York: I.B. Tauris, 2014)

Wilson, Sandra (ed.), *Nation and Nationalism in Japan* (London: Routledge, 2002).

Wylie, Neville, *Barbed Wire Diplomacy: Britain, Germany and the Politics of Prisoners of War, 1939–45* (Oxford: Oxford University Press, 2011)

Articles and Book Chapters

Beaumont, Joan, 'Rank, Privilege and Prisoners of War,' in *War and Society (Australia)*, 3:1, 1983, pp.67–94

Bosch, Elena, 'The Role of Red Cross Aid in the Prisoners of War Camps on the Siam-Burma Railway', British Empire at War Research Group, Article 2, 2012 <http://britishempireatwar.org/> [accessed 26 March 2018]

Davis, G.H., 'Prisoners of War in Twentieth-Century War Economics,' in *Journal of Contemporary History*. vol.12, 1977, pp.623–634

De Groen, Fran and Helen Masterman-Smith, 'Prisoners on Parade: Japan Party 'B', *History Conference, 2002–Remembering 1942'*, Australian War Memorial

Douglas Allison, A.F., 'The Voyage of the *Fukkai Maru'*, *Blackwood's Magazine*, February 1946, pp.135–43

Elrington, Lieutenant Colonel Mordaunt William, 'With 2nd Loyals in Captivity', *The Lancashire Lad*, September 1949, March 1950, June 1950, December 1950, June 1951, March 1952

Flower, Sibylla Jane, 'British Policy Makers and the Prisoner of War Issue: Perceptions and Responses,' in Ian Gow, Yoichi Hirama and John Chapman (eds), *History of Anglo-Japanese Relations,* vol.3, *The Military Dimension* (Basingstoke: Palgrave Macmillan, 2003)

Flower, Sibylla Jane, 'Memoir and the Prisoner of War Experience: United Kingdom', in Blackburn and Hack, *Forgotten Captives*

Flower, Sibylla Jane, *'Captors and Captives on the Burma Thai Railway' in B. Moore and K. Fedorowich* (eds) *Prisoners of War and their Captors in World War Two (Oxford: OUP, 2006).*

Gill, G., and D.R. Bell, 'Strongyloides Stercoralis Infection in Former Far East Prisoners of War,' in *British Medical Journal*, 8 September 1979 2:6190, pp.572–574

Fox, Jo, 'The Propaganda War,' in Evan Mawdsley (ed.), *The Cambridge History of The Second World War*, vol. 2, Michael Geyer and Adam Tooze (eds), Politics and Ideology (Cambridge: Cambridge University Press, 2015)

Kratoska, Paul H., and Ken'ichi Goto, 'Japanese Occupation of Southeast Asia, 1941–45,' in John W. Hall et al. (eds), *The Cambridge History of Japan*, vol. 6, Peter Duus (ed.), The Twentieth Century (Cambridge: Cambridge University Press, 1988)

Gill, Geoff and D.R.,' Bell, 'Persisting Nutritional Neuropathy among Former War Prisoners,' in *Journal of Neurology, Neurosurgery & Psychiatry* 45:10, October 1982, pp.861–865

Ion, A. Hamish, "Much Ado about Too Few': Aspects of the Treatment of Canadian and Commonwealth POWs and Civilian Internees in Metropolitan Japan, 1941–1945,' in *Defence Studies, The Journal of the Joint Services Command Staff*, 6:3 (2006) pp.292–317

Kita, Yoshito, 'The Japanese Military's Attitude towards International Law and the Treatment of Prisoners of War,' in Ian Gow, Yoichi Hirama and John Chapman (eds), *The History of Anglo-Japanese Relations, 1600–2000*, vol. 3, *The Military Dimension* (Basingstoke: Palgrave Macmillan, 2003)

Kovner, Sarah, 'Allied POWs in Korea', in Barak Kushner and Sherzod Muminov (eds), *The Dismantling of Japan's Empire in East Asia:*

Deimperialization, Postwar Legitimation and Imperial Afterlife (Routledge: Abingdon, 2017)

MacKenzie, S.P., 'Prisoners of War and Civilian Internees: The Asian and Pacific Theatres' in L.E. Lee (ed.), *World War II in the Pacific and the War's Aftermath, with General Themes: A Handbook of Literature and Research* (Westport, CT: Greenwood, 1998)

Mackenzie, S.P., 'Prisoners of War and Civilian Internees: The European and Mediterranean Theatres' in L.E. Lee, (ed.), *World War II in Europe, Africa and the Americas, with General Sources: A Handbook of Literature and Research* (Westport, CT: Greenwood, 1997)

MacKenzie, S.P., 'The Treatment of Prisoners of War in World War II'*: The Journal of Modern History,* 66:3 (September1994), pp.487–520

Robson, D., et al, 'Consequences of Captivity: Health Effects of Far East Imprisonment in World War II,' in *QJM: An International Journal of Medicine*, 102: 2, 1 February 2009, pp.7–96

Sweeting, A.J., 'Prisoners of the Japanese', in Lionel Wigmore, *Australia in the War of 1939–45*: vol. 4, *The Japanese Thrust* (Canberra: Australian War Memorial, 1957)

Towle, Philip, 'Japanese Culture and the Treatment of POWs in the Asian-Pacific War', in Sibylle Scheipers (ed.), *Prisoners in War* (Oxford: Oxford University Press, 2010), pp.141–53

Utsumi, Aiko, 'Changing Japanese views of the Allied *Occupation of Japan and the War Crimes Tribunal' Journal of the Australian War Memorial – Issue 30 <www.awm.gov.au/>* [accessed 12 April 2018]

Utsumi, Aiko, 'Japan's World War II POW Policy: Indifference and Irresponsibility' in *The Asia-Pacific Journal* 3:5, 19 May 2005 <https://apjjf.org/-Utsumi-Aiko/article.html>[accessed 4 April 2018]

Yap, Felicia, 'Prisoners of War and Civilian Internees of the Japanese in British Asia: The Similarities and Contrasts of Experience', in *Journal of Contemporary History*, 47:2, April 2012, pp.317–346

Theses

Laurent, Christophe, 'Les Obstacles Rencontrés par le C.I.C.R. dans son Activité en Extrême Orient (1941–1945)', Master's thesis, University of Lausanne, 2003

Robbins, Jane M.J., 'Tokyo Calling: Japanese Broadcasting 1937–45', PhD Thesis, Sheffield University, 2006

Official Publications

Hansard

Norwood, James and Emily Shek, 'Camps in Areas Other Than the Four Principal Islands of Japan, Liaison and Research Branch American Prisoner of War Information Bureau', 1946

Satow, H., and M.J. Sée, 'The Work of the Prisoners of War Department during the Second World War, London: Foreign Office', 1950

Archives

Churchill Archives Centre

GBR/0014/HUHT Digest of Narrative of Private Nuttall, 2nd [Battalion] Loyal Regiment, Papers of Sir Cecil Charles Hughes-Hallett).

International Committee of the Red Cross, Geneva

ACICR, G 8/76, I – IX, Délégation au Japon, Correspondance, 1942–1945.

ACICR G 85/ Gouvernement, Japon, 1939 – Mai 1950.

ACICR, G17, Camps – liste des effectifs – Courrier des délégations CICR, Asie

Digital Archive

V-P-HIST-E-02330, Letter of thanks to Colonel Noguchi

V-P-HIST-E-04272, Photo graph of Purana Qila

Imperial War Museum, London

Documents

1133 Private Papers of A.V. Toze.

4969 Instructions issued to Allied Prisoners of War on their Arrival in Korea, September 1942.

6377 Private Papers of Robert Peaty

Private Papers of Captain John Jesson (these papers have not yet been catalogued and therefore lack a reference)

Photographs

HU 58744 – HU 58753, A.V. Toze Collection Scenes at Keijo POW camp:

HU 95190– HU 95197 Scenes at Changi POW camp, L.V. Headley Collection

Sound (Oral History)
4630 Thomas, Ivor George, 5 August 1980
4986 Hanson, Douglas Parker, 23 June 1981
6058 Roberts, Jack, 8 February 1982
8302 Fraser, Daniel McLair, 9 September 1984
6058 Roberts, Jack, 8 February 1982

The National Archives at Kew, London

CAB/66/42/34 Publicity concerning Japanese treatment of British Prisoners of War and Civilian Internees

CO/980/204 Publicity and Press Releases on POW and Internment Camps

CO/980/205 Setting up an enquiry centre for information regarding POWs in the Far East

FCO 21/3529 Unit 731(Mukden): claims by former British prisoners of war (POWs);

FO 371/31840 Committee of Enquiry into the Treatment of British Subjects in Japanese controlled territories

FO/916 782 POW and Internees in Japanese Hands

HO/215/94 1943 International Red Cross Visits to Camps, Keijo, Korea.

NA DEFE 68/1231 Experiments on Prisoners of War by Unit 731 of the Imperial Army

WO 32/10739 Prisoners of War: Propaganda (Code 91(C)): Publicity about conditions of prisoners of war in the Far East

WO/ 32/9906 British POWs publicity and press announcements

WO/32/9890 Imperial Prisoners of War Committee – summary of action taken in matters relating to POWs

WO163/152 Imperial POW Committee 1941–4 3

WO163/582 Imperial POW Committee Minutes, summary of action, progress reports 1941–1947

WO/163/588 Imperial Prisoners of War Committee, Sub-Committee 'A', Meetings, 1941–1952

WO224/195 Korea: Keijo, Jinsen and Chosen: P.O.W. Camps and Hospitals

WO 252/997. Allied Geographical Section, South West Pacific Area: Special Reports: Korea: Kyongsong.

WO/345 Japanese index cards of Allied Prisoners of War and Internees, Second World War, 1942–1945.

WO/361/1208 Far East: Korea; Loyal Regiment; Court of Enquiry held at Keijo (Seoul)POW camp
WO/361/2020 Prisoners of War, Far East: Allied POWs transferred to Korea.
WO/361 /2067 Prisoners of War, Far East: parties transferred overseas; "B' and 'Special'.

The National Archives at Lancashire Infantry Museum, Preston

846/2.1.87 Harry Kingsley Collection, Keijo, FEPOW
846/2.2.151 P.O.W camp – Keijo, Korea, Orders and instructions to POW's dropped by American aircraft following defeat of Japanese forces.
846/2.2.165 Miscellaneous [including J Lever diary]

Liddell Hart Military Archives, King's College London

GB0099 KCLMA, Procter, Maj John Harold (1917–1950), Personal documents and Photograph album.

Private Collections

Australia

Merrie Bott, Diary of Private Arthur Kerr,

United Kingdom

Richard Baker, Lieutenant G. S. Baker archive: diaries, workbooks, correspondence, memorabilia, photographs.
Alison Jesson, John Jesson archive, Journals, sketches, correspondence
Sherpa, Helen, Diaries of Major Conrad Rigby, 1941–1945

USA

Phil Karshis, Lieutenant-Colonel (later Brigadier) Mordaunt William Elrington archives, transcript of interview, photographs, account of Malaya campaign.

Index